The Black Image
in the New Deal

The Politics of FSA Photography

The Black Image in the New Deal

The Politics of FSA Photography

Nicholas Natanson

THE UNIVERSITY OF TENNESSEE PRESS
KNOXVILLE

Library of Congress Cataloging in Publication Data
Natanson, Nicholas, 1955–
        The Black image in the New Deal: the politics of FSA photography/
    Nicholas Natanson.
            p. c m.
    Includes bibliographical references and index
    ISBN 0-87049-723-5 (cloth: alk. pa.).
    ISBN 0-87049-724-3 (pbk.: alk. pa.)
        1. Afro-Americans—Pictorial works. 2. Photography, Documen-
    tary—United States—History—20th century. 3. United States. Farm
    Security Administration. 4. United States—Social conditions—
    1933–1945. I. Title.

    E185.6.N245 1992
        973'.0496073—dc20   91-14344   CIP

Contents

Figures

Acknowledgments

Many individuals, at institutions across the country, helped make this project possible. I extend my thanks to my Ph.D. dissertation advisor at the University of Iowa, John Raeburn, for his faith and inspiration, not to mention his extensive chapter-by-chapter comments on the manuscript that formed the basis for this book. It was in Professor Raeburn's seminar on *Let Us Now Praise Famous Men*, six years ago, that the essential idea for the present study was born. The other members of my committee at the University of Iowa—Ed Folsom, Rich Horwitz, Albert Stone, Shelton Stromquist, and, before his tragic death, Jonathan Walton—contributed immensely to this project and to my many research and writing endeavors during the course of my graduate career.

Also instrumental was the support of the Prints and Photographs staff at the Library of Congress. Members of the reference staff—Leroy Bellamy, Jerry Kearns, Mary Ison, George Hobart, Maja Felaco, and Marilyn Ibach—were consistently generous with their time and knowledge. Others in the Prints and Photographs Division contributed their expertise at key points: Annette Melville, Elisabeth Betz Parker, Helena Zinkham, Beverly Brannan, and (from the Library's American Folklife Center) Carl Fleischhauer.

In my capacity as a researcher at the National Archives—prior to my employment at that institution—I received some useful reference tips from Barbara Burger and other members of the Still Picture Branch staff; and Jill Sherman and her colleagues at the Missouri Historical Society Pictorial Branch went above and beyond the call of duty in solving a mystery concerning some non-FSA photos of the 1939 New Madrid highway demonstration. Rudy Vetter, Washington, D.C., pho-

tographer, provided stellar assistance in the gathering of certain reproductions. Significant help with permissions came from Jim Huffman of
the Schomburg Center for Research in Black Culture; Kurt Jasielonis
of the Tampa–Hillsborough County, Florida, Library; Ellen Hollyday
of the Harmon Foundation; Ellen Wright; and from photographers
Robert McNeill, Louise Rosskam, and the late Aaron Siskind.

My parents, Maurice and Lois Natanson, my brother Charles, and
my sister Kathy, helped give me the courage to resist the formidable
intellectual winds of Marxism and post-structuralism. And my supreme
thanks go to Barbara Orbach, member of the Library of Congress Prints
and Photographs staff, American Studies innovator, intellectual and
personal companion extraordinaire. Our story together goes far beyond these chapters.

Politics and Culture:
New Deals, Old Deals

October 1939. Marion Post Wolcott's first extended exposure to the Deep South had been less than ingratiating. As she swung through Florida, Alabama, and Mississippi, she complained to Farm Security Administration (FSA) photography director Roy Stryker about small-minded local officials, about a stifling cultural environment, about racism and sexism, even about "polite reform women . . . with their unrealistic and sentimental way of handling [problems]. . . . After a whole day of that crap and listening to them playing Jesus I could just plain puke!"[1]

For a photographer experiencing this sort of distaste, there were rich possibilities in a scene encountered in Belzoni, Mississippi. "Negro Man Entering a Movie Theatre By 'Colored' Entrance," as Wolcott's pointed caption suggested, was no ordinary glance at a small-town entertainment (fig. 1.1). Through its accretion of detail, the photograph both exposes and questions the conventional: the cheerful message of a Dr. Pepper sign ("GOOD FOR LIFE!"), the smiling movie-poster face of Cowboy Bob Steele, the prize advertised by a cash-night sign ($400), and—amid these promises of opportunity and adventure—the somber reality of segregation signs for bathrooms and seating. The isolation of the lone customer, literally dwarfed by the messages surrounding him, adds to the irony; little here seems especially "good" for the black man, as the Jim Crow sign points him toward a deeply shaded, distinctly unappealing area at the top of the stairs. Cash, cowboys, the upward path—myths become hauntingly empty. The long afternoon shadows through the image also create an eerie sense of doubleness, as if underlining the bifurcated nature of Belzoni society.

Fig. 1.1. Marion Post Wolcott. "Negro Man Entering a Movie Theatre by 'Colored' Entrance," Belzoni, Miss. 1939. FSA. Library of Congress.

Further ironies, of which Wolcott may or may not have been fully aware, emerge within the context of film history. Playing at the Belzoni theater was "Feud of the Range," part of a bumper crop of Hollywood westerns in 1939. Bob Steele, along with the likes of Gene Autry, Roy Rogers, and Tex Ritter, were riding, shooting, and often singing their way through one utterly predictable adventure after another. "Feud" appears to have been particularly banal; even *Variety*, not known for its effete tastes, called it a "hoary Western that won't pull much business . . . and will cost Bob Steele most of his following."[2] The "hoary Western" has pulled at least one customer in Belzoni. (Was he arriving early or late for the show, or could it have been that most Belzonians stayed away from Cowboy Bob?) His being black suggests the profound irony of mass-culture romanticism, and of a particularly low-grade sort at that, being "consumed" by members of a race whom most mass-culture creators had done their best to denigrate or exclude. Hence the photograph's special edge: while it is possible that the black man was genuinely interested in Cowboy Bob, it is also quite possible that he was opting to see whatever movie was available—with precious little available that spoke to his experience. No pitiful victim (he will undoubtedly derive some pleasure from the afternoon escape), but no stalwart hero either, the man participates in a realm of mass culture where the very nature of black consumer "participation" is bounded, ambiguous, and troubling.

An obscure town, a forgotten movie—an FSA masterpiece, one that functions within a larger series whole: in her Belzoni coverage, Wolcott shows black and white farmers pursuing, with careful separateness, the same Saturday-afternoon-in-town rituals (shopping, socializing, business with cotton merchants); the theater image feeds a sense of shared yet unshared culture. While there are indications of economic change in some of the Belzoni scenes (blacks waiting outside the headquarters of a "Staple Cotton Cooperative Association"), the theater image underlines the gap between economic and social progress. Finally, while Wolcott's portraits around town explore black individuality, the "Negro man" entering the theater remains a distant, more anonymous figure—and that is precisely the point. In the psychology of Jim Crow, the man's blackness, and not the man, is what counts.

If Wolcott's perceptiveness in Belzoni crossed racial lines, what of the black coverage in the much larger photo-documentary project of which Wolcott, and the Belzoni series, was only a part? From 1935 to 1942, photographers for the Historical Section of the New Deal's Resettlement Administration/Farm Security Administration produced some sixty thousand printed images of American life on the countryside, in small towns, and, to a lesser extent, in big cities.[3] The shifting cast of camerapeople included, among the major contributors, Wolcott; Ben Shahn; Walker Evans; Carl Mydans; Arthur Rothstein; Dorothea Lange; Russell Lee; Jack Delano; John Collier, Jr.; John Vachon; Edwin Rosskam; Marjory Collins; Arthur Siegel; Paul Carter; Edwin Locke; and the black photographer brought on just before the Historical Section was absorbed into the Office of War Information, Gordon Parks. Immensely productive, and more widely publicized in its time than any documentary undertaking before or since, the project's directions were multiple: exposure of the ill fed, ill clothed, ill housed in need of agency assistance; documentation of RA/FSA accomplishments in rural rehabilitation and resettlement; exploration of social, economic, and cultural processes that were not necessarily rooted in the depression; coverage of America's conversion, in FDR's words, from "Dr. Recovery" to "Dr. Win the War." "The most permanent and the most fleeting," as photographer/editor Rosskam described the file in 1940, "the most gay and the most tragic—the cow barn, the migrant's tent, the tractor in the field and the jalopy on the road, the weathered faces of men, . . . the faces of children and the faces of animals. . . . In rows of filing cabinets, they wait for today's planner and tomorrow's historian."[4]

In light of this documentary range, black life would certainly have been a potential subject for Historical Section inquiry. Yet when we consider one of the best-known published FSA photo collections— important in shaping the traditional view of "classic" FSA images— Archibald MacLeish's *Land of the Free* (1938), we find precious few black faces; it is Lange's white migrant mother, Rothstein's white Oklahomans plodding through the dust storm, Lee's white tenant children standing to eat a humble Christmas repast, Shahn's white rehabilitation client with furrowed brow, Evans's white tenant family portrait that receive the prominent play. Or we consider Historical Section Director Roy Stryker's instructions to Lange in June 1937: "Regarding the tenancy pictures," he replied to her inquiry from Texas, "I would suggest that you take both black and white, but place the emphasis on the white tenants, since we know that these will receive much wider use."[5] Four years later, amid preparation of the Richard Wright and Edwin Rosskam photo-book, *12 Million Black Voices*, Stryker was singing a different tune: "We have always been interested in the Negro problems," he boasted to Lee, "have taken pictures portraying these problems ever since we have been in existence, and will probably continue to do it as long as we are in existence." What, we might logically ask, was the *real* FSA tune?[6]

Curiously, for all the scholarship that FSA photography has attracted in recent years, the FSA-and-blacks nexus has never been systematically explored. Works on the project as a whole have certainly included black images, but for many years authors and editors were too concerned with raising hosannas for Stryker and his photographers to offer much in the way of hard analysis. Where such analysis is more in evidence, as in William Stott's *Documentary Expression and Thirties America* (1973), the FSA portion of the Smithsonian Institution's *Official Images: New Deal Photography* (1987), Carl Fleischhauer and Beverly Brannan's *Documenting America* (1988), and the FSA section of Maren Stange's *Symbols of Ideal Life: Social Documentary Photography in America, 1890–1950* (1989), the racial angle remains relatively underdeveloped.[7] Studies of individual FSA camerapeople and of FSA work in particular states have often had too many years or too many miles to cover for any prolonged racial stops. In the case of Parks, the bulk of whose lifetime photographic production has concerned blacks, retrospectives have dealt only passingly with the context out of which his FSA work emerged. Recent work by James Curtis on Walker Evans and by Sally Stein, F. Jack Hurley, Andrea Fisher, and others on Marion Post Wolcott provides a beginning for analysis of FSA racial coverage—but only a beginning.[8] We must inquire whether the "gems" discussed by these recent commentators were interesting exceptions or parts of a broad pattern of racial attentiveness in the FSA file.

The question actually becomes a spate of questions. Did blacks gain the numerical representation in the FSA file that their share of the national population, and their respective shares of regional populations, warranted? To the extent that FSA photographers were including blacks among their subjects, FSAers were not alone. How did the FSA work conform to or defy the patterns of black portrayal established by other 1930s–40s camerapeople, whether politically left or mainstream, whether government sponsored or private, whether white or black? Does the FSA case support the contention of one black historian that "Afro-American photographers will have borne—and must continue to bear—the overwhelming burden of responsibility" for photographing blacks "as people, as real human beings?"[9] A photograph of a rehabilitated black farmhouse was hardly on the same order as a photograph of a tenement, or, in turn, one of a segregation sign. How frequently did FSA photographers venture beyond FSA solutions—the politically safest black subject-matter during the depression—and address issues bearing on economic and racial hierarchies? And what does the inclusion or exclusion of certain sorts of images suggest about the influence of Roy Stryker, or of Farm Security administrators Rexford Tugwell, Will Alexander, and C. B. Baldwin, on the documentary product? Finally, there was the matter of putting pictures to work. To what extent did FSA black images reach the public arena? That is, how were they used, or misused, in newspapers, magazines, photo-books, museum exhibitions, traveling shows; and what sorts of responses did the published or exhibited photographs engender? Were FSA visions of blacks in turn reenvisioned in politically and culturally significant ways?

In confronting these questions, we will be testing the depth of what many commentators have been accustomed to call, with images of whites in mind, the "special" achievement of FSA photography—sensitivity to place, respect for cultural integrity, feel for individual dignity and character, commitment to the understanding of economic, social, and cultural settings. "If there's one great thing I can say for the file," as Stryker boasted two decades later, "one of the greatest prides that I have: I can think of no time that [any of the FSA photographers] ever showed any disrespect [for their subjects], ever looked down upon anyone, ever ridicul[ed] . . . anything that looked funny."[10] In confronting these questions, we will be testing the possibilities for imaginative racial thinking in a New Deal environment whose "newness" for black America has been a matter of considerable historical debate. A truly new deal, an old deal in a new disguise, a trickle that eventually became the great river of the civil rights movement—whatever the possible conclusions, New Deal pictorial activity must be considered in the final reckoning. Finally, in confronting these questions, one will be evaluating not simply a set of cultural artifacts from the depression and early war years but a cultural process of image production, selection and utilization, and impact—part of the larger historical operation, as Thomas Bender has sketched it, in which "some groups and some values [are] so much, or so little, represented in [American] public life. . . . [One needs to ask] whether the interests and values of particular groups are justly represented in society, and

[to] ask, as well, whether the public denies the legitimacy of some groups' most deeply held beliefs, whether about morality, art, or politics."[11] In an era that could produce both *Native Son* and *Gone with the Wind*, both the March on Washington movement and the consistent defeat of federal anti-lynching bills, the question of black representation, cultural as much as political, went to the very heart of what Gunnar Myrdal would shortly be calling the "American Dilemma."

James Agee mused early in his now-classic joint venture with Walker Evans, *Let Us Now Praise Famous Men*: "In the immediate world, everything is to be discerned, for him who can discern it . . . without either dissection into science, or digestion into art, but with the whole of consciousness, seeking to perceive it as it stands. . . . This is why the camera seems to me, next to unassisted and weaponless consciousness, the central instrument of our time." But Agee's faith in photographic vision was not unqualified, for in the very next phrase he complains of camera misuse, "which has spread so nearly universal a corruption of sight that I know of less than a dozen alive whose eyes I can trust even so much as my own."[12] For scholars employing and interpreting photographic evidence, the issue goes beyond Agee's implicit distinction between responsible and irresponsible camera-wielders. We shall confront a number of methodological problems in the course of this study; for the present, several general observations are in order.

As visual texts, as "readable" documents, photographs are both supremely compelling and supremely slippery—emerging as odd syntheses of what has been captured by intention (the photographer's, often mixed with the subject's) and what has developed through serendipity, or though "subliminal vision," as photo-historian Richard Whelan calls it. If we are interpreting what may be partly accidental, the problem of avoiding reckless readings becomes particularly difficult. "Photographs invite interpretation," Alan Trachtenberg points out, "but the interpreter needs some controls upon his own imagination, some limits and a boundary between sense and nonsense."[13] We should attempt, Trachtenberg and others suggest, to "frame" the photograph, to place it in a historical and cultural context as a way of grasping what Roland Barthes would call the image's "historical grammar of icono-

graphic connotation . . . gestures, attitudes, expressions, effects en-
dowed with certain meanings by virtue of practice of a certain society."[14] In the case of the FSA, we have the advantage of working with
fairly specific temporal and geographical information for each photograph, and, in some cases, with photographers' notes on social and
economic conditions at a particular site. From letters, field notes, and
interviews, we can tender educated guesses about the sort of serendipi-
ties more likely for one photographer than for another. For example,
some recent scholars have seen in Wolcott's innocently titled "Advertisement on the Side of a Drug Store, Wendell, North Carolina" a
deeper sociological drama: the sidewalk enactment of Jim Crow rituals, with two black men appearing to step carefully out of the path of a
white woman (fig. 1.2).[15] From our knowledge of Wolcott's written
criticism of small-town Southern folkways, from our knowledge of her
sociologically advanced reading interests of the time, from our knowledge of her other photographic ventures, the notion of a deeper significance to the North Carolina image becomes at least arguable.

Still, the linking of a particular frame with a particular scene remains a risky act. In the Wolcott photograph, it is entirely possible
that the blacks were carefully avoiding the white woman—apparently
holding a baby—just as they would have stepped out of the way of *any*
woman with a toddler. Perhaps concern about upsetting the baby's
balance, rather than observance of racial custom, functioned as the
central motivation here. It is quite possible that racial codes in Wendell, North Carolina, were not as tight in 1939 as they were in Deep
South towns; in "framing," we sometimes run the danger of imputing
characteristics of the regional or national to the local. What's more,
"gestures, attitudes, expressions" might have been ambiguous even for
the Wendell residents in question: symbolic cultural processes do not
always work with the airtight efficiency that photo-historians have
often assumed. If a certain mystery haunts daily social interaction, the
mystery is only heightened in an artificially frozen moment of that
interaction. Finally, it is possible that those commentators who have
argued most passionately for the "Jim Crow" reading, Sally Stein and
Andrea Fisher, have merely imposed their feminist framework—FSA/

OWI female photographers as leaders of a documentary counterculture, uniquely sensitive to gender as well as to racial oppression—on an image that has less to do with oppression than with changes in small-town commerce.

Ultimately, the process of framing demands a level of experiential reconstruction that, in most cases, simply cannot be reached. The process remains, like the ethnographic "deep reading" of which Clifford Geertz writes, "intrinsically incomplete. . . . And, worse than that, the more deeply it goes the less complete it is."[16] We must accept this limitation. At the same time, however, me must be wary of interpretive escape routes: purely aesthetic analysis, ignoring the very raison d'être of 1930s–40s documentary photography; psychoanalytic analysis, yielding some breathtaking conjectures but requiring utter allegiance to a theoretical system that remains suspiciously circular; or structuralist and post-structuralist analysis, energized by a rhetoric that

Fig. 1.2. Marion Post Wolcott. "Advertisement on the Side of a Drugstore Window," Wendell, N.C. 1939. FSA. Library of Congress.

tends to obscure as much as it clarifies, and that too often verges on what even one commentator sympathetic to the movement, Edith Kurzweil, acknowledges to be "semantic games."[17]

Despite its limitations, historical framing, when performed with a sensitivity to multiple connotations in a given image, and when performed with a recognition of the photographic *series* significance that we shall explore in coming chapters, can at least begin to draw out the richness of the photographer's encounter with place and person, and, through that richness, the play of cultural ideas. But beyond the problem of photographic reading lies that of documentary truth. Photography, John Szarkowski warns credulous viewers, amounts to a massive "quot[ing] out of context": through decisions on camera distance, angle, framing, lighting, timing, and, later in the process, printing and cropping, the photographer—sometimes in company with the photo-editor—constructs as much as reflects reality. In a similar vein, Russel Nye reminds historical absolutists that history "never stops—the historian stops it."[18] Selecting from a mass of raw data, unable to purge from the selecting mind the force of social, cultural, and political biases, the historian *creates* as much as *recovers* a past. These propositions about photography and history leave the photo-historian in an unenviable position. In seeking to evaluate the historical quality of photographic representation, he or she seeks to reconstruct the historical situation, only to find that the act of reconstruction involves further artistic invention. What's more, the photo-historian's understanding of historical reality may well be influenced by the very documentary materials whose accuracy is in question.

Faced with these considerations, some current photo-historians have chosen to focus less on historical truthfulness and more on rhetorical invention, utilization, and empowerment. Subjective constructions are unmasked, culturally and politically. "The truth *effect* of documentary," Andrea Fisher argues, "rests with a rhetoric woven around the image, continually traversing its production and its reading" (emphasis mine).[19] Certainly the work of Fisher, Maren Stange, Sally Stein, Pete Daniel, James Curtis, Allan Sekula, Peter Seixas, Victor Burgin, and other revisionists has served a valuable demythologizing purpose, advancing William Stott's early 1970s effort to turn the study of documentary photography away from the thinly veiled hero worship, the biographical celebration, that has often characterized the field. And certainly the revisionist work, frequently exploring photographic markets and marketing, has helped to illuminate a long-ignored part of cultural creation.

Yet some tendencies of the revisionists have revealed notable shortcomings: treating every photographic act as the product of a well-formed ideology (a suspicious determinism, particularly evident in the work of Stange and Curtis, leaving little room for the possibility of experimentation and diversity); equating photographic meaning or significance with market function (ignoring distinct stages of visualization and revisualization); ignoring pivotal issues of representative sampling when dealing with large and diverse collections; and employing neo-Marxist and neo-structuralist critical tools without acknowledging, or questioning, their ideological underpinnings.

Sekula's revisionist treatment of Lewis Hine typifies the problem. Dismissing the individual-toughness theme in Hine's work as a form of mysticism that serves "bourgeois" purposes, Sekula argues: "The celebration of abstract humanity becomes, in any given political situation, the celebration of the dignity of the passive victim. This is the final outcome of the appropriation of the photographic image for liberal political ends; the oppressed are granted a bogus subjecthood when such status can be secured only from within, on their own terms."[20] What those "terms," what real "subjecthood" might be, Sekula refuses to indicate. He is too sophisticated a Marxist, one suspects, to demand the simplistic "wounded proletarian" or "indignant proletarian" subjecthood; however, he remains too much a Marxist to think of working-class subjects in terms other than the "oppressed." By his very choice of words, Sekula gives away his own appropriation of working-class identities.

Ultimately, if "bourgeois" assumptions have their limitations, the paradigm underlying the arguments of Sekula, Stange, and other revisionists is fraught with profound difficulties: New Left radicalism, with its essentially romantic faith in the working-class proclivities for "correct" class consciousness, its alternating claims of critical distance and ideological commitment, its inability to deal with the historical phenomena of mixed motives and conflict within the individual, and its inheritance, from the 1930s left, of a notorious double standard in evaluating the historic behavior of the totalitarian left and the totalitarian right. As for the post-Marxist, post-modernist skepticism evoked by some revisionists, that alternative has its own curse—"the Pyrrhic victory of Angst over bourgeois liberalism," as Denis Donoghue has described its mark in the literary realm.[21]

Revisionists are fond of rejecting what Alan Trachtenberg has called the "tyranny of any fixed version" of photographic truth or photographic meaning.[22] But for all the power of Trachtenberg's phrasing, fixities are not so easily jettisoned. While one may wish to refer to photographs as subjective fictions—or, in Barthes's terminology, "authentications" of subjective experience—one flinches from accepting the further proposition that all "fictions," and all interpretations of those fictions, are created equal.[23] The absence of standards for evaluating photographic acts raises logical problems: currently fashionable frameworks of demythologizing can, in turn, be demythologized, leading us to the brink of an intellectual nightmare. "And thus entails," as philosopher Maurice Mandelbaum describes the regress, "a further statement which must also be estimated [according to conditioning factors] and on and on indefinitely."[24]

Other problems result, as well, from rejecting the kind of intellectual assumptions that make not only photo-historical judgments but political and moral judgments possible. While photo-historical revisionists may enjoy quoting Foucault and applying post-structuralist strategies, they may not enjoy the long-range implications. As Michael Walzer has pointed out: "To abolish power systems is to abolish both moral and scientific categories: away with them all! But what will be left? . . . There is for [Foucault] no such thing as a free human subject, no natural man or woman. Men and women are always social creations, the products of codes and disciplines. And so Foucault's radical abolitionism, if it is serious, is not anarchist so much as nihilist. For on his own arguments, either there will be nothing left at all, nothing visibly human; or new codes and disciplines will be produced, and Foucault gives us no reason to expect that these will be any better than the ones we now live with. Nor, for that matter, does he give us any way of knowing what 'better' might mean."[25]

Inquiries into rhetorical strategies, however revealing, do not eliminate the larger truth issue. Can the racism, for example, of a 9 October 1938 *Louisville Courier-Journal* feature on the Old South (enlarged photograph of a broadly grinning, shiny-eyed black youth grasping a handful of cotton in the field, with accompanying text noting that the "visitor sees . . . a sentimental picture of Negroes singing in the sunny fields, serene and stately manor houses") simply be classified as an alternative discursive mode, an alternative truth "effect" that happened to have the advantage of powerful interests promoting it?[26] Can the problem of racism be neatly separated from a problem of historical distortion—or the notion of distortion separated from an implicit assumption of a fixed reality being distorted?

And so one is left with a paradox. A standard for documentary truth—however problematical—needs to be known. Or at the very least, it needs to be guessed at. The photographic investigator, sorting through a multitude of images that might reveal or conceal the past, cannot afford simply to toy with the diversity of "pasts." As even Trachtenberg, implicitly acknowledging the pulls of relativism and absolutism, concluded in a study of Civil War photographs: "The real war lies in our own effort to win it away from the clutch of historicizing ideologies, to recover a connected history. . . . The real war inhabits the albums of war only as we choose to wage it there."[27]

For the purposes of this study, my sense of a connected history of black America in the 1930s through the 1940s rests on three assumptions. First, there can be no question that blacks faced a special burden during the depression era—reflected in the southern rule of Jim Crow and disenfranchisement; in southern as well as northern unemployment, housing, and health statistics; in levels of fear, and degrees of subjugation, that lay beyond quantification.

Second, there can be no question that the Rooseveltian "black deal" emerged as the product of conflicting currents. There was FDR's eminently pragmatic liberalism, which allowed for the appointment of more than one hundred black advisors to cabinet departments and relief agencies, but, at the same time, placed what he considered "national" (i.e., white) priorities above minority concerns. The road to passage of New Deal legislation led through the very same southern congressional powerhouses who were most resistant to racial change; FDR needed the support of Arkansas Senator Joseph Robinson more than he needed the support of the NAACP's Walter White. FDR's was certainly not the only voice of caution in the executive branch. For every genuine racial progressive—Eleanor Roosevelt, Secretary of the Interior Harold Ickes, National Youth Administration Director Aubrey Williams, U.S. Housing Authority Chief Nathan Straus, and Farm Security Director Will Alexander—there was Vice-President John Nance Garner, Secretary of Agriculture Henry Wallace, political advisor Louis Howe, or another powerful advocate of the status quo. Finally, there were the hundreds of local administrators of New Deal programs for whom racial discrimination was second nature. National administrators, even when they were willing, had difficulty countering the impact of attitudes such as that expressed by one Georgia official: "There will be no negroes pushing wheelbarrows and boys driving trucks for forty cents an hour when the good white men and white women, working in the fields alongside these roads, can hardly earn forty cents a day."[28] As a result, federal assistance to blacks came more slowly, and less consistently, than it did for whites.

But, third, the reality of black history in the thirties and forties amounted to more than a litany of injustices. Here I would apply a root assumption about American minority experiences, drawn from historians and sociologists who have focused on varied groups and eras: John Blassingame's construction of community function in ante-bellum black history, Herbert Gutman's concept of cultural resistance to oppression in late nineteenth- to early twentieth-century labor history, and notions of order amid apparent disorder explored in the twentieth-century urban investigations of William Whyte, John Dollard, and Horace Cayton. In line with such scholarship, I consider to be of more than passing significance the varieties of individual and communal affirmation—the varieties of subtle resistance to degradation—that may not have been expressed in protests, in movements, or even in political consciousness.[29]

On street corners and in courthouse squares, in stores and barber-shops, in churches and lodges, in taverns and juke joints, blacks main-tained worlds of social interaction whose conventions were as central to their lives as the price of cotton or the size of a paycheck. While the tides of racial violence and migration, along with depression and war, certainly affected "culture" in this mundane sense of the term, cultural practices were not merely the function of the era's tragedies. Tradi-tions remained vibrant, including the persistence of sharp cultural di-visions within the black community. Despite all the commentary—radical as well as conservative—that envisioned a standard American black, distinctions rooted in class, religious affiliation, regional back-ground, gender, and skin tone spoke otherwise in the 1930s and 1940s. To confront black America is to recognize the critical omissions made by Richard Wright when he declared, in 1945, that "white America has reduced Negro life in our great cities to a level of experience of so crude and brutal a quality that one could say of it . . . 'it is not that they starve, but that they starve so dreamlessly . . . it is not that they serve, but they have no gods to serve.' "[30] Wright was ignoring black gods. He was ignoring black dreams. Most importantly, he was ignor-ing black choices.

This third assumption of mine, and particularly the notion of choice, will be dismissed by photo-historical revisionists as a "liberal bourgeois" construct. As I have suggested, the alternative paradigms offered, explicitly or (more commonly) implicitly, by the revisionists are hardly more—and in many ways a good bit less—inclusive, scien-tific, or ethical than the model they are intended to replace. In the end, the battle of paradigms cannot possibly be resolved in this study; I make no attempt to conceal my "liberal" interest in individual charac-ter, in the ambiguities of social experience, and in the potential cleav-age, as sociologists Peter Berger and Thomas Luckmann have explored it, between an individual's "visible conduct in the larger community and his invisible self-identification as someone quite different . . . between appearance and reality in the individual's self-apprehen-sion."[31] With the foregoing assumptions in mind, I propose a series of methodological procedures that will at least begin to correct some of the common photo-historical shortcomings.

By establishing a 1930s–40s comparative framework for evaluating black photographic representation, I will seek to avoid the revisionist pattern of (1) bringing 1970s–80s expectations to bear on the visual production of an earlier era; and (2) lumping all New Deal–sponsored photographic activity into a single "middle-class" genre. By using quantitative techniques to evaluate FSA black representation, I will seek to overcome the unsystematic picture file assessment that has characterized revisionist as well as traditionalist scholarship. By analyzing images within their original series context—extending the useful work of Alan Trachtenberg, Carl Fleischhauer, and Beverly Brannan—I will seek to reconstruct the visual complexity that revisionists, in their single-minded determination to unmask "documentary" photography as propaganda, so often ignore. Finally, by carefully tracing the changes in FSA images as they moved from cameras to the public eye, I will seek to correct revisionists' function-equals-meaning simplifications.

To be sure, these procedures will not provide answers to the most fundamental questions about photographic truth-telling and truth-making. And to be sure, these procedures will certainly not satisfy those commentators who wish to create a photo-historical realm—akin to the literary realm in the age of deconstruction—with its own specialized hermeneutical vocabulary. But they will provide a more systematic, less deterministic approach to that notion so often mentioned but so little respected: photographic context.

"Ah done had 'nuff freedom," complains an ex-slave in *Gone with the Wind*. "Ah wants somebody to feed me good vittles regular an' tell me what ter do an' what not ter do, an' look after me when ah gets sick."[32] It is a long way from Margaret Mitchell's fawning dependents to the rebellious slaves of Arna Bontemps's *Black Thunder*, a long way from William Carlos Williams's wagging-waving-weaving-shaking primitives to William Faulkner's wise Dilsey (*The Sound and the Fury*), tormented Joe Christmas (*Light in August*), and determined Lucas Beauchamp (*Go Down, Moses*). It is a long way from the Lord-praising and barroom-scuffling blacks in Thomas Hart Benton's murals to the Christlike lynch martyrs painted by Julius Bloch and Harry Sternberg. It is just as far from Paul Sample's painting of black and white submarine crewmen happily playing cards together to Robert Gwathmey's scene of black parents sending their son off to war under the shadow of a Ku Klux Klan cross. A complex era of black history generated a variety of literary and artistic responses—romantic, reformist, nationalist. Contrasts are evident, as well, in the photographic response to black America. In considering this photographic context for FSA black depiction, one can discern several major tendencies.

One approach exploited popular stereotypes older than the Brady Group photos of Civil War freedmen playing the "happy manservants" for Union officers, older than the medium of photography itself. Here was the poor but contented black, the faithfully servile black. Here was the colorful, naturally rhythmic, emotionally unrestrained black. Here was the hard-gambling, hard-praying black, who, as even the usually sophisticated observer Harry Stack Sullivan once concluded, shows a profound "amiability . . . a timeless, formless optimism about life in general." While a few still photos matched the grotesque characterizations offered by Hollywood, images bearing similar implications appeared frequently in mass-circulation magazines (*Life, Time, Fortune, Saturday Evening Post*, in particular) and Sunday feature sections of newspapers. One finds *Life*, for example, opening its 9 August 1937 issue with a cover photograph of a black farmer driving a wagonload of watermelons to market; interior pictures by Al Burgert showed a grinning black farmhand pushing a watermelon-laden wheelbarrow, as well as a black woman jamming a slice into her mouth with one hand, holding a nursing baby with the other (fig. 1.3). The photo of the watermelon eater was second in a top-to-bottom sequence that began with a politely distant view of white girls enjoying a beachfront watermelon party and ended with a closeup of pigs engaged in their own melon feast. One hardly needed the captions ("Nothing makes a Negro's mouth water like a luscious fresh-picked melon. . . . What melons the Negroes do not consume will find favor with the pigs") to understand the implied hierarchy here.[33]

Similarly, it was not enough for *Life* to include, in its 15 February 1942 feature on Virginia's elegant Homestead Hotel, a photograph of black waiters singing Sunday morning spirituals in the dining room. There was also the John Phillips photo of a smiling waiter carrying a

heavily laden, room-service tray upon his head.[34] The implied connection between service and African heritage had cultural roots two centuries deep. Africanesque waiters, juke-joint dancers taking U.S. Public Health Service blood tests to swing accompaniment, adorable
sharecropper toddlers napping in the cotton patch, a trusty shoeshiner
kneeling to give Harold Ickes a polish at the latter's office desk, a 320-
pound Army trumpeter hamming it up on stage—the permutations
were many.[35] Significantly, such images often accompanied stories that
hinted of the new and potentially troublesome: captive Japanese diplomats staying at the Homestead Hotel, public health service exposure
of appallingly high venereal disease rates, the rise of Southern
agribusiness, Ickes the racial liberal, wartime black demands.

   Amid text that sent mixed signals, these visuals reestablished ground
that was familiar to a great many white viewers, not only from film but
from advertisements and posters. This was a white man's Negro, com-
fortably predictable in an unpredictable age, enviably happy in an
unhappy age, consistently entertaining in a mortifying age. This was
the black perfectly suited to the powerful current of cultural conservatism—discernible in sources ranging from public murals to the Lynds'
Middletown interviews to citizens' letters to the president—that was
as central to the 1930s as political and economic upheaval. Even when,
as in Life's 3 October 1938 spread on America's "minority problem,"
Luce publications made some attempt to puncture racial myths, there
was an all-too-fond and all-too-lengthy lingering on the old conventions. Thus, the opening image for the Life feature was a garish closeup,
from Eisenstaedt Pictures, of an open-mouthed church singer, with the
accompanying explanation: "In the Congo jungle, a black girl like this
would be moaning a murky tribal chant . . . [but here] her ecstatic face
becomes the face of the American Negro, finding in music and religion her soul's two greatest consolations."[36] In the very act of discussing America's "minority problem," Life unwittingly revealed its own
complicity in that problem.

———————

Fig. 1.3. (Opposite): Al P. Burgert. From Life. 9 Aug. 1937. Original
photographs at the Tampa-Hillsborough County, Florida, Library.
Reproduced by permission of the Tampa-Hillsborough County Library.

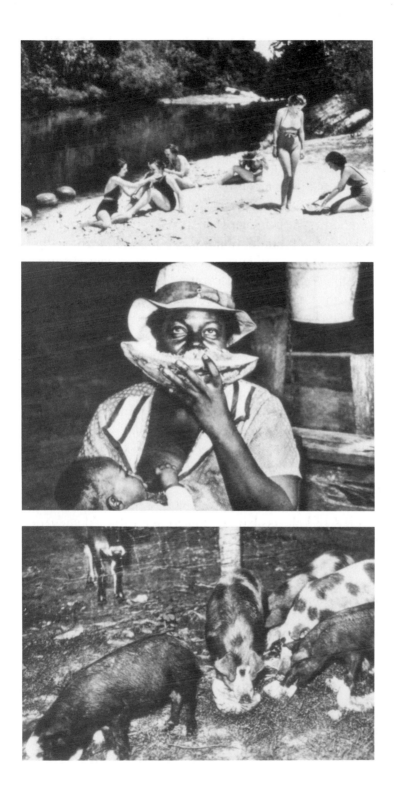

One must make some qualifications here. Such imagery was not always strictly demeaning. Undeniable skill, and probably considerable pride, lay in the Homestead waiter's routine, while the Army trumpeter was displaying more than his corpulence. What's more, even the watermelon pictures represented a positive alternative to the Negrophobic perceptions inherent in the actions of lynch mobs and explicit in the rhetoric of Theodore Bilbo, Gerald L. K. Smith, and other race-baiting demagogues. *Life* was at least accepting its "American Negro" as a valid part of the nation's life, and as more than that during the war, when "Negro distinctiveness" could be seen as emblematic of the ethnic variety that an American democracy cherished but that a European or Asian fascist order sought to extinguish. Such acceptance was not afforded Bilbo's "nigger," a nuisance at best and a threat at worst, prompting the Mississippi Senator to revive ancient ideas of black resettlement. Finally, one should note progress during this period, at least in the case of the Luce publications. The most demeaning stereotypes, such as the watermelon eater, were less likely to appear in the later years, which also saw a more sustained seriousness in the occasional "minority problem" investigations that *were* published.

Nevertheless, the basic assumptions embedded in "colorful Negro" imagery—that blacks were best suited for subservient labor or entertainment roles in American society and were naturally less inclined than whites to take problems seriously—hardly encouraged much careful thought about black needs and concerns, not to mention the personalities operating behind the smiles. To the extent that *Life* and similar publications dealt primarily in *surfaces* with all ethnic groups, blacks stood to suffer most from such treatment. In very practical terms, assumptions about a "happy-go-lucky" orientation only helped New Deal foes see what they wanted to see when they observed black participation in employment and rehabilitation programs. "The [New Deal officials] put [blacks] out at this CCC camp, where they [blacks] spend their time scouting around in the woods trying to hide from work," complained one Greene County, Georgia, official in 1939. "They put them on this WPA and let them go to sleep on their shovels. They put them out on these farms with a brand new plow and a good mule, and $10 worth of seed and fertilizer, and let them waste it."[37]

The "colorful black" also found his way into the 1930s–40s files of various photographic sponsoring or collecting units within the U.S. Department of Agriculture—the Office of the Secretary of Agriculture, the Extension Service, the Soil Conservation Service, the Bureau of Agricultural Economics, and the Agricultural Adjustment Administration. Department photographers had a field day, for example, with the arrival of Jamaican guest agricultural workers in 1943: baskets carried on heads, toothy grins at the dinner table, guitars slung over shoulders on the way to the dining hall. When blacks were not colorful in these files, they were as loyal and diligent, but essentially anonymous, as they were in USDA photographs of earlier decades. Only infrequently did William Forsythe, George W. Ackerman, Ed Hunton, L.C. Harmon, and other USDA photographers show blacks outside the fields, processing plants, or federal labor camps, and rarely was there an intimation about the impact of job status on the quality of life. Captions provided little assistance in this regard. Indeed, it is with the sense of a surprising exception that one reads the statement, accompanying one of Harmon's 1941 cotton-harvest shots from the Mississippi Delta, that "Negro children often start picking when they are old enough to walk." Even in the work setting, closeups of individual blacks were much less frequent than closeups of whites: rather than black laborers, black labor—a homogeneous background presence—worked the land. And when blacks were given more prominence, their identities were more frequently linked with *the crop* than were white identities. Hence Harmon's 1941 portrait of the Mississippi peanut-harvest hand, "George" (fig. 1.4): face aglow, turning sweetly toward the camera, the hired man of the R. G. Prescott farm grasps a peanut vine firmly at his chest. The grasping is not without dual implications, in the sense that "George" both shows his commitment to the harvest and lays a certain claim to its bounty. Loyalty deserves rewards, but loyalty does not demand rewards. Therein lies the safeness of this image. Therein lies the safeness of a great many department images taken, ironically, in a strikingly unsafe era for Southern agriculture. Just as the portrait makes it difficult to imagine

Fig. 1.4. L. C. Harmon. "George, Hired Man on Farm, with Sample of This Year's Crop of Peanuts," Rankin County, Miss. 1941. Office of the Secretary of Agriculture. National Archives.

"George" as fundamentally distinct from the next hired man, the portrait makes it difficult to imagine any "George" joining the Southern Tenant Farmers Union.

Life's references to Africanesque waiters and Congo chants suggest another, related, tendency in black portrayal. Interest in the black American-African nexus was not only a matter of entertainment, nor was it limited to popular-culture channels. While Melville Herskovits's investigations of African continuities in American slave culture highlighted a new wave of scholarly interest in primitivism, less anthropologically inclined literature turned a romantic eye upon the "noble primitive." Like the "noble savage" who had long inhabited the high-literary imagination, the 1930s figure was one of statuesque beauty, "classic," as the *Springfield Union-Republican* art critic Elizabeth McCausland described an Aaron Siskind photograph of a black boy's head, "like an African Negro sculpture."[38] But there were refinements. Unlike the mysterious, peripatetic Queequeg of old, the 1930s figure was solidly rooted in the land, in an enduring community, in a set of traditions that, while distinctive, could be fathomed by an outsider. The "noble savage" had become something of a noble agrarian. As Julia Peterkin, observing descendants of the Gullahs in South Carolina, wrote in *Roll, Jordan, Roll* (1934): "The Negroes hold fast to the old ways and beliefs acquired by their forefathers through years of experience. . . . Undisturbed by the machine age, they live close to the earth which feeds them, free from the fear of starving in the midst of plenty. . . . They find happiness in the present instead of looking for it always in tomorrow and again tomorrow or in something still to be discovered."[39] Tomorrow, in short, had brought the depression.

Peterkin's ecstatic preindustrial vision found its complement in Doris Ulmann's ninety photographs for *Roll, Jordan, Roll*. Better known for her work among Southern white mountain folk, Ulmann applied a similarly celebratory approach to black rustics. The volume's opening photograph, a soft-focus portrait of an old woman ringing a church bell, set the pictorial tone. Grace, gentleness, serenity, religiosity glow in these images, figuratively and literally. One notes the white-robed church members standing in the river to perform a baptism, their slightly blurred figures blending with the soft lights playing off the river surface. One notes the shining faces, the handsome bodies of the workers attending their plows, their cotton sacks, their fishing nets, their cooking pots. Simple folk, at peace with nature and themselves, fill these frames majestically—nary a machine present, nary a machine needed (fig. 1.5). When one compares Ulmann's treatment of this group with earlier photographic work done among similarly situated South Carolina blacks—for example, Leigh Richmond Miner's 1910s–20s images taken on St. Helena's Island, with their accent on education, on interaction between the community and the outside world—one recognizes just how much Ulmann there was in this agrarian idyll.

On the opposite end of the spectrum from the "noble primitives," the "loyal Georges," the "colorful Negroes," one finds the black-as-extreme-victim. Predictably, left-oriented photographers contributed notably. For example, in Morris Engel's 4 May 1941 Harlem tenement exposé for PM, the photographer used such tendentious effects as a zooming closeup of a tenant's hand plucking out a flimsy wad that the landlord had used to "plug" rat holes, or another closeup, eerie in its off-center angle, of a tenant estimating the size of the water bugs infesting her kitchen. "I'm afraid of them," the woman was quoted in the caption. "I have to get my husband to kill them."[40] The exposé took on an almost science-fiction quality, with the human rendered helpless by an unseen creature whose viewpoint (staring up from a dark hole) would seem to match the camera's. But victimology was not merely the stuff of the radical left.

In its very status as a best-seller, the radically inclined Margaret Bourke-White and Erskine Caldwell's You Have Seen Their Faces (1937) became a part of the mainstream experience. Bourke-White's woeful Southern faces were seen, but the techniques that helped get them seen were also, from another standpoint, highly problematical. If Morris Engel's fancy camera angles verged a bit too much on the leering and the thrilling, You Have Seen Their Faces pointed up graver dangers in the "black victim" genre.

There is a critical difference between an image of the hard pressed and an image of the pathetic. Both may jar the conscience, both may invite action, but while the former at least leaves open the possibility that the middle-class or upper-class viewer will adopt an attitude other

Fig. 1.5. Doris Ulmann. From *Roll, Jordan, Roll*, 1933. Original photograph in the Photographs and Prints Division, Schomburg Center for Research in Black Culture, New York Public Library. Reproduced by permission of the New York Public Library and the Astor, Lenox, and Tilden Foundations.

than condescension, the latter effectively closes off that possibility. Visions of the pathetic reinforce customary relationships between the powerful and the powerless. Bourke-White's black subjects, to a much greater extent than her whites, fall into the pathetic category. Consider the physical positions in which blacks appear in *You Have Seen Their Faces*. Lying, sprawling, crouching, kneeling, huddling blacks are everywhere, from the convict asleep in leg-irons to the little girl huddled, animal-like, in front of a sign advertising "live baits such is [*sic*] miners crickets roches [*sic*]." Camera angles and lighting accentuate the hopelessly distorted. The deformed lad sitting, limbs askew, in the rocking chair peers up from a world of menacing shadows, including his sister's directly above him on the wall. On another page, the pregnant farmwoman's body seems to balloon into the viewer's space. The photographic result of Bourke-White's unannounced visit to a College Grove, Tennessee, black church service proved as disturbing as her modus operandi. The fundamentalist preacher all but leaps out of the picture, mouth open, bulging eyes lit up by Bourke-White's flash, face like a cross between a minstrel and a ghoul. Even black *culture* has become distorted, the religious turned into the lurid. By contrast, in her treatment of a fundamentalist *white* service, Bourke-White shows energetic rituals at a distance that both preserves the dignity of the participants and allows the viewer to reach a variety of possible conclusions.[41]

Hence, particularly for black subjects, an angry camera becomes a demeaning camera, with the effect intensified by Caldwell's fictionalized quotations used in the captions. "I got more children now than I know what to do with," the pregnant woman is made to say, "but they keep coming along like watermelons in the summertime." And below the closeup of a tobacco farmer sprawled apathetically on his bundles in the warehouse: "The auction boss talks so fast a colored man can't hardly ever tell how much his tobacco crop sells for" (fig. 1.6).[42] Amid the implicit protest, one finds the return of conventional associations here: slow on the mental intake, fast on the reproductive outtake, watermelon-conscious through and through. Caldwell and Bourke-White probably would have rejected the notion of "natural" black tendencies, but *You Have Seen Their Faces* suggests that, by reason of environment if not nature, these tendencies have developed nevertheless. Stereotypes, banished from the front door, creep in through the back. In a sense, viewers in 1937 had already seen these faces, or at least imagined them. What of the ex-slaves who did not wear foolish grins, or the farmers who were not fatalistic, or the share-cropper mothers who were not bloated? What of the black interac-tions other than those at church or in a relief line? And what of black religion apart from the grotesque? Rarely found in the Caldwell–Bourke-White parade of hideousness is also what is missing from most of the late-1930s–40s U.S. Housing Authority "before rehabilitation" slum views, whose utter hopelessness was meant to be juxtaposed with inspiring "after rehabilitation" follow-ups (figs. 1.7, 1.8). Absent is any impression of functioning minds, capable of creating the social and

Fig. 1.6. Margaret Bourke-White. From *You Have Seen Their Faces.* "The Auction Boss Talks So Fast a Colored Man Can't Hardly Ever Tell How Much His Tobacco Crop Sells For." Statesboro, Ga. 1937. Copyright © Margaret Bourke-White Estate.

Fig. 1.7. Richard Oliver. Slum dwelling, before clearance. Macon, Ga. 1940. U.S. Housing Authority. National Archives.

cultural patterns that, as sociologist James Borchert has written of black alley life in Washington, D.C., "helped . . . mitigate, circumvent, and occasionally avoid the disasters that confronted [residents] daily, as well as providing meaning, form, substance, and pleasure for their lives."[43] Victims, no less than "colorful darkies," could too easily end up depersonalized.

"These pictures lack artistic value," complained one Harlem resident about a 1939 photo-exhibition concerning his neighborhood. "They only show the lower living conditions of Harlem. Get pictures that will show Negroes in a better light."[44] Pictures that showed blacks in a particularly rosy light, images of uplift and success, were in fact gotten in the thirties and forties. Such images came from several sources. Black studio photographers catered to the needs of the black

Fig. 1.8. Richard Oliver. New housing project. Macon, Ga. U.S. Housing Authority. National Archives.

elite. Photographers for black newspapers and black-oriented foundations looked to cultivate what the *Chicago Defender* was fond of calling "Race Pride." And photographers for a host of federal relief/rehabilitation agencies sought to showcase New Deal accomplishments among blacks. If the final source was new, the first two were not. Portraits of the "talented tenth" had been the staple of black studios since the earliest days of American photography, and these subjects continued to dominate the depression-era work of such leading camerapeople as: James Van DerZee and Winifred Hall Allen in New York; Addison and Robert Scurlock in Washington, D.C.; Emma King Woodard in Dallas; Paul Poole in Atlanta; Richard Roberts in Columbia, South Carolina; and Leonard Hyman and Prentice Herman Polk at Alabama's Tuskegee Institute. What Van DerZee developed with his elegantly appointed scenes and Poole with his soft focusing, what Roberts developed with his classically composed family groups and Polk with his warmly lit faces, were polished versions of a polished portion of black society (fig. 1.9). Of course, severe economic pressures on many of these studios in the 1930s discouraged photographic work among nonpaying (i.e., working-class) subjects. (These photographers did some work among non-elites, though at least in the cases of Van DerZee and Polk the images were problematical. Van DerZee's street scenes, even those outside relief stations, remained all too polished while Polk's portraits of rural folk near Tuskegee too often slipped into rustic cuteness. How many black portrait photographers may have been more adventurous in nonstudio work deserves more attention.)[45]

Market forces had their distinct pull: "The No. 1 priority for most black photographers in those days was to make money," the Washington, D.C., black photographer Robert McNeill recounted recently. "You made the pictures that the subjects would buy. [Addison] Scurlock used to say, 'if you didn't see the face, you lost the dollar.' And generally, what people wanted were the conventional shots. It's like that old cartoon I used to have up on my wall . . . person comes into a photographic studio, and says, 'I want a picture of me as I ain't.' When you had bills to pay, a family to support, you weren't in a good position to say no."[46] But in the case of Van DerZee—and, one suspects, others—the economic factor was not the only driving force in the creation of style. As Van DerZee explained his approach many years later: "All the photos in these [1960s–70s] books these people give me—I can't understand the object of making them. Pictures of four marked-up walls, people with clothes hanging off them. They seem to me to show a lot of misery and a lot of negligence. Photographers today don't do any retouching. I always try to depict people at their best, but nowadays photographers seem to believe in 'tell it as it is.' "[47]

Telling it "as it should be" often revealed more about notions of decorum than about individual character. Thus, the fashionable Harlemites, posing for Van DerZee in their raccoon coats next to a stylish automobile, show only the slightest of emotions (fig. 1.9). Even in Van DerZee's particularly opulent world, one finds the note of polite reserve that, repeated time and again in the work of other portraitists, lay at the core of black "class." "It is not poverty that outrages [the] sensibilities [of the upper tenth]," reported Horace Cayton and St. Clair Drake in *Black Metropolis* (1945), "but lack of public decorum—ignorance, boisterousness, uncouthness, low behavior."[48] Asserting a world untouched by the depression, asserting a world that defied traditional white assumptions about black behavior, these portraits often ended up as rigidly stylized as their "colorful darky" and "pathetic victim" opposites.

Newspaper photographers obviously ranged outside the elegant sitting room. But striking here is the extent to which even the most politically militant black weeklies continued to accent the visually upbeat in the 1930s–40s. While the standard "police file" pictures (murders, trials, fires, etc.) found their way into black newspapers, and while there was some attention to antidiscrimination meetings and

Fig. 1.9. James Van DerZee. "Couple in Raccoon Coats," New York City. 1932. Copyright © 1969 by James Van DerZee. All rights reserved.

pickets, there was no outpouring of "problem" shots. When the *New Orleans Call*'s Nat Harris, the *California Eagle*'s Vera Jackson, the *Chicago Defender*'s Daniel Day and James Gushiniere, and the *Pittsburgh Courier*'s Billy Rowe and Emmanuel F. Joseph did their frequent feature coverages, they were not ordinarily concerned with the common workplace, home, or street—or, if they were, these newspapers were not ordinarily choosing to publish such shots.[49]

For example, when the *Courier* sent Rowe to Mississippi in February 1940 for a photo-feature on the Natchez and Vicksburg black communities, the resulting five-picture spread included shots of the Dumas Drug Store ("said to be the finest colored drug store in the state"), a prominent Vicksburg dentist, a one-time Vicksburg postal employee who had become a successful physician, the Brunfield High School Marching Band, and the black-owned Robbins Funeral Home. All were testaments, in one way or another, to black ambition and organizational skill as well as professional and business acumen. When the *Defender* sent correspondent/photographer Dan Burley to cover the January–February 1937 floods in the Midwest and South, the resulting pictures took a rather different tack from the text. Visuals emphasized black contributions to the relief effort—black Red Cross officials issuing boat permits in Evansville, Indiana, or volunteers from the DeMoyne College football team policing a refugee center in Memphis—while the text explored charges of racial discrimination in refugee assistance and forced black labor on the levees. What whites could do, newspaper visuals assured, blacks could do just as well: community volunteers made good, military enlistees made grade, business entrepreneurs made miracles, artists made magic. "They're Stimulating, Sparkling, and Real," noted the headline above a 1938 *New York Amsterdam News* photo-feature on jazz composer Bob Howard and colleagues. Often a bit *too* good to be real—noble poses, yearbook smiles, monumentalizing camera angles produced role-model *types* more often than they presented individuals. If personalities were often submerged in the process, so was any questioning of an essentially conservative value system underlying the definition of success. With some exception made for "special" black musical and artistic talents, blacks were to be, in this view, better whites than whites.

Fig. 1.10. Kenneth Space. "Queen of Honor, Formal Dance," Xavier
University, New Orleans. 1936. Reproduced by permission of Harmon
Foundation.

Upbeat themes extended to the work of photographers commissioned by such black-oriented institutions as the Harmon Foundation,
which in 1936 sent the white New York photographer and filmmaker
Kenneth Space into the heart of the Deep South to document black
life. Over two-thirds of the Space file concerns the talented tenth,
particularly the intellectual elite at Atlanta and Howard universities,
Talladega College, and other black institutions. By presenting a considerable range of intellectual and artistic endeavors on these cam-

puses, the Space file countered conventional associations of black higher education with agricultural, domestic science, and theological training. No Bible-thumping aggies were these collegians: dental labs and social-work classes, snappy dressers, camera clubs, and sorority functions mirrored the scene at white colleges (fig. 1.10). Well-groomed, Space's subjects were also hardworking; the emphasis on student jobs, underscoring the limited financial resources of many of the students, also supplied a particularly virtuous tone to campus life. What whites could accomplish, blacks could accomplish without the same head start.

To be sure, all was not purely tendentious here, for Space managed to avoid the stiffness characteristic of so much black-success depiction. But even with Space's unusually natural visions, the point remains that the photographer gave overwhelming documentary priority to a narrow slice of black experience. What's more, Space's depiction of happy, productive campus environments raises a certain paradox. If these scenes were testaments to black intelligence and determination, they could also be seen, from another standpoint, as testaments to the success of a "separate-but-equal" educational structure in the South. In the very era of major legal challenges to collegiate Jim Crow (i.e., *Missouri ex rel Gaines v. Canada*, reaching the Supreme Court in 1938), all appeared well at Talladega. In fact, such was the very impression given in *Life's* October 1938 feature on blacks, which included a photograph of a spirited Talladega College dance class taken by none other than Kenneth Space.

On the government photography front, project shots—designed to justify the use of funds that many New Deal critics did not want spent on poor people in general and blacks in particular—dominated the principal photo-files of the Federal Emergency Relief Administration, Public Works Administration, Works Progress Administration, National Youth Administration, Civilian Conservation Corps, U.S. Public Health Service, and related 1930s–40s agencies. Dedication and discipline served as the thematic keynotes for black subjects: the black laborer bent attentively over a sprinkler apparatus in a Washington, D.C., WPA airport repair project; black children, expectant and cooperative, being registered at a Charleston, South Carolina, typhoid in-

Fig. 1.11. Unidentified National Youth Administration photographer. "Work Experience in the Operation of Office Machines by NYA Girls," Washington, D.C. Ca. 1940. National Archives.

oculation clinic; the black photo-lab trainee who, the NYA caption notes, "has started a small community business of his own."

Such depictions were not always free of condescension: hence, the WPA shot of a 105-year-old ex-slave in a Columbus, Ohio, adult literacy class, standing next to a blackboard upon which he has just written his name. One is not so terribly far, with this image, from the notion of the white man's burden. Depictions could also be rather heavy-handed, as in the NYA photo of black girls learning the operation of an office machine in Washington, D.C., with a portrait of none other than Lincoln hanging on the wall just above them (fig. 1.11). At times, there was worse, particularly in WPA Southern work. One observes Oscar Jordan's 1936 shot of black women singing spirituals while working on a moss-mattress project in Savannah, Georgia (fig. 1.12), or Jordan's caption reference to "three-year-old pickaninnies" in Montgomery, Alabama. "Uncle Jess Dolly, negro, and his ox, Tom, who hauled sand for WPA curb and gutter work," explained the caption for a 1937 W. Lincoln Highton photo from Columbus, Alabama; never were humans and animals given equal credit in a WPA white image. What's more, there was not always sufficient questioning of conventional assumptions about black accomplishments. "Success," in Woodrow Wilson's 1938 image of a WPA household training graduate serving drinks to white ladies in Durham, North Carolina, may well have been greater in the white photographer's mind than the black subject's. That the New Deal could put blacks to work while reaffirming deeply entrenched economic and cultural structures constituted an effective sales pitch in the 1930s, as these Jordan, Highton, and Wilson shots illustrate. Hence, while project photography helped to counter the image of blacks "falling asleep" over WPA shovels, while

Fig. 1.12. Oscar Jordan. "Mattress Making." Savannah, Ga. 1936. Works Progress Administration. National Archives.

even the most patronizing of these photos avoided the pictorial extremes of *Life* or *Fortune*, while the files gave at least tentative recognition to blacks in professional (teacher, doctor, nurse) or creative (studio art, music, theater) roles, definite limits to documentary imaginativeness emerged here. Just as the FERA-black or WPA-black nexus was problematical in economic-assistance terms, it also proved problematical in photographic terms.

One should make special note here of the NYA file. It was one thing for project photography to show blacks benefiting from New Deal programs. It was quite another for such photography to suggest that New Deal programs were placing blacks and whites together, on equal footing, in the same work or training sites. The difference touched on the very definition of the New Deal, and in this respect the work of Barbara Wright, Dan Nichols, and the other white NYA camerapeople represented a departure from the project norm. Out of every five images showing black NYA enrollees, one also included white enrollees. True, the settings were usually Chicago or Detroit, not Birmingham, but the interracial proportion was still significantly higher than that found in WPA, USHA, or FERA photography in northern cities. In a series from an NYA cafeteria in Chicago, blacks and whites appear in both the serving and receiving lines—the angle of one shot (a young black man shown prominently in the immediate foreground, loading his tray opposite a *white* female server) raises connotations of a revision in traditional racial roles (fig. 1.13). Similarly, a wave-to-the-camera crowd shot from a mechanical training site in Detroit shows blacks and whites grasping one another's shoulders, hoisting one another into view; the closeup effect, eliminating the particulars of the NYA environment, creates the impression of youth racial harmony prevailing anywhere and everywhere. Self-conscious poses, artificial arrangements, yes—but integrated shots, nevertheless. So it was that racial progressivism and documentary cheeriness both came into play in the NYA file; only in a corner of one of the interracial cafeteria scenes, in which a black coffee-tender assumes what is almost a mockingly exaggerated service pose, does one find the cheeriness subverting itself (fig. 1.14). While whites exchange direct and convincing glances along the serving line, the black coffee-pourer, set off physically as well as psychologically from her colleagues, remains all the more distant in her strikingly artificial "enthusiasm," perhaps revealing in the process the doubts and tensions lying within and beyond the NYA setting.

While there is no evidence that the NYA photographic staff received repeated instructions to produce interracial images, the agency atmosphere—influenced by a genuine racial liberal at the top, Aubrey Williams, along with a particularly aggressive black advisor, Mary McLeod Bethune—encouraged such experimentation. It was the same atmosphere that often produced NYA press releases making pointed mention of full black participation in residential work projects. And it was the same atmosphere that led state program administrators to take unusual care in explaining racial discrepancies. As West Virginia ad-

Fig. 1.13. Unidentified National Youth Administration photographer. "Food Service Employees at NYA Lunch Counter," Chicago. Ca. 1940. National Archives.

ministrator Glenn S. Callaghan noted in a 24 September 1940 telegram to national information director Herbert Little: "Six Negro youths taking aviation mechanics training at West Virginia State College. South Charleston (NYA residential project) none. Reason—did not choose this training. 25 had eight weeks training previously."[50]

Somewhat touchy in the turn-of-the-1940s context, government images of interracial work sites became more acceptable with the arrival of war. In this sense, the NYA file anticipated the racial cooperation theme that photographers for war information agencies (the Office of Emergency Management, the U.S. Office of the Coordinator of Information, and the Office of War Information, into which the OEM and OCI were absorbed in 1942) struck frequently after Pearl Harbor. Howard Liberman's "Americans All" series, taken at a California

Fig. 1.14. Unidentified National Youth Administration photographer. "Food Service Employees at NYA Lunch Counter," Chicago. Ca. 1940. National Archives.

Fig. 1.15. Howard Liberman, "Americans All," Long Beach, Calif. 1942. Office of War Information. Library of Congress.

bomber plant for the OWI in July 1942, epitomized the trend In one shot, black and white metal workers are shown laboring side by side over the wing of a P-47 pursuit plane. In another, carefully posed black, Latino, and Chinese workers rub shoulders as they gaze heavenward at a newly constructed plane's test flight (fig. 1.15). "In the armed forces and on the production line," one of the captions lectures, "Americans of every race and creed fight shoulder to shoulder to defeat the forces which threaten to destroy their liberties." Soaring camera angles, closeups highlighting determined faces and skilled hands, underline the point: New Deal beneficiaries had turned into national assets, the "uplifted" black into the "valuable" black. With the establishment of an aggressive Negro Press Section within the OWI (headed by the black editor Theodore Poston, and including the ambitious young black photographer Roger Smith), with the release of two glossy OWI Domestic Branch pamphlets, "Negroes and the War" and "Manpower: One-Tenth of a Nation," images of black strength and interracial cooperation gained added circulation. As one of the OWI's leading white photographers, Alfred Palmer, later recalled: "Poston and I were pretty much in tune; we'd go out for a drink, and talk about the themes we wanted to emphasize in pictures. We wanted to show blacks doing front-line assembly jobs with intelligence, with ability; and we wanted to show them with the kind of dramatic closeups that would tell a story in a single image. Things had changed since Pearl Harbor: when I had been out in the field photographing defense plants [for the OEM] in 1940–1941, the only blacks I'd see in those places were the guys pushing brooms."[51]

"Negroes and the War," incorporating the writing of moderate black commentator Chandler Owen, pictures from an assortment of government agencies and private news services, and editorial layout contributions from Stryker's former FSA unit transferred to the OWI, reflected both the strengths and deficiencies of the nationalist genre. Photos of black and white auto workers ratifying a CIO contract, and of black and white schoolchildren eating federally sponsored lunches together, suggested new directions in American democracy. Photos of black Army officers training enlistees, of a parachute factory's black manager, of black government personnel in Washington, suggested new opportunities for assertiveness that were, in fact, opened by the war. Heavy-handed as the camera work was, sociologically significant stories emerged here, from the expansion of the black medical profession to the movement of black women into nondomestic jobs.

"We are not ashamed of working with our hands," noted Owen, "but a progressing world now offers many of us a chance to prove ourselves in varied jobs and occupations." Owen's tone was carefully nonthreatening, as it had to be, but there was a point at which the textually or pictorially nonthreatening became the retreating. "Negroes and the War" too often reached that point. Acknowledging, again passingly, the Navy's "past" refusal to admit blacks on an equal basis, the pamphlet simply ignored the continuing issue of a segregated military. Acknowledging, at the very outset, that black progress had been "too slow," the pamphlet never described the nature of black concerns. In such fashion, the work continually backed away from the implications that it could not help but raise. And so it was with much nationalist material: the desperate assuredness of the imagery (Joe Louis pictured in military garb on the back cover of "Negroes and the War," declaring: "We'll win 'cause we're on God's side") belied a host of tensions and contradictions. Of course, "safe" nationalism was a relative concept at the OWI; as mild as "Negroes and the War" was, even it rankled some conservatives, who were apt to oppose any OWI foray on the racial subject, and who were also apt to suspect Negro Press Section head Poston and others of radical sympathies. Voices of paternalism were not silent. "Nothing brings more pride to the average Negro reader," advised one OWI consultant, "than a picture showing him guarding some white man's property."[52] The OWI Overseas Branch was even more cautious, with but one of the 124 "Portrait of America" photo-sets featuring blacks.

Nationalist imagery opened certain doors but avoided others. At the very least, Liberman's metalworker was a cut above Highton's Uncle Jess Dolly, who was in turn a cut above Bourke-White's grinning old-timer, who "forgot to remember how old I is." But what about black life away from the specialized environments of the defense factory, the NYA training site, the WPA work site, or, for that matter, the college campus? What about the complex lives not captured in the various *types* surveyed thus far? This was the more formidable challenge for 1930s–40s photographers—for reform-minded photographers whose first instinct was often to try to *shock*, for government agency photographers whose first priority was often to *celebrate*, for black photographers who were often encouraged to *glorify*. Agency pressures and photographers' biases were not the only obstacles: in many situations, black subjects undoubtedly found the presentation of type to be necessary, or alternatively, advantageous.

How to avoid the predictable? To some extent, one can look here to the uncharacteristic images from agencies whose more typical work has already been reviewed. Peter Sekaer's 1938–39 work for the USHA

Fig. 1.16. Peter Sekaer. Slum District, New Orleans. 1939. U.S. Housing Authority. National Archives.

transcended the "before-and-after" norm: views of New Orleans, Memphis, and Washington, D.C., side streets emphasize not the decrepit conditions but the richness and mystery of "unrehabilitated" life (fig. 1.16). Set in deep shadows, Sekaer's elliptical visions of stoop-sitters in conversation, children at play, outdoor cobblers and washer-women at work, rebuff easy conclusions about degraded denizens of black slums. Just as important, these visions undercut standard assumptions about the documentary photographer's (and photo viewer's) privileged entry into, privileged understanding of poorer neighborhoods. Sekaer's "befores" do not imply "afters," and that is their achievement. Lewis Hine's work for the WPA's National Research Project, a 1936–37 survey of fourteen eastern industrial communities, produced black portraits that were few in number but remarkable in quality. The engaging portrait of a Scott's Run, West Virginia, coal miner at rest—confident smile, eyes meeting the camera intelligently, smoking pipe cocked expertly at the side of the mouth—has the unpleading quality that is so notable in Hine's classic white working-class studies of earlier de-

Fig. 1.17. Robert McNeill. "New Car," South Richmond, Va. 1938.
Collection of Robert McNeill. Reproduced by permission of Robert McNeill.

cades. Warmer than Sekaer's visions, Hine's images nevertheless steered clear of romanticism. Indeed, in the shot of a young resident who is doing his own photographing of dreary row houses in High Point, North Carolina, Hine goes beyond warm engagement to raise intriguing questions about whose perspective is most important in defining working-class black life. (Few of the communities selected for the National Research Project had significant black populations. When Hine had more opportunity to photograph blacks during the depression, as in his 1931 coverage of Red Cross drought relief efforts in Arkansas, he did so, and came up with some provocative views of interracial relief lines. Such work calls for a scholarly reassessment not only of Hine-and-blacks but of Hine's 1930s photography in toto).[53]

Photography for other special WPA ventures—Federal Arts Project and Federal Writers' Project studies—also produced more imaginative images, such as the slice-of-life street scenes by Robert McNeill in Richmond, Virginia. McNeill, a black photographer who gathered images in 1938 for the WPA historical volume, *The Negro in Virginia*, captured a sense of spontaneity that was rarely found in the work of the camerapeople, black or white, surveyed previously. When McNeill focused on a group of young Richmonders standing around a new automobile that one of them had just purchased, the result was nearly as far from the work of Billy Rowe as it was from the work of Margaret Bourke-White (fig. 1.17). McNeill might easily have chosen to shoot this scene from the ground up, heightening the stature of the young men. He did not. McNeill might easily have chosen to leave out two or more of the figures, making the apparent car-owner (foot on the running board, hand inside the window) the crux of the picture. He did not. Alternatively, McNeill might have chosen to show more of the surrounding working-class neighborhood, creating an accent on progress in the midst of a humble environment. He did not. Rather than paragons of black success, rather than symbols of Race Pride, these are young men enjoying the conversation, the feel of a new car, and the attention of two young women on a porch in the background. To the extent that McNeill's subjects are responding to the camera (no hidden-camera tricks here), they seem to be responding as individuals, not race- or class-role players.

If the photography of McNeill, Sekaer, and Hine suggested possibilities for uncondescending, nonworshipful documentation of common black life, so did the work of the New York photographers, largely white, associated with the Photo League. The league's roots, lying with the Communist party–directed Workers' Film and Photo League of the early 1930s, were not promising in this regard. Yet the league's group productions, more often than not, steered clear of the victimology or hero-worship conventions. Case in point was the "Harlem Document," assembled largely between 1936 and 1939 under the direction of Aaron Siskind and, though never published in full, exhibited widely in New York. True, the assemblage (followed in 1940 by the related series, "The Most Crowded Block") included damning tenement and domestic-labor pictures, some of which were later published, to the accompaniment of sensationalistic captions, in *Look*. However, the visions of Siskind, Sid Grossman, Jack Mendelsohn, Richard Lyon, Harold Corsini, and the other contributors were not limited to straight muckraking.

There is irony, but no simple indictment, in the "Most Crowded Block" view of a man asleep in his bedroom, walls plastered with pin-ups of *white* movie stars (fig. 1.18). There is disquietude, but not hopelessness, in the "Harlem Document" view of the merchant gazing pensively out of his shop window, surrounded by a clutter of unsold knickknacks. There is the haunting, but also the humorous, in Siskind's view of young boys, attired in men's hats and long coats, rolling dice on a tree stump. The Photo League's Harlem is a harsh environment, as well it might be, but it is not a place that bludgeons the souls of its inhabitants. In contrast to the earlier Workers' Film and Photo League material, the Harlem stories allow their subjects, as well as their viewers, some spiritual and intellectual breathing room; proof was partly in the variety of impressions registered by Harlemites when the "Document" was exhibited on its subjects' turf. The subtle visions of the "Harlem Document" and "The Most Crowded Block" were also educated visions. The undertaking was not simply a matter of a few curious photographers spending an hour or two in the "heart of darkness." *Photo Notes*, the league's publication, described the role of "project consultants on statistics and economic information," and

Siskind would later recall the "visits to the scene, the casual conversations, and more formal interviews—talking, listening, looking, looking. . . . You read what's been written, and dig out the facts and figures for your own writing. . . . And finally, the pictures themselves, each one planned, talked, taken, examined in terms of the whole."[54] To be sure, the final coverage was not nearly so systematic as might be suggested by Siskind's comments, though it did not fall any shorter of the promise than Photo League studies of white neighborhoods. And Siskind, in particular, sometimes overindulged a sense of the alluring poetry of Harlem life. Despite such limitations, however, the "Harlem Document" and "The Most Crowded Block" constituted proof that white photographers could approach not just individual blacks but an entire black community with care and imagination.

Fig. 1.18. Aaron Siskind. From "The Most Crowded Block," New York City. 1940. Aaron Siskind Collection, Library of Congress. Reproduced by permission of Aaron Siskind.

McNeill. Hine. Sekaer. The Photo Leaguers. Other exceptions, such as Irving Rusinow, whose explorations of economic and religious life in Putnam County, Georgia, part of a USDA Bureau of Agricultural Economics community studies series in 1941, combined the naturalism of McNeill with a broader sociological reach, or Helen Levitt, whose studies of black and white children's sidewalk drawings, taken for the New York City Federal Arts Project, were remarkably unpatronizing. These photographers hardly constituted a concerted movement, yet there is at least an indirect connection via the organization and the photographers of prime interest for this study. Sekaer had accompanied Walker Evans through portions of the latter's 1935–36 southeastern tour and later was the curator of an FSA exhibit for the College Art Association; there is certainly a strong touch of Evans in Sekaer's photographic meditations. McNeill remembers being much taken with FSA photography, particularly an Arthur Rothstein view of blacks in a dance hall, at the time of his own government work.[55] The Bureau of Agricultural Economics community studies team that included Rusinow also included Dorothea Lange. Hine, the old warhorse of documentary photography, admired the work of the younger FSAers and corresponded with Stryker. The Photo League exhibited FSA work, sponsored lectures by Stryker and his camerapeople, and paid frequent tribute to the FSA in *Photo Notes*. In fact, league membership included, at various points, Rothstein, Rosskam, and Shahn. "If you have organized [what] looks like a 'Veterans of the FSA Section,' " Shahn wrote the league in July 1940, "may I join too?"[56] If the reports in *Photo Notes* were correct, FSA visitors to the League gallery, and particularly Lange, took considerable interest in the Harlem Document.

Could Lange and the others have perceived in the Harlem Document the sort of approach that the FSA had already taken to the documentation of the black experience? Amid the exceptions to the generally type-ridden presentation of blacks in the 1930s–40s, could the FSA have been the *grand* exception, the touchstone for innovation? We return, with a sense of the perils of the photo-historical territory, to the Farm Security Administration.

2

FSA Photography:
Administrative Contexts,
Quantitative Measures

In late October 1938, a group of prominent farmers in Adams County, Mississippi, submitted a petition, endorsed by the county's board of supervisors, to Mississippi's congressional delegation. It had nothing to do with cotton prices, nothing to do with acreage reduction programs, nothing to do with flood control efforts in the wake of the previous winter's Mississippi River disasters. Rather, the petition concerned a certain assistant rural rehabilitation agent employed by— and, the farmers emphasized, *in*— the Farm Security Administration office in Natchez. Morelee Frazier was a black man. And that did not sit well with the Farmers Bureau, the self-styled guardian of tradition in this history-soaked corner of southwestern Mississippi. Since "young white ladies are employed in this office and other offices of the Court House and are forced to come in contact with this negro," argued the petitioners, "the placing of a negro in this position [is] against the best interest and public welfare of this county and its citizenship." The petitioners demanded Frazier's immediate removal, as well as that of his white supervisor, who had allegedly approved the appointment. "Be it further resolved . . . that [the present supervisor] be . . . replaced with a man . . . who is competent and equipped to carry on the duties of the office and who understands the needs and interests of [the] citizenship and that his assistant be a white man."[1]

Mississippi legislators, leery of the New Deal in general and the FSA in particular, were eager to fan the flames of controversy. "You are a Southerner," Congressman Dan McGehee wrote the then–FSA National Deputy Administrator C.B. Baldwin, "and can readily appreciate the resentment that will be expressed if a negro is placed in any of the county FSA offices." Senator Theodore Bilbo, predictably enough, was more bombastic. "I do not know who is responsible for this outrage," Bilbo warned an FSA state administrator, "but you, as a good Mississippian, should clean out this situation at once. . . . Mississippi is still a white man's country and we do not want any negroes bumping up against our white girls in the official life of the state."[2] FSA officials responded swiftly. The national office's letter to McGehee sought to justify the Frazier appointment on traditional, separate-but-equal grounds (black rehab agents working with black clients, white agents with white clients), assuring the congressman that the black assistant spent all his time in the field and had no occasion to come into contact with white office employees. Even the matter of the letter's signature appears to have been handled cautiously. With Baldwin out of the office at the time, the letter might logically have been signed by the FSA chief, Will Alexander. But Alexander was a well-known racial progressive: "[Milo] Perkins should sign the letters rather than Dr. Alexander," an office memo advised.[3] In the meantime, FSA Regional Director T. Roy Reid was assuring Bilbo that "it is not the desire of this office to place a negro worker where it is objectionable to the people."[4] His implication that "the people" did not include Frazier's black clients must have assuaged Bilbo. And so must have Morelee Frazier's removal from his Adams County assignment within a week of the original complaint. Frazier's erstwhile boss remained, though now with an all-white staff.

The Adams County tempest hardly constituted a major event in the history of the Farm Security Administration. But the episode illustrates several important points about the organization of which the documentary photography unit was a part. In the first place, controversy, racial and nonracial, seemed to follow the Farm Security Administration more doggedly than it did most New Deal agencies. The troubled existence went back to the FSA's pre-1937 status as the Resettlement Administration. Created in May 1935 by an executive order rather than an act of congress—a point that critics never failed to raise—the Resettlement Administration consolidated and expanded an array of experimental programs initiated under various administrative auspices in the New Deal's early years. From the Federal Emergency Relief Administration and the Agricultural Adjustment Administration came programs of land-use planning and farm-debt adjustment. From FERA and the Department of Interior's Subsistence Homesteads Division came the program of planned communities—cooperative or semicooperative farm projects for resettled tenants, and, on what proved to be a smaller scale, "greenbelt" communities for destitute urbanites. And from FERA's Division of Rural Rehabilitation and Stranded Populations came the program of loans, grants, and guidance for tenants and sharecroppers, as well as federally operated camps for migrant agricultural laborers. That the RA was committing such time and money to a segment of the rural population the agricultural establishment was apt to call "lazy" and "shiftless," that the RA was seeking to alter timeworn patterns of tenant dependence on landlord finances and wisdom, raised conservative hackles; the impulse for centralized planning, much in evidence in the resettlement program, spurred even more bitter resentment.

A typical example of such conservative bile appeared in a February 1936 *Washington Post* series on the Resettlement Administration, entitled, caustically enough, "Utopia Unlimited." "Occupying all or parts of 19 Washington buildings," began investigator Felix Bruner, "are administrative directors and staff of one of the most far-flung experiments in paternalistic government ever attempted in the U.S. [The activities] of this organization, which is really a government within a government of the U.S., do not require Congressional sanction or approval. It . . . virtually rules the lives of hundreds of thousands of people, who are told how much they can spend for food, for clothing, for rent, what crops they shall plant, . . . how they shall conduct the most minute details of their lives. At the head is a man who once wrote, 'I shall roll up my sleeves and make over America.' "[5] The man was Rexford Tugwell—"Professor" Rexford Tugwell, as the *Washington Post* series called him, in a reminder that Tugwell's background lay in the classrooms of Columbia University, not the farms of America; "Rex the Red," as other critics, inside and outside government, dubbed him. It was not just Tugwell's ideas about greenbelt towns and cooperative farming, about forcing landlords to share acreage reduction payments with their tenants, about expanding federal regulation of

patent medicines and other items of prime interest to agrarian con-
sumers, that disturbed mainstreamers in the U.S. Department of Agriculture, Congress, and the business world. It was also Tugwell's combative style, his irascible personality. Tugwell was hardly a smooth
political diplomat, and this left him, and the Resettlement Administration generally, open to abuse even beyond the predictable *Washington Post* sort. "Tugwell Has Staff of 12,089 to Create 5,012 Relief Jobs,
Pays His Aides $1,750,000 a Month While Workers on Projects Get
$300,000," charged *The New York Times* (17 November 1935) in a
pot-shot that ignored the fact that it was not the RA's main purpose
to create relief jobs.[6]

Tugwell's resignation at the end of 1936 was probably inevitable;
leadership of the agency passed to better diplomats in Alexander
(1937–40) and Baldwin (1940–42). Congress sanctioned, via the
Bankhead-Jones Farm Tenancy Act of 1937, a reconstituted Farm Security Administration, and the agency's general emphasis shifted from
agrarian experimentation to consolidation of economic progress. With
the addition of the tenant-purchase program, designed to turn promis-
ing tenants into landowners (though it ultimately involved only
12,000 tenants, a fraction of the 695,000 tenants who received standard rehabilitation loans during the course of the RA/FSA), the FSA
made a more direct appeal to traditional family-farm values. Even with
these changes, however, the FSA never shed its trouble-making image, particularly in the South. There, when conservatives perceived
FSA-promoted economic change, they tended to perceive racial
change just around the corner. On a purely analytic level, of course,
matters of race and class were not neatly separable; add an irrational
element, and they were hardly separable at all. As Ruby Pugh, wife of
a dry-goods merchant and member of the school board in Columbus,
Mississippi, complained to the FSA national office in 1941: "I know
that government lending without security, and wastefulness in general, is killing what little thrift and initiative our negroes had to start
with. I know that the aim of this administration is to force racial
equality on us here in the South and the farm program is the biggest
weapon they have." That "our negroes" were actually not benefiting
from FSA programs to the same degree as whites—low-income white

farmers in Mississippi were seven times more likely than blacks to receive standard rehabilitation loans—proved irrelevant to Mrs. Pugh or, for that matter, to Mr. J. J. Pugh, who had warned earlier that the end result of FSA involvement would be "the negroes in school with our children and Mrs. Roosevelt dictating what Communistic racial equality things they shall be taught."[7]

The very fact, complained Milton Tainter of the Louisiana Farm Bureau the same year, that FSA officials in Washington were willing to grant an audience to "six negroes" from the radical Farmers Union tended to make local blacks uppity: "Any type of government assistance to these people that tended to grant them certain privileges which were out of the ordinary when compared to previous governments tended to make the [racial] situation more serious than it [would have been]."[8] Similarly, when Congressional investigation of the FSA as a "non-essential government expenditure" in 1942—an ultimately fatal assault spearheaded by the National Farm Bureau in cooperation with Tennessee Senator Kenneth McKellar and other longtime FSA foes on Capitol Hill—brought out charges that agency loans were being used to pay the poll taxes of white clients in Hale County, Alabama, conservatives were quick to describe even darker scenarios. The issue, affirmed a January 1942 editorial in Alabama's *Greensboro Watchman*, "is a matter of deep and fundamental principles. We contend, along with Judge [Robert] Greene, that federal money is being used in this manner to buy the control of our elections—and we contend further that it is merely the entering wedge by which the ballot would be thrown open to both races, in the Black Belt as well as throughout the state."[9]

From its birth to its death, from its relations with the Pughs and the *Watchman* to its relations with the Extension Service and other federal farm agencies, the RA/FSA attracted more than its share of negative attention. But, as the Morelee Frazier episode also suggests, FSA leaders were not unwilling to give ground, particularly on racial issues. Tugwell, for all his idealism and stubbornness, never gave racial questions a high priority; broad economic problems, not the particular needs of a minority group, set this upstate New York native's imagination aflame. Will Alexander's commitment to racial progress was undeniable: the ex–Methodist minister had long been a driving force behind the Commission on Inter-racial Cooperation, had served as president of Dillard University, had helped direct the Rosenwald Fund, and had worked with Arthur Raper, Charles Johnson, Edwin Embree, Walter White, and others seeking to awaken interest in racial justice. Yet Alexander, raised in southern Missouri and trained for the ministry in Tennessee, remained a pragmatist. He was quick to remind more militant liberals that, as he wrote in 1922, "America is an aggregate of Gopher Prairies, large and small, and the idea of better race relations must be made to take root in the hard soil of their Main Streets." He was quick to urge blacks to become, as he described in a 1934 address at Howard University, "more class conscious and less race conscious." He was not one to approve of the March on Washington movement, or to savor the reformer Lillian Smith's 1944 novel about an interracial love affair, *Strange Fruit*. "Left free, human beings group themselves according to their tastes, interests, and cultural backgrounds," Alexander assured *Harper's* readers in 1945. "Even without arbitrary segregation, common interests and common backgrounds would probably lead most American Negroes to develop their own way of living and find much of their associations among themselves, as other groups do."[10]

Seeking more patience from an Adam Clayton Powell while he sought more commitment from a Franklin Delano Roosevelt, Alexander pursued a careful liberalism that was shared, for the most part, by his FSA successor. "Beanie" Baldwin, raised in a liberal Virginia business family, educated at Virginia Polytechnic Institute, experienced in the railroad and electrical supply businesses before coming to Washington, had always been more comfortable as a manager than as a social activist. Other Southern liberals in the FSA national and regional offices—Robert Hudgens, T. Roy Reid—were also reluctant to lead the agency into a racial crusade. Hence, while Alexander, Baldwin, and others deplored the considerable differential between white and black access to FSA loans in most southern states, they did not press the issue in any sustained fashion. Blacks were more likely to be applying for FSA loans in 1940 than they had been in 1937, but they were not more likely to be getting them. Hence, when FSA plans

to resettle blacks near Orangeburg, South Carolina, drew heated protests from local whites in 1937, Hudgens authorized a "protective" belt
of land surrounding the black settlement to assure absolute racial separation. And hence, while the FSA made black appointments—the
moderate Joseph H. B. Evans, succeeded in 1940 by Constance Daniel,
as race advisor in the national office; race advisors in the southern
regional offices; assistant farm supervisors (forty-one by 1941); home
management advisors (fifty-five); and nurses (serving in ten medical
associations)—in sufficient numbers to gain favorable comment even
from the *Chicago Defender*, there was only one instance, that of William Walker in the all-black Aberdeen Homesteads of Newport News,
Virginia, of a black appointed to a head supervisory role. None of the
FSA's ten all-black *agricultural* settlements had a black chief. "Not
even the FSA," Baldwin put it later, "was foolhardy enough to try to
force that down the throats of the field organization."[11] When push
came to shove, black assistants could be jettisoned, as well.

This is not to suggest that Alexander, Baldwin, and their colleagues
were obsessed with public relations. But they were well aware of the
agency's image problem, and they made efforts to improve it. One of
Alexander's first acts as FSA chief was a major shake-up in the Information Division. "I [wanted to] clean out all the publicity crowd we
had had," Alexander explained later. "Over the years they had never
told the complete story of what we were doing. . . . I wanted to tell our
story in a thousand communities in America—to the newspapers and
bankers and businessmen—and interpret our work to the people themselves. I knew we would have some sympathy then."[12] Under the direction of ex-novelist John Franklin Carter (brother of FSA photographer Paul) and, briefly at the end of 1936, M. E. Gilfond, the division
had produced some handsome materials for select audiences, including
a much-praised 1936 Resettlement Administration annual report. But,
with the notable exception of the Pare Lorentz film celebrating government-induced agrarian teamwork, "The Plow That Broke the
Plains," the division had been less successful in exploiting mass-media
channels.

Alexander's new appointee was John Fischer, a Texas-born Rhodes
scholar, a Senate reporter for Associated Press, a man with a feel both

for ideas and ways to get them into the public forum. Under the guidance of Fischer and by 1940, top assistant Jack Bryan, the Harvard-educated star journalist from the *Memphis Press-Scimitar*, the division greatly increased its volume of press releases, pamphlets, reports, traveling exhibits, radio spots, and slide shows. The FSA endeavored to sell itself as energetically as other New Deal agencies did: again and again, materials dramatized how the agency had transformed rural eyesores into well-tended farms, and hopeless tenants into healthy, productive, modern agrarians. Experimentalism was given a folksy, populist tone, cooperation reconciled with the ultimate (and safely mainstream) goal of self-sufficiency. "They need our help," as one 1941 exhibit on nutrition declared, "to help themselves." Not surprisingly, the tenant-purchase program drew special attention, quite out of proportion, in fact, to its modest share (13 percent) of the FSA budget. The international crisis of the 1940s gave the division another safe pitch: in one 1941 exhibit, "Home-Grown Food" was equated with "Strength for America." What the public did not know about more radical aspects of FSA activity, Fischer and late-1941 successor Bryan reasoned, would not hurt the public. Thus, when a Texas FSA official sent the national office a draft of a 1942 public report on agency objectives, Bryan crossed out a reference to "encouraging low-income farmers to organize the proper farmers' organizations to make them articulate in political and economic affairs."[13]

On the subject of race, Fischer and Bryan were progressives—but also political and administrative realists. Remembers Ed Trapnell, the FSA regional information chief in Raleigh (1940–42): "Within the agency, I always found the attitude on the race question open and constructive. If there were any really badly-prejudiced people, I never encountered them. Bryan, a brilliant writer and the guy who really helped shape the character of the entire [information] operation, had helped me learn a great deal about black conditions in the Delta when we were both working for the *Press-Scimitar*. But of course at the FSA we all had to be awfully careful not to make things worse than [they] already were [for blacks] in the areas where the agency was trying to upgrade the poorest of the poor."[14]

The key here was careful targeting of publicity materials. Fischer, for example, appears to have steered the efforts of publicity-minded race advisor Constance Daniel in a safe direction—channeling black-related news releases and other materials to black (or notably enlightened white) audiences. As Fischer noted in an October 1940 memo to regional information chiefs: "Mrs. Daniel has established fine outlets with the Negro press. . . . Whenever you get any dope on Negro borrowers or projects, we would appreciate your sending it to us, so Mrs. Daniel will work up a release and arrange for its distribution. . . . Incidentally, you may have information on Negro borrowers in your files that you don't consider worth a release, but which would be very valuable to Mrs. Daniel as material for talks, etc."[15] Daniel appears to have done much of the copywriting herself, from short releases to major spreads, such as that appearing in the April 1940 issue of the NAACP's *Crisis* ("Security for Farmers"). How heavily Daniel's writing was edited by Fischer and Bryan cannot be determined, but the final product generally minimized discussion of special black burdens, particularly noneconomic ones. Only in the final paragraph of the long *Crisis* piece, for instance, did Daniel list the factors working against black farmers: "less opportunity than most to acquire productive land, less access to credit, less [exposure] to education, progressive thinking, and normal community life." (Precisely what "progressive thinking" or "normal community life" entailed, the article never discussed.)[16] Daniel knew how to play the publicity game: in a June 1940 memo to Stryker on Florida migrant coverage, she dwelt not on race relations but the FSA before-and-after progress theme: "Shacks in canal area [of Okeechobee, Florida], with small children in front . . . FSA camp scenes—facility house showing migrant wives washing and ironing and 'neighboring' over tubs, ironing boards."[17]

Even with these sorts of bland project coverages, regional information officials recognized the relatively specialized media market for black-related materials. "Black newspaper editors wanted any pictures, showing improvement in black lives, they could get," recalls Trapnell. "I never even had to suggest stories to them. [Outside the black press] you knew which papers to try, the few with the more progressive editors . . . the *Louisville Courier-Journal*, or the *Nashville Tennesseean*. They were unusual—the *Courier-Journal*, which published a story I did on the FSA program with Marion [Post Wolcott]'s photos, must have been the only [big-city] paper in the world to allow a government publicity man to do the actual writing of a [proposed] feature story."[18] As we will see in chapter 6, regional information chiefs were sometimes apt to consider black-related materials outright liabilities for general audiences.

Contained within the Information Division was Roy Stryker's photographic unit, officially designated the Historical Section. Given a modest charge upon creation by Tugwell in July 1935—"to make accurate descriptions of the various . . . phases of the Resettlement Administration, particularly with regard to the historical, sociological, and economic aspects of the several programs and their accomplishments"—the section very quickly pushed beyond those bounds. Stryker never saw himself taking orders from RA/FSA information chiefs, or, for that matter, from Tugwell, Alexander, or Baldwin. FSA officials, for their part, recognized and respected Stryker's independence. Tugwell, who had known Stryker as a student, teaching colleague, and research collaborator at Columbia University, trusted his judgment. Alexander left the Historical Section untouched in the Information Division shake-up of 1937, as did Baldwin amid the congressional attacks of 1942. Yet Stryker remained acutely aware of agency needs, and it was precisely this awareness that helped keep him on generally amicable terms with FSA administrators. As keen as he was on developing a documentary alternative to what he later called the "goddamn newspaper pictures," Stryker stood as no intellectual dreamer. He knew how precarious the agency's budget was, and, in turn, the section's budget, which teetered on the brink of nothingness at one point in late 1937. He recognized the depth of opposition to FSA reforms that, by and large, he believed in. He also learned quickly that his section's products could generate controversy that would haunt him, the agency, and the Roosevelt administration.

Russell Lee's 1937 photograph of a young Iowa tenant mother—labelled "Tenant Madonna" by an overzealous FSA copywriter and then published in the *Des Moines Register* with a similarly excessive caption—outraged religiously sensitive Iowans and stirred trouble elsewhere in the Midwest. The previous year's furor over Arthur Rothstein's allegedly faked Dakota drought pictures extended well beyond a single region. Charges originally brought by the *Fargo Forum* and half-conceded by the Historical Section, that Rothstein had moved a steer's skull to create particularly dramatic shots, were trumpeted by papers across the country as Republicans tried to embarrass FDR in the heat of the presidential campaign. Complaints about a portable skull led to disputations about government expenditures for "publicity adventures" (*Chicago Tribune*, August 29), remonstrations about an RA "publicity machine" that also included "Ben Shahn, formerly a leader of the left-wing painters of the John Reed Club" (*New York Herald-Tribune*, August 29), and speculations about other RA photographic manipulations (*New York Sun*, August 29).[19] Waste, communism, deception—it had not taken much to elicit the old bugaboos. "Look," Stryker mused later, "they were not after me, but you see [if] they could get their finger on me, they could smear everybody [in the agency]."[20] The Information Division needed skull-less positive press, and time and again Stryker reminded his photographers in the field to get the material for such press. There were times, in fact, when Fischer communicated his desires directly to Stryker's camerapeople. "If you have any time," Fischer wrote Lee in September 1938, "I wish you would talk to Mr. Schwander, in the FSA office at New Orleans, about making some pictures for us on the tenant purchase activities in that region. He told me that some interesting material was available at the Asa Bridwell Farm in Rapides Parish, where 10 families have taken over a plantation under the tenant-purchase program. . . . We are extremely anxious to build up before and after files on both T-P and rehabilitation. If you have time to stop at Lake Dick, we are badly in need of a complete photographic story of this project."[21] As the depression years turned into the war years, Stryker made no bones about his desire to curry favor with politicians apt to think of a non-war-information photographic unit as a government extravagance. (The point will be explored more fully in chapter 5.)

It is no coincidence that nearly one-fifth of the RA/FSA photographs concerned subjects useful for agency promotion efforts: agency construction and land-clearing projects, activities in completed resettlement projects and migrant labor camps, rehabilitation and tenant purchase loan recipients on improved farms, clients being assisted by the agency's farm, home management, and medical advisors. RA/FSA photographers were generally not enthusiastic about taking these shots. "Same old hash," as John Vachon described a set of his pictures from Ohio's Greenhills Homestead, "women hanging clothes on the line, children sliding down slides, etc."[22] But, with the exception of Walker Evans, this was material that they collected in considerable quantity. And even Evans experienced demands for project photography. "I am sure you will be tired of hearing me clamor for more pictures," Stryker warned him in 1936, "but I assure you that this clamor is due to the insistence behind it. The only way that I can protect you from being put out to do project photography . . . will be that you turn in a lot of pictures."[23] It is also no coincidence, as we will find in chapter 5, that even the file's nonproject portion bore an increasingly upbeat tone in the 1940s. "We must have at once," Stryker urged Lee in February 1942, "pictures of men, women, children who appear as if they really believe in the U.S. Get people with a little spirit. Too many in our file now paint the U.S. as an old person's home and that just about everyone is too old to work and too malnourished to care what happens."[24] That there was a good deal more to the RA/FSA file than agency public relations and nationalist pap has been appreciated by commentators over the years; that Stryker worked hard to protect his administrative flank with such routine shots has been less frequently noted.

Stryker's reminders to his photographers about getting agency publicity shots included occasional references to black projects. "I have been checking over the good Negro projects," Stryker wrote Wolcott on 14 April 1939. "Prairie Farms is in Alabama, not very far from Gee's Bend. Talk to Constance [Daniel] about this, and plan to do it later when convenient. If you go anywhere near Flint River in Georgia, stop in and plan to do a story on this project." (When Wolcott was slow in getting these pictures to Washington, Stryker pressed: "Very necessary that we have them, in order to quiet the Administrator's office.")[25] There were not many such references, however. Even rarer, at least in the 1930s, were references to potential black subjects outside the project context. When, for example, the RA/FSA photo-director prepared a list of recommended shooting subjects for Evans's tour of the Deep South in January 1936, he seemed to mention every-thing—from soil erosion to old plantation mansions, from tourist camps to steel mills, from a U.S. Tire Company model town to Clemson College—except the subject of blacks. By contrast, a shoot-ing outline prepared by *Evans* the previous year made specific refer-ences to black life. Perhaps Stryker simply assumed that his photogra-phers needed little encouragement to cover black life; yet it is evident, from Stryker's lengthy correspondence with his camerapeople in the field, that there were numerous subjects on which the photographers hardly required prompting and on which, nevertheless, Stryker com-mented. Lee needed no reminder, when he shot his November 1939 story on the predominantly white town of San Augustine, Texas, to do "portraits of citizens about town . . . the character of people/character of town connection," but the project clearly excited Stryker.[26] When, four months earlier, Lee had written Stryker from Oklahoma, "Would you like a story on the Negro day-laborer? They are in the majority around here, but the Negroes seldom migrate west," Stryker never responded.[27] If Stryker was excited about coverage of any minority group in Lee's Texas and Oklahoma work, it was Mexicans, not blacks.

Stryker's apparent lack of enthusiasm about black subject-matter is worth considering. Especially before the 1940s, when Viking Press pub-lished the Historical Section–Richard Wright collaboration (*12 Mil-lion Black Voices*), Stryker tended to see black material as notably less usable than white images. What is more, a policy of promoting black images might have been viewed as encouragement for pictures liable to spark controversy as explosive as the Rothstein skull crisis. "Would like to do some work on disenfranchisement in the South, as the result of the poll tax," Lange wrote Stryker in May 1938. "Dynamite on this one!"[28] Dynamite, to be sure: Stryker did not respond.

If encouraging nonproject black shots promised trouble, so did the presence of a black photographer on the staff. When Gordon Parks came aboard in the summer of 1942, he was taken on not as a salaried FSA staffer but as a Rosenwald Fund intern, and Stryker appeared reluctant to approve even the internship arrangement. "I don't think he wanted to take me because of the conditions that existed there at the time," Parks later reflected. "It was an all-Southern laboratory; D.C., in 1942, was not the easiest place in the world for a Negro to get along. It wasn't going to make Roy's task any easier and I think they [Rosenwald Fund officials] had to prevail upon him . . . to take me. [Stryker] just felt that I was going to walk into lots of trouble and he had enough trouble of his own. But finally he said, 'OK, well, send him on.' "[29] One of the lab assistants and eventual photographer for Stryker at the OWI, Esther Bubley, later confirmed the hostility toward Parks among the technical personnel: "The people in the darkroom were practically frothing at the mouth, they were so opposed to a black photographer. They sounded like a bunch of rednecks. It's amazing they didn't just destroy Parks's negatives."[30]

But, even apart from the problem of controversy, Roy Emerson Stryker does not appear to have been one of those unusual 1930s–40s progressives for whom black affairs constituted a leading concern. This is not to suggest that Stryker was unenlightened on race. In one of his few responses to photographers' reports of southern racial conditions, Stryker lamented to Jack Delano (April 1941): "I guess you will have to develop some calluses if you are going to stay in the South. At least, that is what everyone else seems to do. I'm afraid I would have some difficulty doing it, though."[31] Nor is this to deny that Stryker showed some courage in overcoming hesitations about Parks, whom he later kept on as a paid photographer when the Historical Section was transferred to the Office of War Information. In fact, Stryker's 1940–41 office staff included two young blacks from Washington, D.C., Walter Payton and Robert Williams, who worked as exhibits assistants. "Walter and I had applied for the jobs through civil service," recalled Williams later. "But Stryker had to OK the appointments, and that showed some character in those days. He dealt pretty fairly with us; as a supervisor, on a scale of eight to ten, I'd give him an eight. He was a real taskmaster, he demanded professionalism, he demanded perfection—but as long as you worked within his guidelines, it was fine. Of course, if your work was no good, he'd slap you down, but there was never a racial motivation."[32] The point is simply that for Stryker, whose geographical roots lay in Montrose, Colorado, and whose spiritual roots lay in a memory of western small-town neighbor-liness and kinship with nature, passions lay in realms other than race.

In his staffing decisions, in his temporal and geographical plotting of photographers' trips, in his provision of background information and contacts, in his multitudinous communications to his people in the field, Stryker played an important part in the shaping of the photo file. But he did not control his photographers' minds. "You weren't bound by the shooting scripts," Marion Post Wolcott remembered. "You went off on all kinds of tangents."[33] While black "tangents" did not excite Stryker, quite the opposite appeared to be the case for many of his camerapeople. Letters and field notes suggest not only consider-able interest in black life but an investigative intensity on the subject.

Here was Arthur Rothstein, reporting from Belle Glade, Florida, in January 1937 about the hidden costs of an apparent black wage advan-tage in the local bean fields. "The negroes who pick the beans get 30 cents, 10 cents more than the white rate [for other crops]. The higher rate is due to the fact that the pickers suffer from a bad skin disease called 'mucker itch.' In most sections, the negroes are forced to work. They had a strike at Belle Glade once, but after the sheriff beat up a few of them and threatened to run the rest out of town, they went back to work."[34] Here were Walker Evans and Edwin Locke in Febru-ary 1937 in the Arkansas flood refugee camps, reportedly being as painstaking with black subjects as they were with white: "They [black refugees in inferior camps] are not happy-go-lucky about it, but dazed," Locke wrote, refuting accounts of cheerful black refugees in *The New York Times* and other newspapers. "There is a good deal of illness: excruciating coughs, pneumonia, and influenza cases lying in a dark cotton warehouse. I shot in there with the Leica, but Walker said it was too dark. He brought photo-flashes and shot with the 4x5, but is afraid that the exposures were wrong. He will undoubtedly want to go back."[35]

Here was Marion Post Wolcott, visiting an all-black community in Orange County, North Carolina, in September 1939, noting that al-though the residents seemed relatively natural in their dealings with white visitors, "none of the prescribed forms were violated. . . . A further suggestion in connection with studying this community is a comparison of race attitudes and relations in this place with those in the ordinary bi-racial neighborhoods."[36] And John Collier, Jr., in September 1941, described discrimination not in Mississippi or North Carolina but in Connecticut: "Some folks from Hartford were talking to the FSA representative, and I overheard him say that as far as he was concerned, there were not going to be negroes allowed on the [defense housing] project and that he had orders from higher up to forward any Negro applications on to Washington as a means of passing the buck."[37]

In some cases, photographers' interest in black America may have stemmed from background influences and experiences. For Shahn and Lange, well-known pre-FSA contacts with Communist party art organizations in New York (Shahn) or with radical agrarian organizations in California (Lange, through her investigative partner and eventual husband, Paul Taylor) probably encouraged attention to oppressed minority groups. Walker Evans had photographed extensively among dark-skinned Cubans while collaborating with journalist Carleton Beals on *The Crime of Cuba* (1933). Caribbean work may also have sharpened minority-group interest for Edwin Rosskam, the German-born artist and world traveler whom Stryker hired off the *Philadelphia Record* as a photo-editing specialist in 1938. Commissioned by *Life* the year before to do a photo-story on Puerto Rico, Rosskam spent two months probing the island's political and economic troubles, incurring the wrath of *Life*'s conservative editors in the process.[38]

John Collier, Jr., son of FDR's progressive administrator of Indian affairs, had developed an early feel for minority concerns, later clashed with Stryker, who opposed his desire to give thorough coverage to Indian life, and greeted the publication of *12 Million Black Voices* with a cry for more. "If only," the photographer wrote Stryker, "there was such a publication every month."[39] Marion Post Wolcott, although employed just prior to her FSA tenure as a staff photographer for the notably stodgy *Philadelphia Inquirer*, had been exposed to progressive ideas through her mother's birth-control activism, through colleagues at the University of Vienna and New York's New School for Social

Research, and through contacts (similar to those made by Marjory Collins) with New York avant-garde filmmakers and photographers. Arthur Siegel, one of the final arrivals (along with Collins and Gordon Parks) at the Historical Section in 1942, was a Detroit-based photography teacher and feature documentarian who had photographed that city's black section on an assignment for *Life*, and later contributed much of the unpublished material from that assignment, including a gripping series on the 1942 Sojourner Truth housing project riots, to the RA/FSA/OWI files. Siegel had investigated the urban black Midwest; Parks, as a railroad porter, musician, fashion photographer, and aspiring documentarian in Minneapolis and Chicago, had lived it.

But in the case of other Historical Section photographers, the background connections to black subject-matter were much less clear. For example, Russell Lee, the small-town midwestern native and chemical engineer–turned–photographer, took a long and winding route to documentary interest in blacks. In fact, Lee's Texas-born wife and frequent FSA traveling companion brought the wrong sort of racial "interest" to Russell's attention. While observing young black children laboring in the Louisiana strawberry fields in April 1939, Jean Lee turned immediately to nostalgic memories of the cotton harvest in Texas: "No time of the year was so gay, so exciting, so filled with promise as cotton picking time. And still today when I see the wagons filled with cotton moving to the gin and the new baled cotton stands thick in the gin-yard, I feel an inward glow that all's right with the world."[40] Russell, to his credit, remained unconvinced. Ultimately, the photographer's experimental cast of mind, more than any specific background influences, prevailed—as it did for Arthur Rothstein, fresh out of Columbia University with a technical camera training; Paul Carter, out of Dartmouth with the same; Carl Mydans, who had cut his journalistic teeth in predominantly white Boston; Jack Delano, the prize Philadelphia drawing student; Edwin Locke, the aspiring New York novelist and Stryker protegee; and John Vachon, who, as he admitted later, "had never been to California, or Florida, or hardly anyplace else except Minnesota and Washington, D.C."[41]

If FSA photographers, and not just the predictable ones, showed considerable initiative in visiting black sites and in recording written impressions of black life, how extensively did they actually *photograph* blacks? Numbers may not tell all, but in the context of a series-oriented photographic file, they at least provide a measure of the depth of commitment to particular subjects; and in the context of a file used so frequently for exhibits, books, and media spreads, statistics provide a necessary foundation for comparing image availability with eventual photo-editing decisions. After all, the criticism that an editor bypassed one-tenth of the file is of a different order than the complaint that an editor overlooked a few remarkable images.

One-tenth of the file, as it turns out, is no arbitrary figure. Of approximately 60,250 noncolor prints taken in the continental United States under Resettlement Administration–Farm Security Administration auspices, 6,070, or 10.1 percent, included discernible black figures or their dwellings.[42] That proportion was very much in line with representation of blacks in the continental United States population (9.8 percent in 1940), only slightly below the proportion of blacks among the nation's RA/FSA standard rehabilitation loan recipients (12.5 percent between 1935 and 1939) or the proportion of blacks among total United States farmers (12.6 percent). Given that Stryker hardly encouraged attention to blacks during much of his tenure, given that the Information Division as a whole could make wider use of white than black images, and given that other non-Anglo minority groups tended to be underrepresented in the file (Native Americans, Mexican Americans, Chinese Americans, and, before the last-minute flurry during the 1942 relocation crisis, Japanese Americans), this level of black representation is striking.[43]

Significantly, the RA/FSA representation compares very favorably with black proportions in other New Deal agency photographic files. In the case of the Works Progress Administration, black representation in the agency's largest file (the Washington Office Information Division file, with 2,100 black-related photos among 25,000 total, or 8.4 percent) was below both black representation in the United States population and black representation in the agency's national workforce (16 percent in 1940). In the case of the National Youth Administration, blacks had 7.3 percent representation in the agency's national information file (225 black-related among 3,050) and 5 percent representation in the combined state information files (337 black-related among 6,680)—again, below general population representation and agency work-force representation (11 percent nationally in 1940). The FSA-NYA comparison reveals particularly the strength of FSA black photographic representation since the NYA was the very New Deal agency where black administrative voices were most prominent.

Of the rehabilitation agency photo-files, only the U.S. Housing Authority's showed a black presence as strong as the FSA's: between 1937 and 1942, one-third of the dwellings built by the USHA went to blacks; 32 percent of the agency's photographs from these years included blacks. Among non-FSA agricultural agencies, the USDA Bureau of Agricultural Economics file, even with the inclusion of Irving Rusinow's intensive black community study from Georgia, had only 7.4 percent black representation during the 1930s–40s (370 of 5,000 photos), and the U.S. Extension Service's principal 1930s–40s file had a similar level at 8.3 percent (1,175 out of 14,200 photos). As for the vast general file of the Office of the Secretary of Agriculture, blacks proved well represented in certain work-oriented sections—"Migratory Farm Labor" (nearly 50 percent of 110 photos), "Cotton" (24 percent of 550 photos), "Celery" (44 percent of 50 photos)—though much of this material was shot in the 1940s, well *after* Stryker's crew had tackled these subjects. Other sections of this agricultural file show very few black faces, leaving the overall black representation (approximately 7 percent of 23,000 images) lower than the RA/FSA proportion.

The Office of War Information during Stryker's tenure from October 1942 to October 1943 also provides an important model for comparison with the RA/FSA. OWI Domestic Branch photographers included two blacks on the regular staff (Parks, and beginning in December 1942, Roger Smith, who moved from news photography for the *Chicago Defender*, *Washington Afro-American*, and other black papers to the war agency's Negro Press Section), and at least one black free-lancer (Emmanuel F. Joseph, an Oakland, California, cameraman also noted for his work with the *Pittsburgh Courier* in the early 1940s).

And with the "valuable black war contributor" theme in full bloom, there was administrative incentive for black subject-matter. Yet, even with these advantageous factors, black representation in the OWI Domestic Branch files (those compiled by the units that ultimately became part of the branch's united Division of Photography in early 1943) turned out to be no greater than in the RA/FSA file. In fact, it lagged behind slightly (8.6 percent of 16,600 photos). Relative to other government photo collections, then, the absence until the final few months of a black photographer on the RA/FSA staff did not seriously hamper the production of black-related photographs. Of the war agencies besides the OWI, only one, the Office of the Coordinator of Information (March–August 1942), had a black file representation matching or bettering the FSA proportion. With major coverage of black housing projects and health facilities in Chicago, black emergency office workers and war-related school activities in Washington, D.C., and black military training in Kansas and North Carolina, the OCI file incorporated 22 percent black representation (720 of 3,200 photos). The photographers hired on a free-lance basis for this project bore familiar names: Jack Delano, John Collier, Jr., Arthur Rothstein, Marjory Collins.

In sheer numbers of black photographs, the FSA file was unrivaled among federal government collections of the depression and war era, unprecedented among government collections of earlier eras. In proportional terms, the FSA file had *few* contemporaneous equals; if there were federal government precedents for one-tenth representation, they were not the more prominent collections, such as the 1900s–20s files of the Bureau of Agricultural Economics (3.5 percent black of 3,100 photos). Taken as a whole, RA/FSA black coverage was of historic proportions—but was black representation relatively steady through the course of the RA/FSA years? Or did the file gain its historic significance as the result of a late flurry of black photos? Certainly the large 1941 concentrations of black photos for the book projects in Chicago (Wright and Rosskam's *12 Million Black Voices*) and Greene County, Georgia (Raper and Delano's *Tenants of the Almighty*), the solid contributions from a freshly arrived Parks in summer 1942 helped to make the black proportion in the final two years combined (11.6 percent) somewhat higher than the black proportion in the first six years combined (9.7 percent). The difference, however, was hardly monumental. Had Stryker's unit ceased operations after 1939, the black proportion would have been 10.2 percent, almost exactly what it was for the complete file. In yearly production, the black proportion was never higher in any year than it was in the very first (18.9 percent, with Shahn leading the way). The proportion plummeted in 1936 (3.8 percent); rose in 1937 (7.5 percent), 1938 (10.5 percent), and 1939 (13.1 percent); dropped off notably in 1940 (7.9 percent); rose again in 1941 (13 percent); and dropped again in 1942 (8.4 percent). Long before Gordon Parks arrived on the scene, long before the Chicago and Greene County projects, the RA/FSA black file was thriving.

Analysis of temporal distribution leads, in turn, to consideration of geographical distribution. In assessing regional figures, one must remember an important fact about the entire FSA collection. Just as agency programs were weighted toward the tenant-laden South and the migrant-laden West, the photographic collection *as a whole* was weighted toward the same regions. Thus, while 11 percent of the United States population lived in the West (1940 census), the region was represented in 21.9 percent of the total RA/FSA photos, and while the South held 31.5 percent of the country's population, it was represented in 42.4 percent of the photos. On the other side of the coin, North Central states composed 30.3 percent of the population but only 22.8 percent of the photos; Northeastern states 27.2 percent of the population, only 12.9 percent of the photos. Did the pattern carry over to the black portion of the file? In the Northeast, yes: the lag between regional share of national black population (10.7 percent) and regional share of national black photos (5.2 percent) was similar to the general lag. In other important regions of black population (North Central and South), yes—but only until 1941. With the massive infusion of North Central black photos from the Chicago series, the final ratios of black photos to black population were much more in line than they were for whites. The South held 77 percent of the nation's black population and 80.1 percent of all black pictures; and the North Central region held 11 percent of the nation's blacks and 14.2 percent of the black photos. In short, the general FSA photo-

graphic orientation away from the Northeast and North Central regions affected blacks and whites equally—and, in the case of the North
Central states, blacks ended up somewhat overrepresented.[44]

To look at the regional figures another way: equally important was
whether the percentage of black photographs out of all photographs
taken within a given region corresponded to the region's black population. In the South, blacks were a tad underrepresented in the file.
While blacks constituted 23.8 percent of the region's population—
and equivalent percentages of farm operators (23 percent), RA/FSA
standard rehabilitation loan recipients (23 percent), and resettlement
project residents (25 percent) in the region excluding Delaware, Maryland, and the District of Columbia—they appeared in 19.3 percent of
the southern photos. In the Northeast, the proportions were in close
correspondence, with blacks constituting 3.8 percent of the region's
population and appearing in 4.1 percent of the region's photos. As for
the North Central states, the Chicago series helped produce black
overrepresentation—3.5 percent of the region's population, 6.3 percent of the region's photographs. Within each region, state representations (black population in the state versus black photos taken in the
state) varied considerably.

Blacks were notably overrepresented in the Missouri photo-file and
somewhat underrepresented in the Ohio file; they were notably
overrepresented in New Jersey, somewhat underrepresented in New
York and Pennsylvania. In four of the nine upper South states—Arkansas, West Virginia, Maryland, and Oklahoma—black photo percentages exceeded population percentages, with Oklahoma (7.4 percent of population, 17.1 percent of photos) and Arkansas (24.8 percent
of population, 29.3 percent of photos) leading the way. In only one of
the seven lower South states (Georgia) did the percentage of black
photos equal or better the percentage of black residents; the margin of
underrepresentation was smallest in Florida (27.1 percent black population, 25.1 percent black photos), greatest in Alabama (34.7 percent
population, 22.4 percent photos) and Louisiana (35.9 percent population, 21.7 percent photos). Hence, representation fell off somewhat in
southern areas with the highest concentrations of black population,

but *not to a degree* that rendered the national balance, one-tenth national population and one-tenth national photos, meaningless.

The most serious disproportion emerges not in regional or state analysis but in urban/nonurban breakdown. While 33 percent of the nation's blacks lived in cities of at least fifty thousand in 1940, only 18.7 percent of the RA/FSA black photos came from such locales. Of that urban photo bloc, over one-third came in a single 1941 burst from Chicago, and nearly two-thirds came in the final three years of the documentary project. By contrast, the black portion of the Office of War Information file assembled during Stryker's tenure was 55 percent urban, the black portion of the Office of the Coordinator of Information file 81 percent urban, and the black portions of principal Works Progress Administration and National Youth Administration files over 70 percent urban. A central part of the twentieth-century black experience, the move from the countryside to the cities was not, in purely quantitative terms, a central part of the RA/FSA black depiction. However, in light of the rural focus of RA/FSA programs—and, conversely, the urban accent of WPA and NYA programs and the industrial and Washington–nerve-center orientation of OCI and OWI publicity—the big-city gap is entirely understandable. If the urban black photographic shortcoming was large, the urban nonblack gap (34.1 percent of whites living in big cities, 15.3 percent of photos including whites taken in such locales) was even larger. In fact, Historical Section photographers were aware of the weakness. Delano and Rosskam even prepared a lengthy memo to Stryker in late 1941 proposing a systematic investigation of big-city life. "We have pictures of farmer's meetings . . . and town meetings, but we are almost completely lacking in the urban counterpart," the photographers pointed out. "The same holds true of home life, or office life and even of the worker's life except for slum and a few housing project pictures."[45]

The Delano-Rosskam idea, however, was never fully carried out under FSA auspices. "I would have liked a little more urban stuff," Stryker recounted much later. "I was very sorry we couldn't do more stuff in the cities. We didn't. It was expensive living in the cities. It was expensive to work there. We had a charter, we stayed with our charter."[46] Had Stryker been as passionately interested in the American city as he was in the American small town, he probably would have been more willing to bend the "charter"; one suspects that, at root, Stryker was in the city but not of the city. Of the relatively small percentage of RA/FSA pictures taken in big cities, blacks were included in a reasonable portion overall (blacks constituting 9.5 percent of all big-city residents and appearing in 12.4 percent of all big-city photos), though the city-by-city results were uneven. Blacks were extremely overrepresented in the Chicago file, somewhat underrepresented in the Detroit and New York City photographs. Blacks were very well represented in the photos from the upper South and lower Midwest cities of St. Louis, Memphis, Durham, Arlington, Norfolk, and Baltimore, less well represented in New Orleans, strikingly underrepresented in the photos from other lower South cities such as Atlanta, Birmingham, Charleston, Miami, and Mobile. In Washington, D.C., Stryker's "backyard" where more RA/FSA photos were taken than in any other city, a late flurry from Parks and Collins narrowed the margin of black photographic underrepresentation, though the proportion of black photos still trailed the proportion of black residents in the nation's capital by nine percentage points.

Parks, all of whose 142 FSA photographs were taken of Washington, D.C., blacks, obviously led all the FSA camerapeople in percentage of photos devoted to black subject-matter. Beyond Parks, the best assessment of individual attention to blacks can be made by computing the percentage of black photos out of all photos taken by *each* photographer *in states* where he or she had a reasonable chance of encountering black faces.

Using this approach, we find Lange (31.1 percent), Wolcott (23.6 percent), Shahn (10.2 percent, increasing to 25.4 percent if one excludes his rurally oriented Ohio trip), Rosskam (23.5 percent), Evans (17.5 percent), and Collier (13.7 percent)—those who, as we noted earlier, had particularly favorable backgrounds—making important contributions. But if Lange and Wolcott figured as vital forces in the black collection, equally so did Delano (31.4 percent). Evans's percentage was nearly matched by those of Lee (17 percent) and Locke (15.4 percent). Among the other photographers, Carter (11 percent),

Collins (10.2 percent), Mydans (8.2 percent), Vachon (7.8 percent), and Rothstein (7.3 percent) trailed somewhat; Siegel, much of whose FSA work was done in the rural, nonblack portion of Michigan, was further behind at 4.4 percent. When one looks at photographers' black production in a selected group of states with nearly equal black population levels—North Carolina, Georgia, Alabama, Louisiana, all between 34 and 38% black—one finds a similar configuration: Delano (45.7 percent of his photos in these states black), Wolcott (31.9 percent), and Lange (31.9 percent) the highest-percentage performers, Shahn (23.8 percent), Evans (20.8 percent), and Lee (17.4 percent) on the next tier. Vachon (15.5 percent) and Rothstein (12.5 percent) again trailed, but not by nearly as much. (Collier dropped off to 8.2 percent; Collins, Mydans, Locke, Rosskam, Carter, and Siegel did little or no photographing of any sort in these states.)

Hence, while it is evident from these calculations that certain RA/FSA photographers made more frequent black contributions than others, it also appears that: (1) black-file leadership was not simply a Shahn-Lange-Evans-Wolcott affair, (2) the quantitative roles of Delano and Lee were pivotal, and (3) the contributions of the nonleaders were by no means infinitesimal. Just as a range of photographers made references to blacks in their letters and field notes, a range of photographers did significant amounts of black picture-taking. In particular cases—Mydans in the District of Columbia in 1935, Rothstein in Missouri in 1939, Vachon in Pennsylvania steel country in 1941—even the nonleaders photographed blacks at rates in excess of local black populations. A fair degree of multiple-photographer participation also characterized what FSA urban black coverage there was. If Parks's work was 100 percent urban, so was the black photography of Rosskam. Mydans's black coverage was nearly 70 percent big-city, Lee's 29.7 percent, Vachon's 24.2 percent, Collier's 15 percent. Just as FSA black photography in general did not revolve around Gordon Parks, neither did FSA urban black photography in particular.

Also crucial to an assessment of the RA/FSA black file is the breakdown by subject. Although subject classification can be a tricky affair, quantification based on such classification promises an alternative to the game that so many FSA commentators have played: finding the subject types the commentator *wants* to find in the vast file, then conceiving of the file in terms of those handy "discoveries."

In seeking to characterize the cloth from which a great many FSA suits can be cut, one finds that over half the black photographs (56.9 percent) concerned the working and housing situations of low-income agrarians, whether tenants, sharecroppers, day laborers, or agency clients. That such subjects would have been represented by a major bloc is not surprising, given the functions of the sponsoring agency. That the figure is not considerably *higher* begins to suggest that the characteristic breadth of the FSA file carried over to the black photographs. Images pertaining directly to agency work did not dominate this agrarian portion of the black collection—much in contrast to the emphases in WPA, NYA, CCC, and other rehabilitation-agency black photography. Photographs of activities in RA/FSA resettlement projects and migrant camps (or group demonstrations away from such sites) constituted 16 percent of the black photographs, photos of farmers identified as rehabilitation or tenant-purchase clients another 6 percent. The combined percentage is still well under that of photos taken of agrarians *not* enrolled in agency programs (34.9 percent). The relative proportions of enrollees to nonenrollees correspond to those for photos of white low-income agrarians. In short, while RA/FSA camerapeople photographed black beneficiaries of agency projects, they did not emphasize this "safest" of black subject-matter any more than they stressed white project shooting.

One logically inquires whether certain of Stryker's photographers were more likely than others to take black shots relating directly to RA/FSA programs. Among the photographers who worked on the countryside, percentages did vary. Collier, with 49.7 percent of his black shots touching on agency work, Wolcott (29.7 percent), and Vachon (25.1 percent) were above the group average while Delano (18.9 percent), Lee (16.9 percent), and Mydans (16.2 percent) were somewhat below, with Rothstein, Lange, Evans, and Shahn much farther below. In general, the photographers who did much of their work in the later years of the Historical Section assumed greater responsibility for black public relations: these were the photographers employed when Stryker began making note of black projects in his assignments, and when the agency began attending to the problems of eastern migrant laborers. Wolcott, in fact, carried a particularly heavy public relations load for white as well as black programs. To suggest that Wolcott was more likely than Lange to take project shots is not to contend, however, that Wolcott limited herself to rural pap. Her percentage of photos of agrarian blacks unaided by the FSA (29 percent, with relatively few of an especially upbeat nature) was nearly equal to her percentage of agency client photos. Wolcott's nonenrollee black photos, as well as those of the other RA/FSA photographers, bore significance in another way. Such work was divided evenly among shots in the fields and shots in domestic environments, in contrast to Department of Agriculture photography, which was 85 percent field oriented. In the FSA file, agrarian blacks had dimensions other that picker, puller, hoer.

If RA/FSA photographers ventured beyond the fields, they also ventured beyond farmers and farmworkers. Nearly 19 percent of the black photographs (a bloc only slightly smaller than that devoted to project shots) concerns laboring and housing conditions for working-class blacks off the farm—agricultural processing workers, fishing industry laborers, construction workers, stevedores, coal miners and steelworkers, sawmill and turpentine hands, armaments workers, domestics, cooks, waiters. Of course, the urban underrepresentation had its impact here: it is no coincidence that agricultural processors (particularly cotton-gin and tobacco warehouse laborers) were better represented than steelworkers. Only when workers from RA/FSA building projects are included in the "construction worker" category does the latter approach the level of representation accorded agricultural processing. Urban underrepresentation also limited the coverage, direct or indirect, of black unemployment. Indirect references—urban slum shots— amounted to some five hundred photos, a significant portion of the non–farm working/housing category but a sliver of the black collection as a whole. What's more, housing shots and work shots were not always in equal proportion, particularly in some of the more dangerous professions. As with whites, we see coal miners at home, but not on the job. A file on hazards of the workplace, a 1930s update of the 1900s–10s factory and mine investigations of Lewis Hine, the FSA collection was not; references to dangerous work conditions came in non-workplace photographing contexts, as in Delano's May 1941 coverage from Heard County, Georgia, of the funeral of a nineteen-year-old black sawmill worker. Still, one should note the quantitative strengths of the non–farm work/housing portion of the FSA black collection, as contrasted with other government photo-files: its attention to workers in nontraining, nonpublic employment situations (as opposed to the uplifted-by-Uncle-Sam situations predominant in the NYA and WPA files); its attention to some of the more forgotten members of the rural and small-town work force, such as turpentine hands and shellfish cleaners; its inclusion of Chicago, Washington, D.C., and other city slum shots from sites *not* designated for slum clearance (as opposed to the before-and-after orientation of the USHA file).

From the cotton plantations of the Mississippi Delta to Chicago's south side, economically troubled blacks were certainly in abundance in the RA/FSA file. Well they might have been. But attention to social and cultural life was also quantitatively significant. Nearly one in every five RA/FSA black photos concerned a less immediately problematical aspect of common black life: religious activity (4 percent of the file); recreational activity in dance halls, taverns, theaters, parks, fairgrounds (5 percent); interactions on sidewalks and in stores, barbershops, auction houses, train stations, and other public places (10 percent). Among the principal files of other federal agencies, this degree of attention to social and cultural activity away from project sites was matched only by the OWI Domestic Branch during Stryker's tenure (24 percent, with a major boost from Parks).

As for RA/FSA coverage of the higher echelons of black society—from landowners to educators, from business leaders to physicians—the general lack of urban coverage again had an impact, limiting the amount of photographer exposure to the largest concentrations of the black establishment. The Chicago series was an exception, albeit a glowing one that merits closer examination in chapter 5. If one is looking for images of black college life in the RA/FSA file, one will be hard-pressed to find them in the 5 percent bloc of photos pertaining to black education. It was not until their OCI and OWI days that

Rothstein and Parks did extensive work at Atlanta and Howard universities, Tuskegee Institute, and Bethune-Cookman College. Among pictures taken of farmers whose tenure status was identified, landowners were underrepresented (6 percent of the photos of non–FSA-aided agrarians, versus 13 percent of black agrarians in actual life), though it is possible that landowners appeared in the many scenes of Saturday afternoon in town where farmer status was not indicated. Representation of FSA black personnel was adequate (principally teachers, doctors, nurses, and home economics advisors in resettlement communities, and also including the black manager of Newport News's Aberdeen Homesteads), though photographers did little with black farm advisors—the Morelee Fraziers—away from the all-black settlements. Despite these weak spots, however, RA/FSA inclusion of non–working-class blacks amounted to nearly 8 percent of the files, not a bad stab at the talented tenth. The quantitative strength of FSA documentary work *in general* was not middle-class coverage, particularly before the 1940s; black coverage reflected the general pattern.

The RA/FSA black assemblage intersected with the white file in literal terms: 11 percent of the images showing blacks also included white faces. Approximately one-third of these interracial images pertained to agency activities, either the construction of homesteads or the actual rendering of services. However, the majority of the RA/FSA interracial shots came in nonagency labor, market, or street settings. As a record of everyday racial coexistence (with varying degrees of interaction) outside the government site, the RA/FSA file was quantitatively unmatched by any government collection, except the OWI during Stryker's tenure. In regard to the nonmetropolitan South, the RA/FSA file stood in a government class of its own. A qualitative factor should be acknowledged here: to say that Stryker's photographers went out of their way to amass particularly controversial images of an interracial nature would be an exaggeration. Vachon's photograph of black male and white female agricultural labor strikers standing shoulder to shoulder in solidarity (Morrisville, Pennsylvania, 1938) was a rarity for Vachon as it was for the collection as a whole, and the same can be said of Lange's pungent, centuries-embracing "A Plantation Owner," Clarksdale, Mississippi (fig. 6.1). Much less dramatic shots filled this category, though, as we will see in coming chapters, important racial messages could emerge in seemingly mundane situations.

"Notice," Wolcott emphasized in her field notes for a November 1939 court-day coverage from Oxford, North Carolina, "many farmers in the [courtroom] audience and the segregation of Negroes on one side and whites on the other."[47] Here, what was *implicit* in scenes of separate black and white social groups on the street, views of all-black schools, or views of all-black projects, becomes a more *direct* exposure of legal Jim Crow. How many such direct references—images of clearly divided public meeting or waiting rooms, images of segregation signs, or captions referring explicitly to segregation policies—ended up in the RA/FSA file? Not more than forty, hardly constituting a sustained thematic interest. In light of the photographers' generally perceptive written comments on race, in light of their sensitivity to the importance of public signs in general, a higher total might have been expected. Still, scattered as these references were, they at least appeared, and, as suggested with the image in figure 1.1, were often handled in imaginative fashion. Such references did not appear in the principal photo-files of other government agencies, save for a much smaller group in the OWI file (most of these, interestingly enough, coming not from Parks or Smith but from Esther Bubley, a Wisconsin-born, Minnesota-educated white photographer). Such references did not appear in the files of the special government projects that sent Hine to West Virginia and North Carolina, Rusinow to Putnam County, Georgia, and McNeill to Virginia. And such references did not appear, even in the non-"talented tenth" portions, in such private files as the Harmon Foundation–Kenneth Space collection. Virtually all the RA/FSA photographers who spent time in the South contributed a few images of this sort. Significantly, in light of the earlier discussion of "predictables" and "unpredictables" among photographers depicting black-related subjects, leadership in the category of direct segregation references did not come from Parks, Shahn, or Lange, and came only in part from Wolcott; Lee was just as important a contributor.

FSA coverage of other crude manifestations of racism proved to be thin. The series on voter disenfranchisement that Lange proposed to

Stryker in 1938 never appeared in the file. In the end, only some
Lange field notes quoting the disenfranchised at Mississippi Delta
Farms (the quotations not included in the final picture captions), a
brief Lange reference to votelessness in the caption for a photograph
of white Texas sharecroppers, Lee's 1939 photograph of a poll-tax sign
in Mineola, Texas, and Delano's suggestive 1940 view of black farmers
sitting idly on Election Day in Stem, North Carolina, represented the
extent of FSA coverage on this issue—which, as Lange correctly noted
in her original proposal to Stryker, was integrally bound up with the
economic problems being addressed by the agency. Evidence of racial
violence remained equally scarce in the file. Apart from Siegel's late
contributions on troubled Detroit, not actually done under government auspices, the only reference came in Lange's captions describing
the violence-scarred backgrounds of some of the Delta Farms residents,
Wolcott's 1940 photo of a Ku Klux Klan historical marker in Yancey-
ville, North Carolina ("Caswell Courthouse . . . Erected About 1861.
Alleged Ku Klux Murder Here, 1870. Led to Martial Law and Kirk-
Holden 'War' "), and Lee's 1938 shot of a New Madrid, Missouri, tree
from which, as he explained in the caption, "several Negroes have
been hung." If the shadow of poverty hung heavily over blacks in the
RA/FSA file, the shadow of terror was all but nonexistent.

Inasmuch as fear of "The Law," and particularly the chain-gang fate
that befell a disproportionate number of southern blacks, also represented an important part of the black experience during these years,
the RA/FSA file again proved quantitatively unimpressive. The single
series concerning chain-gang conditions, Delano's 28 photos from a
Georgia convict camp, was hardly the quantitative answer to John
Spivak's 1932 textual-visual exposé (*Georgia Nigger*), though its qualitative worth—sensitivity not only to prison suffering but the culture
of prison survival—was considerable. As for the more activist black
responses to injustice, the file includes more than a handful of images
(150) concerning radical agrarian protest, from Lange's portraits of
Southern Tenant Farmers Union members at Delta Farms to
Rothstein's coverage of the 1939 Missouri sharecropper demonstration
(led by a black STFU member, Owen Whitfield) to Lee's work on
interracial STFU, Workers' Alliance, and United Canning, Agricul-

tural, Packing, Allied Workers of American organizing in Oklahoma. Such images were not to be found in even the most adventurous of the other government photo-files. At the same time, however, evidence in the RA/FSA file of the burgeoning NAACP, National Urban League, and CIO activism in towns and cities was minimal, as we will see in chapter 5.

Reasons for the dearth of FSA photographs in these racism-and-protest categories will be explored in later chapters; for now, several considerations are appropriate. In certain cases of noncoverage, special factors were at play: voter disenfranchisement, for example, was not a subject that lent itself readily to visual representation. One could certainly picture the condition of poverty that political impotence served to rigidify, but the actual process was better rendered in extended text than in pictures and captions. (One should add here that the general subject of elections, above or below the Mason-Dixon line, received relatively little attention in FSA photography; scenes of voting were not much more plentiful than images suggesting votelessness). In the case of racial violence, the fact that FSA camerapeople were not news-oriented photographers based in particular locales made such documentation less likely. Capturing images of naked terror was no simple affair even for photographers with a thorough knowledge of the local turf, or for photographers who could afford to wait weeks and months to get such shots. (By the 1930s, photographs of lynch victims were often gained through circuitous means: for example, one such Florida picture published in the NAACP's *Crisis* was the result, the NAACP report explained, of a "snapshot taken by a travelling salesman who had the film developed at Melbourne, Alabama, and then gave a copy to a colored police officer.")[48]

Obtaining the sort of caption information that Lange obtained from families of terror victims proved no simple affair, either. If blacks had reason to fear repercussions for talking to photographers about their economic and political circumstances, they had even more reason to be cautious about describing white mob action. "As you will note in the [general] caption," Lee wrote Stryker about a series concerning a black Oklahoma tenant farmer, "there is some information [about co-op activism] which might get him in 'dutch' with the local banker and

businessman should it be released as material supplementing publication. If it should be released, I would suggest it be anonymous or
handled in such a way that it could not definitely be traced to him."[49]

For all these cases, another conceivable factor is intriguing. One
wonders whether many highly controversial photographs might have
been taken by the RA/FSA photographers but not placed in the file. It
is known that Evans, Lange, Shahn, and possibly others withheld negatives from the FSA office. It is also known that a great many negatives
submitted to the office were not selected for *printing* by Stryker. In the
early years, Stryker punched holes in 35 millimeter rejects, discarded
rejects in larger negative sizes, or, in some cases, returned them to the
photographers. After Shahn and others protested against the most
cavalier procedures, Stryker agreed to maintain the unprinted negatives. Some sixty thousand of them are presently interfiled with the
negatives for printed photos in Library of Congress storage areas. What
gems might lie in the "other" FSA collection? At least in Evans's case,
some of the negatives kept by the photographer have been subse-
quently printed, revealing material that is frequently more *spontaneous*
than that in the RA/FSA file but not, in racial terms, more controversial. Unfortunately, a systematic survey of the rejects at the Library of
Congress lies beyond the scope of the present project; a tentative assessment, however, can be offered.

My survey of the rejects for six series with strong potential for politically troublesome material—Rothstein in the strike-torn Birmingham steel and coal district (1937), Vachon at the Morrisville, Pennsylvania, farm workers strike (1938), Delano in Stem, North Carolina,
on election day (1940), Lee at Oklahoma radical agrarian meetings
(1940), Delano at the Greene County, Georgia, convict camp (1941),
Vachon at a Chicago street demonstration (1941)—did not produce
much evidence of Stryker's "cleansing." In the first place, the rejection
rate for these series turned out to be no higher than for series dealing
with less explosive subjects. Second, rejected negatives *generally* contained little visual information that was not contained in the printed
images; near-duplicates proved the norm. In the Vachon agricultural
strike and Delano prison series, the *most* provocative images (i.e., black
and white strikers standing shoulder to shoulder; black convicts

watched by an armed guard, or convicts' hands reaching through the bars overhead, grasping for an elusive freedom) made it into the printed file. Finally, in the two series that held the liveliest rejects, decision to print would not have fundamentally altered the final coverage.

In the case of Rothstein's Alabama series, the printed file contains a single image of a black convict gang working on the road (no chains or guard visible); printing the rejects would have expanded the coverage to five images—again, no chains visible; a white guard shown in two of the rejects, though not with rifle, pistol, or whip prominent. In Vachon's Chicago series, the five file views of pickets in front of realty and dairy company offices would have increased to twelve. A few of the unprinted shots from the Mid-City Realty demonstration—views, for example, showing residents of apartments above the Mid-City office gazing down at the pickets protesting high rents—did suggest that the demonstration attracted more attention than what was suggested in the printed images—a change, but less than radical.

In short, whatever preshooting signals Stryker might have sent to his photographers in the field, he does not appear, from this survey, to have been a determined postshooting censor. To the extent that photographers had physical opportunities to shoot more of the controversial material, the apparent case that they did not do so reflected at least in some instances their adoption, perhaps semiconscious, of Strykeresque caution—and, indirectly, of a tacit New Deal strategy that deemphasized the fundamental racial imbalances and conflicts lying beneath the surface of depression-era suffering. Word of government photographers snooping around convict camps, investigating poll taxes, or getting the dirt on Jim Crow would not have done much to allay the suspicions of state and local authorities whose resistance could make life extremely difficult for the camerapeople, or to allay the fears of Stryker, whose ultimate support the photographers needed. As Delano remembered the tense conditions under which he managed to shoot his very brief series on the Georgia convict camp: "It's true that we did get into the [camp] and we did take the photos. Arthur [Raper] wrangled that, but while we were there we had the feeling that we had better do this and do it fast because we didn't know whether they [prison authorities] meant it or not in the first place."[50] The agency, Stryker, and the photographers (often returning to previously photographed areas) had a stake in Georgia; John Spivak, Margaret Bourke-White, or a photographer from the *New York Post* seeking chain gangs did not. How many times could an FSAer have gotten away with the technique once used by Rothstein in Alabama coal-and-steel country ("You take that film," he reportedly warned an abusive guard in a company town, "and my boss won't stop until he gets you guys") around would-be camera-smashers? In the final reckoning, Rothstein's boss, or his boss's boss, was not in a position to do much "getting."[51] As Delano reflected later: "If I had gone out of my way [in Greene County, Georgia] to emphasize segregation and racial antagonism, I wouldn't have lasted long; I would have found it impossible to work. Local people would have figured that the northerner, the 'foreigner' was trying to butt into their affairs, and to stir up trouble. You had to be careful. . . . I can remember Arthur Raper coming back one evening, telling me he had given a lift into town to a [white] man who turned out to be drunk, and who boasted about having in his possession a severed thumb taken from a lynching victim."[52]

Assuredly, the adventurousness of RA/FSA photographers, however much it exceeded Stryker's, had limits. As was the case with RA/FSA depiction of America in general—making short shrift of industrial strife, or political and economic radicalism, of crime and "justice," of the dark hatreds and fears at the center of the Centervilles, of the structural maladies that predated and would certainly postdate the depression—the depiction of black circumstances was less disturbing than it should have been. The implicit conservatism, the implicit paternalism of New Deal policy-making (creative reform seen as coming from the government, not from grass-roots activists) found its way into aspects of FSA image-making. There were compromises and more compromises: the agency that did not stand by a Morelee Frazier did not, in its photographic ventures, expose fully the nature of the beast that drove Frazier out of Adams County, Mississippi. This was unfortunate. Radical historians will find such shortcomings decisive in their evaluation of FSA photographic "ideology"; Stryker celebrants will undoubtedly meet the radical cry of "cop-out" with the furious retort, "nitpicking!" Neither argument is particularly persuasive. If RA/FSA coverage of black America did not amount to a great leap forward, the numbers suggest that it was at least an important advance. Against administrative odds, the photographers collectively achieved a range and depth of black coverage that was rare in government or private photography. The nature of that advance will be explored further as we turn from statistical to visual readings.

3

The Photo Series: Ben Shahn's
Southern Meditations

Roy Stryker to Arthur Rothstein, story outline, 1939: "Economy of [corn] farmer. . . . Is he self-sufficient through live-at-home program? Is he a specialist? How much waste? How much dependence on non-farm supplies, i.e., clothes, gas, etc.? Farmer goes to town. . . . Why? What to do? Meeting places? Farmers talking to local banker, implement dealer, visit to landlord. . . ."[1]

It was the photographic series as a whole that Stryker conceived in dozens of shooting scripts and hundreds of memos sent to his camera-people in the field—albeit with few direct references to black subjects—and the series as a whole that most of the photographers went to considerable lengths to build. It was the series as a whole that Stryker preserved by allowing as many images to be printed as he did. And it was the concept that even the originator of FSA subject classification, Library of Congress Curator Paul Vanderbilt, acknowledged when he had the images microfilmed in their original series before creating the new organization.

With the FSA photographic series, one reckons, in the concrete terms of a place and a time, with questions of photographic meaning, of inclusion and exclusion, of achievement and limitation. Such will be the reckoning in this study. Three important series varieties will be examined in chapters 3 to 5: the relatively freewheeling coverage of an area (Shahn's 1935 southern trip), coverage of a specific event (Rothstein's 1939 series on a Missouri sharecropper protest), and intensive coverage of a specific community (the joint Lee and Rosskam investigation of south-side Chicago, 1941). In order to place the Lee-Rosskam study in a larger 1940s FSA perspective, there will also be consideration of Parks and Delano series from this period. While the sample stories here are not necessarily all typical of the FSA black file, they will serve useful comparative functions.

"To him that *hath* shall be given, and from him that *hath not* shall be taken away even that which he seems to have." So testified black sociologist Charles S. Johnson about the practical consequences of the Agricultural Adjustment Administration's cotton program, at an AAA hearing in Memphis, 1935.[2] Johnson's critique was hardly what the Memphis audience, dominated by loyal AAA officials, major planters, and shippers, wanted to hear. But, in the larger arena of public discussion that year, Johnson was not the only commentator suggesting that the early New Deal's agricultural centerpiece had produced a decidedly raw deal for Southern tenants and sharecroppers. From varied sources, including an investigation sponsored by the AAA itself, came reports of landowner abuse: planters withholding AAA parity-payment shares from their clients, demoting tenants to sharecropper status in order to minimize payment shares, or simply evicting their tenants and sharecroppers and substituting day laborers who did not have a claim on AAA benefits. The very nature of the political, economic— and racial—structure in many cotton-producing areas militated against an equitable AAA impact. As an evicted sharecropper in Tyronza, Arkansas, complained in a desperate letter to Agriculture Secretary Henry Wallace: "Mr. H. N. Norcross [a powerful planter] is a cut lawyer the way he treated some family [*sic*]. . . . Dear Secretary we need some help and it don't do no good for us to see the County Committee for he tole us if Mr. Norcross says move to move for them was Mr. Norcross houses. . . ."[3]

The issue of the AAA—too little government, for liberal critics; too much government, for some conservative critics, who ultimately persuaded the Supreme Court—burned brightly at mid decade. And there was a more violent side of the story. Southern Tenant Farmers Union agitation on AAA abuses and other matters produced a landowner backlash whose excesses, particularly glaring in the STFU home ground of northeastern Arkansas, generated a wave of national interest in the union. Accounts of selective evictions, beatings, jailings, shootings, and at least one related lynching reached even *The New*

York Times, which ran a five-part series in April 1935 on what the reporter, F. Raymond Daniell, termed the atmosphere of "perfervid hysteria" in Arkansas. With upwards of two-thirds of the STFU membership black, the hysteria was as much racial as economic. "We've had a pretty serious situation here," one of the scions of Marked Tree, Arkansas, told Daniell, "what with the mistering of these niggers and stirring them up to think the government was agoin' to give them each 40 acres. Why, it even got so they held a parade here one day of nigger and white sharecroppers, and a nigger with a cane tried to hold up a car with a white lady in it."[4] Despite intimidation, the STFU pressed on, leading an early autumn cotton-picker strike in areas of Arkansas and Oklahoma. The strike exacerbated tensions, though it ultimately forced wage concessions from planters caught in a pinch at harvest time.

Into a troubled Arkansas, on the heels of the STFU strike, in a year of sharecropper-related political turmoil, came Ben Shahn with his 35-millimeter Leica camera. The painter-turned-photographer had journeyed through West Virginia and Kentucky coal-mining country, through the small towns of western Tennessee, and he would travel on down the delta, through Mississippi and Louisiana. Given the context of political and economic turmoil, given the generally self-defined nature of Shahn's photographic agenda (though the production would eventually wind up in the Historical Section file, Shahn undertook this journey to do photographic research for his own poster-making, sponsored by the Resettlement Administration's Special Skills Division), given his then-recent Communist party connections, and given the sources and tenor of his early-1930s art work (the Sacco-Vanzetti and Tom Mooney series, and the anti-Women's Christian Temperance Union canvas, all tapping news photos), one might have expected a confrontational, perhaps tendentious brand of photography. There had been indications of such an approach in Shahn's West Virginia work, some of it taken in towns affected by a United Mine Workers strike. His now-classic view of a Morgantown deputy's expansive, gun-and-holster-laden rump, and his extended caption for a black miner portrait in nearby Purseglove—detailing, item by item, the company's deductions from the worker's already skimpy paycheck—were the sort of touches that would have pleased Shahn's former colleagues in the Art Front. But the further Shahn journeyed, the less obviously combative his work became. While many of Shahn's Arkansas, Mississippi, and Louisiana views made apparent the need for New Deal programs with a deeper thrust than the AAA or NRA, there were no direct references—in pictures or captions—to benefit-payment denials or evictions, to ex-tenants turned sharecroppers or ex-sharecroppers turned day laborers, to day-laborer wage increases or decreases, to STFU agitation or landlord counteraction.

Shahn did not miss the most troubled regions. He actually passed through the heart of the Arkansas battle zone, Marked Tree. While the photographs taken there contained a few hints of bitterness and polarization (for example, the image of a dilapidated billboard adver-tising the Marked Tree Bank, with the upbeat message—"Bank With Confidence! Owned by Home Folks"—placed in an ironic light by the collapsing signposts, the litter-strewn roadside, and the mention of "tuberculosis" in another sign at the edge of the picture), they hardly amounted to a visual counterpart of The New York Times exposé. Nor was there a suppressed Shahn exposé, censored by Resettlement Ad-ministration authorities; even more so than the rejects noted at the end of the last chapter, the unprinted negatives from Shahn's Arkan-sas trip tended to be technical mistakes rather than items of a politi-cally sensitive nature. Perhaps, instead, Shahn experienced some in-timidation in the field. Places such as Marked Tree were sufficiently hostile to restrict the quantitative and qualitative production of any outside investigator who valued his or her safety. "When Jack Bryan had gone to Marked Tree around that time to do a story for the Mem-phis Press-Scimitar," recalled the journalist–turned–FSA information official Ed Trapnell, "he was arrested and put in jail. The charge was something I had never heard of: 'barratry'—inciting to riot."[5] That Shahn was occasionally accompanied in Arkansas by a politician well known for his opposition to the STFU, Senator Joseph Robinson, may also have inhibited him.

But, in the final analysis, hostile Marked Trees or suspicious Joe Robinsons cannot completely explain Shahn's approach. Shahn was not necessarily seeking the explosive exposé. Prior to his RA involvement, Shahn had seen very little of America outside New York City, and the more he experienced the hinterland, the more fascinated he grew with the designs, the dynamics, the details of American survival. The ordinary, Shahn perceived, could be extraordinary, not merely for what it said about depression-era suffering but for how it revealed individual and cultural identity. "I came to know well so many people of all kinds of belief and temperament, which they maintained with a transcendent indifference to their lot in life," Shahn wrote later. "Theories melted before such experience. . . . There were the poor who were rich in spirit, and the rich who were also sometimes rich in spirit. There was the South and its story-telling art, stories of snakes and storms and haunted houses, enchanting; and yet such tales thriving in the same human shell with hopeless prejudice, bigotry, and ignorance."[6]

Shahn's observation fairly invites the fury of New Left critics, to whom it might represent a failure of radical nerve, a retreat to bourgeois romanticism. Even non-Marxists will find certain implications troubling: indifference was far from an American keynote in 1935. But if Shahn failed to address some of the period's hottest issues, if he did not fully convey the crisis of the mid 1930s, his work was nevertheless probing in other respects. Particularly in his black coverage, extensive throughout the southern tour (nearly half of the 125 Arkansas photographs concerned blacks, for example), Shahn offered subtle insights that challenged misleading assumptions on both the right and the left.

Consider, for example, his cotton-picker series from the Alexander Plantation in Pulaski County, Arkansas. Strike conscious or eviction conscious it was not, but the series departed significantly from the accent on grinners or drones, on the "cute darkies" or human extensions of the cotton plants that characterized so much of the period's cotton harvest photo-coverage. Such coverage included a 1937 *New York Times* picture page ("The South Harvests a Bumper Cotton Crop," with sweeping *Times* and Wide World photos of anonymous bent backs, wide-rimmed hats, and ripe cotton balls covering the Texas landscape), and L. C. Harmon's 1941 USDA photos of the Mississippi cotton harvest, featuring, among other sights, a soft-focus closeup of a young black child, with sparkling eyes, surrounded luxuriantly by fleecy cotton (fig. 3.1). In the first place, Shahn devoted nearly 40 percent of his cotton-picker coverage to workers assembling near a plantation storehouse before work. This prework focus, rarely seen in other coverages, encourages the viewer to consider the laborers separately from the crop. Shahn was willing to go out of his way to capture this angle: "I knew I'd have to be there at 5:30 in the morning when the crew got together," he remembered later.[7] Shifting from large-group portraits to small-group shots to studies of individuals, and sustaining the visual integration through figures who appear to be glancing out of one frame and into the next, Shahn presents a medley of characters as carefully and respectfully as he would later portray the parishioners outside a black church.

Variety here makes for richness. One notes, as one seldom does in field scenes, the considerable differences in the pickers' garb: in 6028-M1, a woman wearing the familiar floppy straw hat; in 6028-M4, a woman sporting a dressier narrow-rimmed hat with peacock decoration; in 6028-M5, a young man with eminently practical clothing—overalls, a simple hat with holes punched for "airing"—and in 6028-M3, a young man looking as if he were ready for Beale Street (fig. 3.2). One notes other differences in self-presentation: in 6029-M5, the eminently formal pose of the older picker, seated on the porch of the storehouse with hands clasped neatly in his lap and a rigid expression on his face; the casual stance of a younger man nearby (6028-M5), regarding the camera nonchalantly as he puffs on a cigarette; the half-open, half-protective look of the woman in 6028-M2, who, though her back is to the camera, glances behind with the beginnings of a smile. "Cotton pickers who receive 60 cents a day," informs one of Shahn's captions, yet Shahn's camera reveals a realm of experience not determined simply by occupational and income status. Even the ways in which the pickers hold their empty sacks suggest differences in outlook. The old-timer in 6029-M5 drapes his sack across his chest and lap, as if to confer upon it the status of vital, and accustomed, partner (fig. 3.3). By contrast, the sharpest dresser in 6028-M3 has flipped a rolled-up sack over his shoulder, concealing most of it from view as he stands with back to the wall (fig. 3.2). The tool of this man's trade becomes more incidental than the lunch pail held in his

Fig. 3.1. L. C. Harmon. "Negro Child in Pile of Cotton, Delta Pine Land Company Plantation," Bolivar County, Miss. 1941. Office of the Secretary of Agriculture. National Archives.

other hand; in fact, he could very easily pass for a man in another line of work. It is the expertly tipped hat, the stylish scarf, the jaunty crossing of the legs, that appear more central to his self-definition. Standing slightly apart from the other laborers, his polished appearance a striking contrast to the dreary building behind (wooden slats across the window, producing a jail-like effect), and his gaze directed away from both the camera and his colleagues, the man seems to be waiting as much for a change of venue (perhaps migration out of cotton country) as for the start of the workday.

We should not go too far, of course, in drawing conclusions based on body language. But the larger point is that Shahn invited speculation about the individual spirit that the labor system—masses assembled; masses sent to the fields to perform the same bending, plucking, pulling motions hour after hour; masses paid at the same rate— was too often assumed to render irrelevant. While such speculation was perhaps disappointing to political militants (Shahn paid relatively little attention to such obvious marks of injustice as gnarled hands, worn kneepads, battered shoes, and desperate faces), the approach nevertheless avoided the condescension that often characterized "wounded proletarian" exposés by liberal journalists in the 1930s. "I have seen the victims of something very like oppression, and I am full of pity for them," as one writer for *The Commonweal* lamented after spending several weeks with a cotton-picking crew. "How terrible to have no chances, to be hemmed in hopelessly from every side!"[8] At the same time, even the most colorful dressers among Shahn's subjects do not fit easily into picturesque black stereotypes: it is the quiet self-containment of the dapper fellow in fig. 3.2, not any strutting or other sign of emotional exuberance, that serves as the keynote.

Restrained, contemplative in the early morning, Shahn's subjects also appear curiously *alone* together. Such disconnectedness is particu-

Fig. 3.2. Ben Shahn. "Cotton Pickers," Pulaski County, Ark. 1935. FSA. Library of Congress.

larly evident in one of the large group shots, 6027-M5 (fig. 3.4), where
the stage-like setting of the porch seems to contain four or five separate presentations: the man in the right-foreground absorbed in rolling
a cigarette, the woman behind him staring off to the side; to the left,
the aforementioned old-timer, remote, statue-like; a man standing
above him, peering more inquisitively at Shahn from behind a post;
and peeking out from the deeper recesses of the porch, two whites who
would appear, from their attire, to be managers. To be sure, the sense
of multiple worlds within a world has an important connection with
Shahn's technical procedures. His Leica, unobtrusive to begin with,
was equipped with an angle finder that enhanced the photographer's
ability to catch subjects unaware. "The angle finder," Shahn explained
later, "lets you look off in another direction when you focus, so it takes
away any self-consciousness people have."[9] In many of the group pictures from 1935, black-related or not, some subjects appear to be aware

'g. 3.3. Ben Shahn. "Cotton Picker," Pulaski County, Ark. 1935. FSA.
'brary of Congress.

of the camera, others not—hence, the divided attentions. But Shahn was not merely after photographic tricks; there were broader cultural implications in the products. Scholars observing the fragmented quality in some of Shahn's better-known white photos, such as "The Terwilligers, Ozark Family, Arkansas," have found therein expressions of depression-era disorder (fig. 3.5). In the nonfamily setting of Fig. 3.4, however, other meanings emerge. While the implicit lack of worker solidarity will undoubtedly violate some photo-historians' prejudices, the appearance of aloneness also carries a connotation of privacy—fleeting and incomplete, yes, but privacy nevertheless amid a work routine that, by its very nature, made a space of one's own (literal and figurative) extremely hard to come by. In the apparent disarray lie possibilities for dignity.

The lack of a vigorous force at the center of the photograph is intriguing as well; one wonders about the possible significance of the

Fig. 3.4. Ben Shahn. "Cotton Pickers at 6:30 A.M.," Pulaski County, Ark. 1935. FSA. Library of Congress.

whites *not* filling the void. Managers and laborers on the same porch could have produced a portrait akin to Lange's "A Plantation Owner" (fig. 6.1), yet in fig. 3.4 and throughout Shahn's cotton-picker series, whites remain in the background. Whether Shahn arranged this, or whether the managers were wary of an association that could later be used as liberal ammunition, the final image is somewhat ambiguous. While the whites are decidedly out of the spotlight, their very presence in the rear (buttons, collars, ties more notable than faces; shadowy figures that manage, in a very subtle fashion, to block "our" entry to the interior of the building) is disquieting. Less assuming than Lange's landowner, they are perhaps more cunning—a quality that some commentators on Lange's photograph found notably lacking in her arrogant Mississippian. "Lange's . . . posed portrait," noted a *Washington Times* columnist, "depict[s] a testy old guy who would obviously brook no contradiction. . . . The background consists of a seated crowd

. 3.5. Ben Shahn. "The Terwilligers, Ozark Family," Boone County, Ark. 1935. FSA.
.rary of Congress.

of young colored men, the faces of whom indicate they have considerably more intelligence than the local czar."[10] In the end, Shahn's group
portrait is no naive retreat from Southern problems. Whites are neither gone nor forgotten; white authority, unflaunted, remains haunting.

Shahn continued the series in the cotton fields. He did not follow
the *same* individuals featured in the waiting scenes, an unfortunate
discontinuity given the interest that the opening coverage raised in
particular lives. But if Shahn was not entirely systematic, he continued
to find ways to visualize a mass experience in immediate, personal
terms. Camera angles, for example, reduced the distance between
viewer and laborer. In 6217-M2, an over-the-shoulder view of a woman
filling her bag, the camera probes her activity without reducing her to
an anonymous pair of hands; the woman's dressy hat and earrings provide a striking, and humanizing, part of the scene. In another shot

Fig. 3.6. Ben Shahn. "Cotton Pickers," Pulaski County, Ark. 1935. FSA.
Library of Congress.

(6220-M3), Shahn views pickers from behind, but not routinely so. Their long sacks trail endlessly, relentlessly, into *our* space, as if to underline the essential connection between a labor experience and cotton "consumption," between sacks dragged through the fields and the clothes on our backs.

Shahn goes beyond creative single images in his effort to counter notions of the distant proletarian mass. The photographer follows *one* picker through a succession of actions, giving the viewer a narrative focal point that was so often missing from even the more sensitive Agriculture Department coverages. The series within a series concerns a young female picker, a subject readily exploitable in left as well as conservative terms, but handled more imaginatively by Shahn. We see the girl at a slight distance, bent over her task. We see her dragging her sack toward the immediate foreground (fig. 3.6). We see her pause to peer at Shahn directly (fig. 3.7). And we see her moving on, passing

g. 3.7. Ben Shahn. "Picking Cotton," Pulaski County, Ark. 1935. FSA.
rary of Congress.

another young girl fingering a cotton ball. These are undramatic actions, to be sure, but, taken together, they suggest the steady demands of this labor. We do not see overt signs of anguish, but we do not have to. The obvious heaviness of the burden in the second frame, the sheer size of the sack, dwarfing the girl's leg, in the fourth frame, are indictment enough. At the same time, there is no suggestion of cuteness or preciousness; the girl concentrates intently on her work in the first two frames, casts a wary, vaguely impatient glance in the third, and busily moves out of the picture in the fourth. This is an adult-child, as particularly evident in the third frame. Photographed close up from a low vantage point, the girl looms prominently over the surrounding field, pickers, and building—an almost monumental angle that seems to increase her age. With her back bent slightly, her head at an awkward tilt, her hair falling raggedly beneath the rim of her cap, she shows something of the costs of the extra "years." Neither wholly crushed by her environment nor wholly secure within it, the girl invites responses other than pity, but certainly other than complacency as well. Again, the comparison with Agriculture Department coverages is revealing. Not only is the young picker in the late–1930s Extension Service photo shown with a rakish grin, but she is filmed at an angle that suggests a dominant figure peering down at her (fig. 3.8). Shahn's angle is fundamentally more respectful; the girl is not a curious specimen but a figure to be met on her own terms. When USDA photographers were not zeroing in on grinning children, they were showing children working alongside their parents, as in several of Harmon's Boliver County, Mississippi, views. The family touch, reassuring from a conservative standpoint (blacks "at home" in the fields), is notably absent from the harder-edged Shahn series.

Shahn's approach was unusual in another respect. While cotton-harvest photos in the USDA files rarely showed blacks in a capacity other than picker or hauler, *all* the nonpickers in Shahn's field scenes are blacks. In fact, nearly half of the sixteen images from this phase of the coverage include a black checker, weigher, or tagger; three of the shots are closeups of such personnel, which provide significant contrasts to those of common laborers. We observe the picker inspecting a cotton ball in her hands, the checker poring over a notebook in his

Fig. 3.8. Unidentified Federal Extension Service photographer. Cotton picker. Ca. 1939. U.S. Department of Agriculture, Extension Service. National Archives.

hands; we observe a picker standing a bit uncomfortably in the camera's eye, a nearby checker establishing a more confident, businesslike presence in front of the cotton wagon. In the course of this coverage, Shahn acknowledges what was too often forgotten by liberals and conservatives alike: first that blacks contributed more than just physical labor in the cotton harvest, and second, that black hierarchies, perhaps more immediately visible in towns and cities, extended to the southern plantation. Stereotypes of the organizationally inept black are clearly rejected, but the series also leaves in doubt the conception of a simple labor/capital dichotomy in a land of "exploitation."

By presenting a broad spectrum of black responses to the camera, Shahn undercut common assumptions about a predictable black mindset. The photographer's most direct examination of racial myths came just before the Arkansas coverage. Interestingly, it came in a context that one would not immediately associate with racial issues.

In Huntingdon, Tennessee, Shahn encountered a traveling medicine show captivating the locals on a Saturday afternoon. The event, of course, was naturally appealing to any investigator of the American scene. Medicine shows, featuring characters the likes of Yellowstone Kit, Doc Rolling Thunder, and Princess Lotus Blossom, and offering remedies for every malady from constipation to tuberculosis, were a colorful—if sleazy—part of small-town tradition. While the heyday of the medicine show had passed, pitchmen still made the rounds, lecturing, dazzling, bamboozling the "yokels." "The thing about pitching medicine is to make a fuss," one veteran told a Federal Writers Project interviewer, "and in any bunch of men you draw, half are going to have aches and pains due to over or under-eating—malnutrition, I believe they call it. And the less education they have, the more they'll believe in the power of a bottle to cure them. People believe what they want to believe."[11] Patent medicines tendered by the pitchmen, or marketed directly by manufacturers, were very much in the news in the mid 1930s, with reformers led by the Resettlement Administration's own Rexford Tugwell seeking to block distribution through a strengthened Pure Food and Drug Act. (There was no more vigilant campaigner than Tugwell, who wrote or inspired congressional bills that touched off furious national debates—even cries of "un-Americanism" from pharmaceutical companies—in 1934 and 1935. It was no coincidence that Shahn and other photographers associated with a Tugwell-directed agency took more than a few shots of "666," "Grove's Chill Tonic," and other patent medicine advertisements on barns, houses, and billboards. Shahn incorporated the devilish "sixes" into one of his photograph-based lithographs that clearly suggested a link between patent medicine fraud and sharecropper poverty.)

But, in the seventeen photos comprising the Huntingdon series, Shahn explored more than local color and local chicanery. Sure enough, the Huntingdon pitchman, unidentified, emerged as appropriately shady with his black top-hat, assorted props, and mysterious bottles. Of greater interest to Shahn was the pitchman's "Negro assistant," as the photographer later remembered him, wearing classic minstrel makeup.[12] As Shahn may have realized, minstrel singing, dancing, and comedy routines had long been part of the medicine-show spectacle; for the average audience, "Mr. Bones" represented a reassuringly familiar counterpoint to the pitchman's high-blown rhetoric and exotic wares. Shahn's minstrel interest went beyond the obvious. No overt clowning, no banjo-playing caught the photographer's eye; in 6164-M3, 6165-M5, and other initial views, the minstrel assumes a businesslike pose, standing rigidly, dutifully next to the pitchman on the makeshift stage. The stereotyped face, displayed in almost perfunctory manner, is made to seem even more *artificial* through Shahn's creative juxtapositions. In 6164-M3, shot from the back of the crowd, Shahn directs our attention not only to the pitchman and his assistant but to another figure rising above the crowd (fig. 3.9). Opposite the stage, a black youth climbs atop a bench, presumably to gain a better view. The resulting contrast between photographically prominent blacks is sharp: the liveliness of the youth, the frozen posture of the minstrel; the youth choosing his perch, the minstrel, in effect, locked into his (the brick wall looming directly behind the stage accentuating the impression of entrapment). But for his makeup, the older black would almost seem ready to be auctioned, the predominantly white crowd pressing forward to inspect the merchandise. What the black youth makes of the "white man's Negro," how necessary denigrating facades might be in the youth's own experience—such questions arise from Shahn's remarkably busy image. In 6165-M5, shot closer to the stage, we see the minstrel in profile (backed by another ethnic type appearing frequently in medicine shows, the full-feathered Indian), but we make more direct contact with a black onlooker who peers acutely at the camera while the rest of the crowd is absorbed in the pitchman's delivery (fig. 3.10). Composition reinforces meaning here. The action occurs along a strong diagonal running from the upper right to the lower left corner; the master of artifice, and his handy black creation, stand at one extreme, and at the other, viewed only by us, is the more authentic black man. Artifice holds the commanding position—for the moment.

Of masks, of men. The distinction emerges not only through comparisons among performers and observers but through the series evolu-

Fig. 3.9. Ben Shahn. "A Medicine Show," Huntingdon, Tenn. 1935. FSA. Library of Congress.

tion of the minstrel himself. The assistant is replaced on stage by an even cruder racist symbol, a garishly clad minstrel dummy manipulated by the pitchman. The crowd is softened up by the routine; one of the locals accepts a medicine sample from the pitchman, who in a gesture summing up the connection between salesmanship and racial myth, offers the bottle in one hand while he clutches the dummy in the other. The one man *not* captivated by the proceedings is the minstrel, shown in 6164-M5 at the edge of the crowd, leaning against a telephone pole with hands in pockets, gazing at us, distracting us from the sight on stage that, in a less venturesome photograph, would have been the riveting focal point (fig. 3.11). Detached from the crowd, detached from his official role filled just as easily by the dummy, the assistant becomes a hauntingly in-between figure, free of the worst manipulations on stage yet still wearing a caricatured face, still distant, literally and psychologically, from the viewer.

Fig. 3.10. Ben Shahn. "A Medicine Show and Audience," Huntingdon, Tenn. 1935. FSA. Library of Congress.

Shahn might easily have stopped there, but in 6167-M4 he moves in for a closer view of the minstrel offstage, and the suggestion of an active consciousness operating behind the mask grows stronger (fig. 3.12). Seated amid some boxes, the assistant turns to face the camera as a man—perhaps surprised, perhaps anxious—rather than as a clown. In fact, the glance is reminiscent of the black onlooker's in the crowd shot (6165-M5), as authenticity begins to gain ground on artifice. The man's positioning, between the dummy resting on a box in the immediate foreground and whites looming ominously against a brick wall in the back, produces a pictorial tension with broader implications. Here, encapsulated, is the beginning of the process that popular rituals were designed to suppress. Here is the emergence—difficult, cautious, cramped, but emergence nevertheless—of the black individual in a world of confining white expectations, of misconceptions as glaring as the dummy's suit, with its uncanny resemblance to a convict's uni-

Fig. 3.11. Ben Shahn. "A Medicine Show," Huntingdon, Tenn. 1935. FSA. Library of Congress.

form. And here is Shahn's struggle, in a corner where he is not necessarily welcome, to expose the multiple layers of cultural identity. (In another photo from the same sequence that Shahn kept for his own files, two white boys appear to the left of the dummy, one glancing with considerable hostility at the camera, as if to bar the investigator from further insights. The resulting triad, encompassing the dummy's lifeless eyes, the black's suddenly expressive eyes, and the white lad's forbidding eyes, is an even stronger summation of ritual, revelation, and resistance.) The one step that Shahn does not take, of course, is depicting the medicine-show assistant *entirely without* his makeup. Perhaps this was a final barrier that a cameraman perceived as a "stranger," or even an invader, could not overcome. Whether because of white resistance or wariness on the black man's own part, this last coup in racial demythologizing had to wait.

In general, Shahn made skillful photographic use of corners and

Fig. 3.12. Ben Shahn. "A Medicine Show Puppet," Huntingdon, Tenn. 1935. FSA. Library of Congress.

edges, of spaces that confined and spaces that separated. Evident in so many of the medicine-show audience shots is the paucity of blacks in the thick of the crowd; blacks hang in the back or to the side, observing well-established social codes. In 6165-M1, the space dividing two young blacks from two older whites standing on the same public bench fairly crackles with tension, one of the blacks assiduously turning away from the nearest white, as if avoiding the slightest chance of physical contact (fig. 3.13). The youth's colleague we have seen before, juxtaposed with the minstrel in 6164-M3. As this follow-up makes clear, onstage rituals have their counterparts, subtler but no less troubling, offstage. Shahn did not focus on legal Jim Crow in Tennessee, but an image such as this does not require any segregation signs in order to drive home the message: the real ill in Huntingdon is not the one that the patent medicine pitchman is offering to cure.

Fig. 3.13. Ben Shahn. "Watching a Medicine Show," Huntingdon, Tenn. 1935. FSA. Library of Congress.

When Shahn was not examining public performances during his southern journey, he was exploring public displays of a different sort, namely signs and advertisements. The pattern had begun in West Virginia and, as noted earlier, continued in Arkansas. In Omar, West Virginia, he had photographed a black miner inspecting a theater marquee advertisement for "Hard Rock Harrigan," then walking away amid a dreary, denuded landscape. One is left to wonder whether the Hollywood melodrama—featuring a tunnel-digging crew, rivalry between "Hard Rock" (George O'Brien) and "Black Jack" Riley (Fred Kohler), mandatory cave-in, rescue of bad guy by good guy, ultimate completion of tunnel—was as hard to take for an actual tunnel-digger in strike-torn, racially divided coal country as it was for a New York reviewer who called the movie a "clinical experiment to discover just how bad a motion picture can be."[13] Was mining romance needed as a break from mining reality, or was romance being rejected in Omar, as well? The image sequence remains intriguingly ambiguous.

But it was in Natchez, Mississippi, that his sign utilization reached its quantitative and qualitative peak. Throughout the Natchez coverage, in which twenty-two of the twenty-three shots were black related, interplays between signs and other elements suggested multiple points of economic and cultural tension: a black man walking past a sagging shed plastered with patent medicine promises; another black seated in front of a slum district barbershop window, with its tantalizing "Money Saving" sign; a woman seated on her front porch with her head down, opposite a discarded traffic sign (shaped like a policeman, and strikingly white) that casts an eerie pall, a residue of official intimidation. Interplays were particularly revealing in Shahn's treatment of the shoeshine subject. Here was a two-photo series within a series (fig. 3.14). First, he provided a fairly staid overview of a sidewalk shoeshine station—crippled black man crouched at the feet of a white customer, other blacks standing politely, perhaps a bit nervously, at a distance from the more confident white; all figures viewed from afar. Then Shahn made a closer inspection in 6094-M5, isolating a single black, considering more carefully the world ignored by the white customer, dispelling the taken-for-grantedness of the previous scene and, in the

Fig. 3.14. Ben Shahn. "A Group of Negroes in Front of a Cafe," Natchez, Miss. 1935. FSA. Library of Congress.

process, offering a meditation on stations, sitters, and advertisements (fig. 3.15).

There is no submissive crouching in the closeup. If a viewer expects a pathetic victim in the one-legged black man seated to the right of the shoeshine station, the man is not accommodating with his natty suspenders, jauntily tipped hat, and vaguely elegant chair. Shahn's portrait is a far sight from a comparable shot taken just a few months later by the WPA's Oscar Jordan, who found a "58-year-old negro, Willie Hooey . . . in the doorway of a warehouse in Montgomery, Alabama, . . . hobbling around on his knees to sweep the pavement around his doorway when it gets too dirty for comfort" (fig. 3.16). But if the viewer expects an entertaining shoeshiner, the kind found frequently in *Life*, Shahn's subject is no more accommodating with his steady, serious gaze that both invites our curiosity and frustrates it. Somewhat disarming with the shadow from his hat obscuring a portion of his

Fig. 3.15. Ben Shahn. "Street Scene," Natchez, Miss. 1935. FSA. Library of Congress.

face, he is a decidedly alert figure, and quite a contrast to the slumped, lolling Natchez characters whom Margaret Bourke-White would depict, two years later, "just sitting in the sun watching the Mississippi go by."[14]

Opposite the man is another evidence of black nonsubmissiveness, a store window sign for a "Joe Louis Celebration." One should remember the early-October 1935 date of the photograph. The "celebration" concerned Louis's dramatic four-round knockout of white star Max Baer in a million-dollar extravaganza at Yankee Stadium that had been one of the most talked about nontitle fights in years. From the standpoint of many blacks, there was good reason for celebration. Baer, the onetime heavyweight champion with a penchant for crowd-pleasing high jinks in the ring (as well as nightclub carousing outside), had the mainstream media and the boxing establishment solidly behind him. But even the presence of the venerable Jack Dempsey in Baer's corner

Fig. 3.16. Oscar Jordan. "Willie Hooey, Crippled Negro, Sweeping Doorway Where He Lives," Montgomery, Ala. 1936. Works Progress Administration. National Archives.

had not prevented the rout by Louis. "The California ex-champion sinks to the canvas after taking a frightful hammering from the fists of the Detroit negro," as Damon Runyan had described the denouement, "and is counted out resting on one knee. Baer's face is a smear of blood. It sprouts from his nose and mouth, damaged by the cutting left hooks and crashing right-hand blows." Louis, who had been fighting for $50 a night a little over a year before, earned $250,000 for the victory; a title fight with reigning champ Jim Braddock was in the offing. White commentators responded to the "Detroit negro" with a mixture of condescension and fear: he was a soft-spoken, respectable sort outside the ring, some writers reported; he was, warned Associated Press correspondent Edward Neil, "the savage, merciless" fighting machine, "with no hint of expression around his broad, pink lips, no light in his dark eyes." Numerous black writers, meanwhile, were proclaiming Louis to be much more than a sports hero.[15] After the Baer fight, a

Chicago Defender editorial compared Louis with Emperor Haile Selassie: "These two men—both young—one a fighter, the other a statesman, have upheld the highest ideals of the Race by the manner in which they have conducted themselves in their respective fields and between them have performed more creditably as representatives of the Race than any two other individuals in the past decade."[16] In Natchez, the fact that the Louis Celebration is being sponsored by a "Harlem" society underscores the connection between boxing conquests and ethnic assertiveness, between the new champion-to-be and the new possibilities opened by black migration to the North. In the heart of the Deep South, signs suggest alternatives.

But the photograph is no simple celebration. The presence of the shoeshine station is a reminder, one of many in the Natchez series, of the low economic and social status in which most blacks remained. Moreover, the Coca-Cola advertisement at the right, looming so much larger than the Louis Celebration and "Rex Nite Club" signs, underlines the relentless march of corporate America. Shahn would comment later on the significance of big-corporate, mass-produced signs penetrating and even dominating the spaces once occupied only by small-business, hand-lettered advertisements; the standardized versus individualized byplay had more than aesthetic implications for the photographer. The slick lineup of Coke bottles in the Natchez sign is emblematic of a white-controlled mass culture that tended either to divert attention away from ethnic cultures or to enfold them. (The juxtaposition of a Louis reference with a mass-culture icon was prophetic: by the early 1940s, the black champion was often cast in the mainstream media as the physically powerful but staunchly loyal, dependable black American.)

There is the final ironic juxtaposition of a one-legged black man with Joe Louis and nightclub dancing signs suggesting leg-oriented activity; pride rubs against the limitations of physical reality as one man's street-corner world becomes distinct from the glamour world of the Brown Bomber. And so it is that the image, considered along with Shahn's other shoeshine shot, presents a series of tensions: transcendence and restriction, ethnic culture and mass culture, self-perception and societal expectation. The lack of a simple resolution, the open-endedness that characterizes form (signs cut off at the right, tipped hat cut off at the top, shoeshine station cut off at the left) as well as content, was hardly what an orthodox Marxist, a racial traditionalist, or, for that matter, a Resettlement Administration publicist would have been seeking that autumn. This is not to imply that Shahn was any paragon of objectivity; one might complain that his very inclusion of the Joe Louis sign was an imposition on the main portrait subject, who deserved to be presented on his own terms. Admittedly, Shahn did his share of manipulating, just as journalists did their share with respect to Louis. But the point remains that, on a side street in Natchez, no less than on the main street of Huntingdon, Shahn was sensitive, and unusually so by 1930s standards, to a range of historical, cultural, and racial meanings embedded in the fabric of the everyday.

4

The Photo-Series: Arthur Rothstein and the Missouri Bootheel

FSA photographers did not ordinarily go hunting for strikes and demonstrations, for the clashes that made headlines during the Great Depression. One might have expected this troubleshooting from Ben Shahn; as we have seen, it did not come to pass. But there were occasions when the "front line" news story seemed to find the FSA photographer. Such a convergence of right time and right place came during Arthur Rothstein's January 1939 visit to New Madrid County, Missouri. Rothstein planned a routine coverage of resettled sharecroppers meeting with advisors on the FSA's LaForge Project. He wound up devoting most of his attention to events, considerably more dramatic, along the area's highways.

The area was Missouri's southeastern tip, aptly dubbed the "Bootheel"—a place, FSA economists were reporting, of "Rich Land, Poor People." Economically and socially, this was the Delta South more than the Midwest: plantation agriculture, cotton based; landless farmers, nine times as numerous as landowners; extensive sharecropper displacement, due to mechanization and planter application of AAA programs; sharecroppers–turned–day laborers, disproportionately black, competing with migrants from Arkansas and Texas for work at depressed wages; racial discrimination and violence as deeply rooted as poverty. "Before a Negro can receive [local] relief," FSA economists found, "he must be in much more desperate straits than a white man. Among many members of the Negro group there was an attitude that relief was not for them."[1] The LaForge Project, composed of sixty white and forty black families and not as rigidly segregated as other mixed settlements, provided some hope, as did the agency's rehabilitation loan program. But FSA resources were vastly outstripped by Bootheel needs, which grew more acute at the end of 1938 when seventy of the largest landowners decided to shift operations from the tenancy system to day labor. Some of the hundreds of sharecroppers affected received formal eviction notices. Most were given to understand that, if they wanted to stay, they could do so only as wage hands. Faced with the prospect of three months of unemployment until cotton chopping in April, and then of trying to support their families on wages of seventy-five cents a day, sharecroppers began heeding the advice of Owen Whitfield, a black Baptist preacher, LaForge resident, and activist for the STFU and United Canning, Agriculture, Packing, and Allied Workers of America. Whitfield urged his followers to demonstrate their plight to the world. And that they did.

On 10 January 1939, some 1,300 embittered sharecroppers and day laborers—later estimated at 90–95 percent black—took their household possessions to the edge of the open road, where they set up crude camps along seventy miles of Highway 61 and thirty-eight miles of Highway 60. Amid their bundles, their bedsteads, and even their kitchen stoves, entire families settled in for what promised to be a difficult stay. "It's gotten so the sharecroppers couldn't stand it any more, that's all," one demonstration leader told a reporter, "and now that we've been thrown out in the cold, we're going to stick together and fight together until something happens."[2] Nature was not accommodating, with winds, snow, and freezing temperatures. Nor were local and state officials, who denied emergency aid to the families, prevented J. R. Butler and other national STFU leaders from lending on-site support, branded the demonstration the work of "subversives" and "Fifth Columnists," and blamed the FSA. LaForge director Hans Baasch, declared a landowner resolution read before the U.S. Senate by Harry Truman, "is reliably reported to have made various communistic remarks leading to this trouble, [such as] 'it will not be long before all the ground in New Madrid County will be owned by the government and given to the poor people when divided into 40-acre tracts.' "[3]

By 13 January, state police, armed with orders from the Missouri health commissioner, began removing the sharecroppers from the highways, scattering them among less visible, but no more hospitable, locales. The largest contingent was moved to a swampy area, adjoining the New Madrid Spillway, known as "Homeless Junction"; there, further controversy arose when the state police confiscated sharecroppers' firearms (mostly hunting pieces), roughing up several blacks in the process. Highway Patrol Officer A. D. Sheppard, defending the strenuous policing of the camp, reportedly told a federal investigator that critics "did not understand what was necessary in handling niggers."[4] Six days later, just as FSA emergency supplies were due to arrive at Homeless Junction, the group was moved again, this time to cramped quarters in a church (ironically, the Sweet Home Baptist Church) where many families remained for another three months.

In spillway camps, out-of-the-way churches, and abandoned dance halls the protest ended in disarray. It was not a total failure. Some landowners, fearing the results of an AAA inquiry, eventually made concessions, allowing a small percentage of the sharecroppers back on pre-eviction terms. The FSA expanded its loan, grant, and housing programs in the area (including construction of the Delmo Labor Homes), despite continuing resistance from local officials. Whitfield, who had fled New Madrid upon receiving death threats the night before the demonstration commenced, worked through the St. Louis Committee for the Rehabilitation of the Sharecropper to settle nearly one hundred displaced families on privately purchased land. At the very least, the protest drew heavy national press coverage at a time when the general subject of sharecroppers was passing out of the limelight. The nation did watch, though the coverage had notable limitations, particularly on the pictorial side. Associated Press photographers, along with camerapeople representing the *St. Louis Post-Dispatch* and other Missouri papers, arrived on the scene not long after the demonstrators; by the morning of the eleventh, pictures were appearing in newspapers ranging from the *Memphis Commercial-Appeal* to the *New York Herald Tribune*, from the *Chicago Daily News* to the *Daily Worker*. Partly because of the common AP picture source (prominent newspapers often sent their own correspondents, but not their own photographers, to Missouri), there tended to be considerable uniformity in pictorial coverage throughout the crisis. The uniformity certainly did not favor black protesters. While blacks constituted the overwhelming majority on the roads, whites tended to receive the closeup views on newspaper pages.

The *Chicago Daily News* employment of AP pictures was indicative in this regard. On the eleventh, readers were given a distant view of blacks trudging across a bridge en route to the highway encampments, and an even more distant shot of black "families and their belongings strung along the road" (fig. 4.1). By contrast, the white scene published that day was intimate, engaging—a family carrying on in makeshift quarters, father holding a young child in his lap, mother feeding the toddler from a pot in the immediate foreground. (Significantly, the *Daily News* saved its punchy, populist caption for the white photo, under which the sharecroppers were described "blam[ing] their plight on [the] government crop control law, which restricts the growth of cotton." Here, by implication, was a natural family group, protesting an unnatural law.) The portrayal of blacks as no more distinct than heaps of furniture, whites as more recognizably and appealingly human, continued in subsequent issues. On the thirteenth, the *Daily News* featured a human-interest shot of a makeshift *white* school on the highway's edge, complete with teacher standing atop a barrel and sharecropper children clustered around slates bearing their lessons. On the fourteenth, the New Madrid coverage returned to the anonymous, with snow emphasized in the foreground ("All Is Not Beautiful in the Snow—Not Near New Madrid"), blacks and their tents merging into the landscape.[5] At least the *Daily News* acknowledged a black presence; there were papers, such as the pivotally located *Washington Post*, that restricted their pictorial coverage *solely* to whites.

When newspapers did bring black faces to the fore, they often exploited stereotypes. There were shades of the picturesque in the AP photo, used in the *St. Louis Globe-Democrat*, of black demonstrators handling a live chicken brought for eventual consumption ("We Eat"), and there were shades of the primitive in the *St. Louis Post-Dispatch* pictures of demonstrators kneeling and bowing their heads in ardent prayer ("Prayer among the grown-ups and bewilderment for the children").[6] The focus on the flock, rather than the prayer leaders, was also important here: newspapers omitted direct coverage of the many Whitfield lieutenants who helped keep the protest going for three days.

Fig. 4.1. Unidentified AP photographer. "Hundreds of Sharecroppers Marched with Their Meager Possessions . . ." New Madrid, Mo. 10 Jan. 1939. Reproduced by permission of Wide World Photos, Inc.

The specter of black *directors* might have been threatening to the average reader, the specter of black followers much less so. "Patient, devout, and inured to poverty and hardship," went the *St. Louis Post-Dispatch* picture-page commentary, "the homeless croppers carried out their demonstration without making trouble."[7]

Hence, newspaper coverage of the highway encampments made extremely unconventional sharecropper activity more palatable, at the expense of the all-important black angle. Depictions of the forced removals also tended to be safe. The focus was on piled possessions, on cars and trucks, rather than on individuals. Not only did this emphasis keep protesters (black as well as white) in the background, but it served to conceal tensions between sharecroppers and state police. For ex-

ample, the lone removal picture run in the *Philadelphia Inquirer* was an
AP selection shot from the back of a highway patrol truck, with the
vast truck bed obscuring the figures of patrolmen and demonstrators.
"The police provided trucks, where necessary, to take families and
their belongings back to the farms or to temporary relief camps," assured the *Inquirer* caption.[8] Or, in the case of the *St. Louis Post-Dispatch*, the interest seemed to be in the range of vehicles used for the
removal (an image of a smiling black sharecropper carting off his
family's possessions in a horse-drawn wagon) rather than the issue of
the dispersal itself.[9] As for the final fate of the protesters, coverage was
generally limited to an overview of the spillway camp—tents, barren
ground, but few discernible faces. Sharecropper-police troubles, camp
suffering, and subsequent dispersals received varying textual treatment—"Sheriff Thwarts Sharecroppers Riot Plot: 500 at Camp Had
Arsenal," the *St. Louis Globe-Democrat* proclaimed; "Terror Reigns
among Evicted Croppers as U.S. Begins Probe," the *Daily Worker* countered—but no visual treatment.[10] It is probable that officials guarding
the spillway camp and other relocation sites discouraged photographers' entry; it is also probable that the news agencies with photographers on hand considered the follow-up story too tangential, too em-
barrassing, or perhaps too black, to justify persistent risk-taking.

Of course, we do not have complete knowledge of what the AP,
Post-Dispatch, and other photographers might have shot that was never
used. There is evidence that one or more photographers actually made
it into the relocation sites: several uncredited photographs (perhaps by
Missouri free-lancers James Turnbull or Peter Keep) showing evacuees
in an abandoned dance hall and in the spillway camp, eventually
wound up in the files of Fannie Cook of the St. Louis Committee for
the Rehabilitation of the Sharecropper. Given this incomplete knowledge, the comparison between published news photographs and the
complete Rothstein file is only half-revealing, for one can never be
certain that any Rothstein departure from the published norm was in
fact unique. Still, the comparison does suggest the extent to which the
FSA cameraman did or did not produce the sort of New Madrid shots
that were favored in the American mainstream.

New Madrid was not Rothstein's first exposure to blacks in difficult economic straits. He had taken hard looks at conditions in Florida, Maryland, and New Jersey migrant camps, in Washington, D.C., slums, and, just prior to the New Madrid story, in midwestern industrial towns. "Unfortunately, all this WPA money is being spent on the usual silly little projects," he had written Stryker from Herring, Illinois. "If the present system is continued, after awhile the visitor to this area will find the ridiculous situation where there are beautiful, well-paved roads with flowers . . . on the borders, elaborate picnic grounds and recreation areas, magnificent schools, resplendent bridges and a population housed in decaying shacks, too poor to be able to drive over the pretty highways, unable to afford picnics, children who cannot go to school because they have no clothes or can't afford to buy textbooks."[11] New Madrid was, however, Rothstein's first encounter with substantial numbers of blacks taking the initiative to protest their situation. Quantitatively, the photographer made no effort to minimize the black presence on the highways. Quite the opposite was the case. In fact, one would be distorting the Rothstein coverage by showcasing his shots of white demonstrators. Of the eighty-seven printed photos comprising Rothstein's New Madrid series, racial identities can be discerned in seventy-four; of this group, sixty shots (81 percent) concerned black demonstrators, twelve concerned whites, and two showed sharecroppers of both races. What's more, of the sixty black images, forty (66 percent) gave their subjects a strong foreground presence, and 16 percent were of the extreme-closeup, pure portrait variety that Rothstein tended to include, in this same proportion, in many of his predominantly white coverages. In short, Rothstein faced the reality, inherently troubling for many newspaper editors, that the move to the highways was essentially a black phenomenon, a matter of "invisible" men and women demanding visibility.

The closer focus on black protesters produced various results. Consider Rothstein's tour of one of the strung-out Highway 60 camps. Moving from one group to another with his 35-millimeter camera, Rothstein at times played up the beleaguered-refugee theme, suitable for prodding consciences and loosening government purse strings. What was a distant whimper in the newspaper photos was an unmistakable cry in such images as 2968-M1 (fig. 4.2) and 2943-M5. In

2968-M1, the lone, stooping figure of the woman—backed by a leaning tower of barrels, bundles, and frames—creates the impression of
impossible burdens, as well as dangerous vulnerability: next stop, disaster. The fact that the woman's posture resembles that of a cotton
picker is perhaps a coincidence, but a handy one for the photographer's
purposes. Additionally, the rope tied over one of the bundles and
stretching into the immediate foreground fairly invites a "hand" from
the viewer. A stoop becomes a crouch in 2943-M5 as another lone
figure, this time a young boy, stares disconsolately at the ashes of a
campfire (fig. 4.3). The empty chair opposite the lad adds to the sense
of loss (no heat, no company); the "American Sunrise" labels on
nearby lard cans lend the requisite irony. Here the American sun illu-
minates a scene of American despair. The only forceful item missing
from this picture is the brand name of the stove, which, one realizes
from an earlier shot, is none other than "Eclipse." With its accent on

Fig. 4.2. Arthur Rothstein. "An Evicted Sharecropper along U.S. Highway 60,"
New Madrid County, Mo. 1939. FSA. Library of Congress.

the downward gaze—viewer peering at the downtrodden figure, down-trodden figure peering at the ground—2943-M5 epitomizes an approach, almost suspiciously perfect in its dramatic thrust, that Rothstein also used for some of his white portraits (for example, in 2951-M3, the boy slumped hopelessly in a chair, hat pulled low over his eyes). Had *The New Republic* published photographs, these images would have fit the account of "shivering, hungry families exhibit[ing] themselves, a sort of specimen social ulcer, to frightened motorists."[12]

But, lest one conclude that the essence of Rothstein's black coverage was the substitution of the black victim for the newspapers' anonymous black, one should note the many highway camp images of a considerably more complex nature. Had Rothstein been interested only in heart tuggers—New Madrid black versions of the FSA classics from the Dust Bowl refugee camps of California—an image such as 2945-M4 would not have made much sense (fig. 4.4). Rather than

Fig. 4.3. Arthur Rothstein. "An Evicted Sharecropper along U.S. Highway 60," New Madrid County, Mo. 1939. FSA. Library of Congress.

emphasizing the pregnant woman's exposure to the elements, the portrait presents husband and wife in a confident, almost commanding pose. Dressed as if for a formal occasion (only the man's mud-stained boots are a concession to the environment), hands thrust jauntily in pant or coat pockets, faces composed, the couple stands firmly in front of the tent and neatly-stacked possessions. Heads rise above the bleak landscape, the woman turns slightly toward the man in a gesture of unity, and, in the process, the subjects take on more the appearance of homeowners than evictees. Composition reinforces this impression of stability, as the curve running from the woman's elbow to the man's hat is echoed in the curve of the tent, rising out of the picture at the left. Simple specimens of social ulcer these figures were not; instead, there is the sense of an insistent order.

Other family shots convey mixed messages. In 2967-M4, for example, the apparent imbalance in the group—women present, one of

Fig. 4.4. Arthur Rothstein. "Evicted Sharecroppers along U.S. Highway 60," New Madrid County, Mo. 1939. FSA. Library of Congress.

them very obviously pregnant; children present; but, except for the old man turned away from the camera in the background, adult males absent—suggests disarray (fig. 4.5). Yet the fur-lined coat, worn by the woman at the right, and the spunky, bemused expressions of the children at the left work against a pitying response on the viewer's part. This ambiguity continues in some of the related closeups. The photographer zeroes in on the aforementioned old man and juxtaposes his sturdy features, his pose of an outdoorsman seated amid the wilderness, and his hard, direct gaze at the camera with the discomforting darkness of the open tent (fig. 4.6). Assertiveness in new surroundings, clarity along with an element of mystery: the portrait does not make it easy to view the man merely as a problem. Rothstein also zeroes in on the fur-coated woman, finding a curious combination of elegance in the outer garment with holes and safety pins in the layer directly beneath (fig. 4.7). There are other tensions here—the woman's

Fig. 4.5. Arthur Rothstein. "Evicted Sharecroppers along U.S. Highway 60," New Madrid County, Mo. 1939. FSA. Library of Congress.

Fig. 4.6. Arthur Rothstein. "An Evicted Sharecropper," New Madrid County, Mo. 1939. FSA. Library of Congress.

Fig. 4.7. Arthur Rothstein. "An Evicted Sharecropper along U.S. Highway 60," New Madrid County, Mo. 1939. FSA. Library of Congress.

head held high despite an anxious expression, her imposing frame set against a stovepipe rising forcefully, a bit ominously, behind her. Her interior shabbiness exposed, the woman has the appearance less of a pleader than someone with very mixed feelings about being an "exhibit." Hers is a personality to be reckoned with, no less than the three men, from another group (2926-M3), who seem to press forward and inspect Rothstein as studiously as he was undoubtedly inspecting them. Tension between black subjects and an inquiring white photographer may well be a subtext in some of these images, but amid the tension, black subjects—no less than whites—emerge as social actors rather than simply figures acted upon, and as thinkers rather than simply figures thought about. The activism that spawned the demonstration in the first place also comes through in Rothstein's faces.

With his interest in the demonstrators' fortitude, Rothstein might have been tempted to play up the religious theme. But, to his credit, the FSAer avoided the "faithful flock" emphasis appearing in the *St. Louis Post-Dispatch*. Wisely, Rothstein did not extend to the New Madrid coverage the "simple people of the Lord" spirit that infused his own Gee's Bend, Alabama, story two years before. The prime subject in one of Rothstein's more striking series within a series clutches not a family Bible but, rather, what appears to be a family clock in its original box (fig. 4.8). Rothstein observes the woman standing alone with the box tucked firmly under her arm, then joining a larger group around the highway patrol truck, and eventually standing alone in the back of the vehicle, gazing fixedly down the highway. The grasping of the nonreligious item has its own symbolic power, conveying both the sense of time running out on the sharecroppers (and perhaps the sharecropping system as a whole) and the sense of timeless endurance by a figure beset from every side. The structure of the mini-narrative is such that the woman does not fade gently into the flock; her expression in the opening closeup is severe, bordering on defiant, with none of the stereotyped softness evident in the *Post-Dispatch* faces. In fact, she is very much the match for Rothstein's stubborn-faced white sharecropper portrayed, in 2929-M3 (fig. 4.9), with hand resting protectively on the family sewing machine. Rothstein's depictions of persistence among the economically uprooted—clock-toting or sewing machine-

Fig. 4.8. Arthur Rothstein. "An Evicted Sharecropper along U.S. Highway 60," New Madrid County, Mo. 1939. FSA. Library of Congress.

Fig. 4.9 Arthur Rothstein. "Evicted Sharecroppers along U.S. Highway 60," New Madrid County, Mo. 1939. FSA. Library of Congress.

gripping pioneers facing a hostile world—thus show a considerable measure of racial evenhandedness. Rothstein's emphasis in both these images on the rugged individual, as opposed to the collectivity, would not be pleasing to Pete Daniel, Maren Stange, and other New Left critics of the FSA. Admittedly, Rothstein's populist symbols could sometimes be somewhat overdrawn. But if Rothstein appeared to be in a noncollectivist mood during his 1939 midwestern tour, he had his reasons. In an account, for Stryker, of a United Mine Workers meeting in Herring, Illinois, Rothstein notes: "The union is very autocratic around here. The rank and file are not allowed to make any criticism and fear that they will be thrown out and lose their jobs if they do. The officers are appointed, not elected, and look and act like the worst kind of bureaucrats."[13]

Rothstein also recognized the multiple implications of continuity and change in New Madrid. In 2923-M4 (fig. 4.10) and 2947-M4 (fig. 4.11), there are subtle reflections of an uneasy alliance between the majority blacks and minority whites on the highway. Consider Rothstein's choices in these related tent-side views. He might easily have concentrated on the cute element in both—namely, the white girl with the jump rope. Such a keynote would have been a newspaper picture-editor's delight. But the photos go beyond the obvious human-interest angle, incorporating a series of provocative juxtapositions. In fig. 4.10, the white girl jumps rope; black children, remaining a safe distance away, eye the activity across a space that seems fraught with danger. These are figures of innocence, figures of not-so-innocent custom. Meanwhile, a black sharecroper stoops to gather a cardboard box next to the tent, fingering the object gingerly as if he might be accused of theft; a white man turns to inspect the action, again from a distance. Finally, a second black adult confers with a better-dressed white in front of the tent, their postures suggesting an awkward formality. A busy scene, fig. 4.10 is revealingly bifurcated, with the compositional line running from the girl's feet to the main tent-pole functioning as a racial divider. In fig. 4.11, blacks and whites are grouped around the same makeshift stove, perhaps an accomplishment in itself; the blacks are even seated, indicating a degree of confidence. Yet note the configuration: blacks on one side of the barrel, whites on the other; whites,

Fig. 4.10 (*Above*) and Fig. 4.11 (*Below*). Arthur Rothstein. "Evicted Sharecroppers' Camp," New Madrid County, Mo. 1939. FSA. Library of Congress.

including the well-dressed man from the aforementioned photo, turned entirely away from their "stove-mates." Bootheel traditions are bent but not broken, as the groups seem to occupy separate worlds much in the same way as Shahn's Tennessee medicine-show watchers. That Rothstein was thinking about the precariousness of interracial cooperation is suggested in his 16 January letter to Stryker, in which the photographer recounts a painful episode witnessed just before he began the demonstration coverage. "At the [annual LaForge] meeting," Rothstein wrote, "two negroes were nominated by the negro population of the project to serve on the board of directors of the co-op. There was an almost electric atmosphere until, to the applause of the white voters, the two negroes 'voluntarily' refused the nomination."[14]

Not long after Rothstein arrived at the highway camps, state police began the removal. On this particularly controversial phase of the New Madrid story, Rothstein's letters were hard-hitting. "[The demonstrators] are much worse off now than they were before the state troopers moved them from the highway," he wrote Stryker. "While they were along the roads, people brought them food and clothing, though the Red Cross refused to do anything under threats of no contributions from the planters. Most of [the demonstrators] are now in open fields or barns well away from the public eye."[15] Some of that probing quality carried over to Rothstein's photography. For example, 2954-M3 is much more than a group portrait of demonstrators awaiting transport (fig. 4.12). Lying in the immediate foreground is a split log with axe still embedded—a provocative suggestion not only of interrupted activity, or of demonstrator assertiveness on occupied territory (a sort of pioneer's laying of claims), but of potential friction between law enforcement officials and protesters. Arrayed behind the log, their faces showing more suspicion than patience, the five blacks appear readier to stand their ground than to cooperate with authorities. In the end, of course, the demonstrators had little choice but to acquiesce in the clearance order, and the immediate burdens of that acquiescence emerge in the Rothstein series, as they did *not* in the newspaper coverage. While vehicles piled high with possessions were treated simply as an accomplished fact in the papers, Rothstein explored the process—with some interpretive bite.

Fig. 4.12. Arthur Rothstein. "Sharecroppers Being Moved Away from the Roadside by Highway Officials to an Area between the Levee and the Mississippi River," New Madrid County, Mo. 1939. FSA. Library of Congress.

In 2975-M2, the photographer incorporates a highway junction sign as an intriguing narrative element in a scene of demonstrators lugging their possessions across a gully and toward the highway patrol trucks (fig. 4.13). The arduous human movement is toward the left of the picture, and it is at the far left that the sign reminds the viewer both of the sharecroppers' present difficulties (one arrow pointing to the right) and their uncertain future (the other arrow pointing to the left, out of the picture, perhaps in the general direction of Homeless Junction). As the next image makes clear, the joining of Missouri roads was not accompanied by a joining of Missouri classes; at these crossroads, the blacks are doing the hauling, the white patrolmen the presiding. Rothstein also uses image sequences for a reconsideration of the super-ficially routine. In 2940-M1, 2940-M3, 2934-M1, and 2934-M2, he moves from fairly standard views of loaded trucks to distinctly un-settling images that juxtapose the highway activity with what appear to

Fig. 4.13. Arthur Rothstein. "State Highway Officials Moving Sharecroppers Away from the Roadside to an Area between the Levee and the Mississippi River," New Madrid County, Mo. 1939. FSA. Library of Congress.

be tombstones. Set in a bleak winter landscape, under isolated trees, the markers of death evoke ominous associations, corresponding to Rothstein's fears about the sharecroppers' post-highway fate. "An especially vicious thing has been done with about 75 negro families," he informed Stryker. "They were dumped in an area inhabited by river rats and other desperate whites along the lost levee who were proud of the fact that no negro dared poke his nose around their part of the country."[16]

Accordingly, the highway patrolmen are not entirely neutral functionaries in Rothstein's photographic rendering. Subtle vignettes say much about the indignities and tensions of the situation. One patrolman (in 2973-M5) pokes through a family's possessions behind the backs of the family members, who concentrate on a sight down the road; another patrolman (2920-M3) exchanges conflicting gestures with a black man who, positioned for loading in the back of a truck, appears the much harder worker, and momentarily the more commanding, of the two (fig. 4.14). The loader points *down* at the trooper, who in turn gestures toward the ground, as if uncomfortable with the black's aggressive posture. In the follow-up to the latter scene, Rothstein gives the loader his due, as the sharecropper poses in front of the truck bearing his handiwork (fig. 4.15). Backed by his carefully stacked possessions, including a broom just above his shoulder, and showing a certain determined orderliness amid the chaotic circumstances, the man effectively beats the officer at the officer's own game. No grinning flunky, even if he falls short of rebelliousness, the loader invites our respect to a much greater degree than does his supervisor. Rothstein goes a step further in 2932-M2, presenting an all too blatant dichotomy of good guys versus bad guys (fig. 4.16). Not only is the patrolman shown as unhelpful here—standing, with hands in pockets, directly behind a group of blacks who struggle mightily to load a heavy piece of furniture—but he is of the cigar-chomping, protrusive-bellied species, very much the Rothstein answer to Shahn's broad-rumped West Virginia deputy or Lange's arrogant Mississippi landowner. Swaggering white villain, black victims—had this image, with its almost cartoon-like quality, been the sum total of Rothstein's coverage of the police intervention, one might charge the FSAer with offering crude didacti-

Fig. 4.14. Arthur Rothstein. "State Highway Officials Moving Sharecroppers Away from the Roadside to an Area between the Levee and the Mississippi River," New Madrid County, Mo. 1939. FSA. Library of Congress.

cism in place of the newspapers' polite runarounds. What we have
seen, however, is that Rothstein was quite capable of subtlety even as
he was producing a pointed narrative. (In most books about the FSA,
or about Rothstein in particular, the cigar-chomping patrolman image
is the one used to "represent" the New Madrid coverage. Actually, one
of the strengths of the series is that the patrolmen do not *always* emerge
as obvious villains. Along with the images mentioned, there are those,
such as 2936-M4 or 2931-M3, in which officers preside without any
particular pushiness.)

In sum, Rothstein's coverage of the highway camps and their dis-
bandment took some imaginative, unpredictable turns—separating
black individuals from the mass, presenting black demonstrators in a
variety of attitudes (not necessarily plaintive), accenting the human
side of a demonstration breakup that was too often viewed in imper-
sonal terms, suggesting tensions that newspaper visuals concealed. Yet
for all these insights, Rothstein's view was by no means comprehen-
sive. There were limitations from the outset. Whether because of technical problems or resistance from the subjects, Rothstein took but a
handful of shots *inside* tents, and, as a result, the sense of round-the-
clock protest, the sense of the camp as a sleeping-eating environment,
was diminished. Interestingly, his few interiors involved a white family; in this regard, Rothstein's white coverage had one measure of intimacy that was lacking on the black side. Additionally, while Rothstein
showed groups of demonstrators conferring around stoves, he offered
no more attention to leaders, black or white, than did the newspapers.
He claimed, to Stryker, that by the time he arrived, "the leaders [had
been] run out of the area by the county sheriff."[17] But this was not
entirely accurate. Whitfield lieutenants were still to be found;
Rothstein, perhaps more in a mood after his UMW experience to see a
spontaneous rising than an organized movement, did not seek them
out. In any case, the photographer did not mention any weeding out
of leaders in his captions.

There is *much* that the captions did not convey. Rothstein's private
communications reflected his recognition that "the situation was created when the planters gave the croppers the alternative of getting off
the land or remaining as day laborers. . . . The move to the highways

Fig. 4.15. Arthur Rothstein. "A Sharecropper Who Was Moved from the Roadside to an Area between the Levee and the Mississippi River by the State Highway Officials," New Madrid County, Mo. 1939. FSA. Library of Congress.

Fig. 4.16. Arthur Rothstein. "State Highway Officials Moving Sharecroppers Away from the Roadside to an Area between the Levee and the Mississippi River," New Madrid County, Mo. 1939. FSA. Library of Congress.

was a public protest against this kind of economic slavery."[18] Yet the captions—in effect, his public statements—referred to the protesters simply as "evicted sharecroppers." Was this the result merely of Rothstein's general tendency toward sketchy caption-writing, in contrast to the habits of Lee, Lange, and Wolcott? Or was Rothstein, perhaps considering future publication possibilities, playing it safe with a caption that described symptoms rather than causes? Whatever the thinking (and perhaps both considerations were at work), the result was that some of the larger, more disturbing dimensions of the New Madrid affair—such as landlord-client conflict over a number of issues, including wage levels—remained hidden in the FSA coverage. And there was another, even more important, missing link.

The momentum that developed in the series as it moved from the protest to the police intervention petered out at the next stop, namely, Homeless Junction. Quantitatively, only eight photos comprised Rothstein's coverage of the sites to which the demonstrators were taken, and the final installment was also a qualitative anticlimax. The virtu-

ally identical views of the New Madrid spillway camp convey something of the area's barrenness and remoteness (the truck tires leaving
deep scars in the marshy ground, with long afternoon shadows intensi-
fying the gloom), yet they remain extremely distant, devoid of the
human engagement that marked the earlier coverage.

If the intention of the state authorities was to return the sharecroppers to an invisible status, Rothstein's spillway photography did not do
much to counteract that effort. Living conditions in the new camp,
conflicts with patrolmen over firearms confiscation and other issues,
the "river rat" problem to which Rothstein referred in his letters, the
subsequent removal of Homeless Junction residents to yet other problematical sites—all went unrecorded on film. It was not until ten
months later, long after the crisis had subsided, that Rothstein's story
picked up again with his visit to a Butler County backwoods settlement composed chiefly of ex-demonstrators. That forty-three–photo
series had a few intriguing wrinkles: an indication that the ever-so-
tenuous cooperation between black and white protesters extended from
the highway camps to the settlement, and the depiction—at long
last—of black leadership (an outdoor meeting of community residents,
directed by blacks). In general, however, the series concentrated on
the safer theme of demonstrators–turned–industrious homesteaders
cutting wood, repairing cabins, drawing water, washing clothes. Lost
in the bustle of homemaking activity was the less inspiring story of
what happened to those demonstrators before they reached the settlement, or what happened to the many demonstrators who never ended
up in this relatively tranquil, self-governing community. Lost as well
was the larger consideration of whether the Bootheel conditions that
had prompted the highway demonstration in the first place had fundamentally changed. Rothstein's follow-up was more than any newspaper offered, but it fell short of the searching investigation that
Rothstein's January passions seemed to demand. "This whole mess,"
the photographer had written Stryker, "is just the beginning of what
will happen as the planters realize that the sharecropper system has
outworn its usefulness."[19]

To be sure, the time constraints, particularly on his first visit in
January, did not encourage a careful tracking of the demonstration's

aftermath. Unlike Russell Lee's visit to the Bootheel the previous year, designed to produce a massive survey of the area's problems and FSA solutions, Rothstein's January trip was a side venture in a tour bearing a very different focus. With the agency's New Madrid file already well stocked before 1939, with sharecropper problems no longer a top priority for FSA photography in general (Stryker's push for small-town coverage was at its peak), there was an administrative rationale for Rothstein *not* lingering on the post-demonstration scene. Assignments in southern Illinois coal towns, and points east, beckoned; in fact, shortly after Rothstein left New Madrid, Stryker was peppering him with documentary suggestions for West Virginia and Pennsylvania.

But, beyond the matter of photographic commitments, there was the matter of controversy. Had Rothstein stayed on and attempted to explore the full Homeless Junction story, he likely would have had to tangle with local authorities. He had stepped on toes in previous photo-stories, but never in an area where the agency had as much at stake as it did in the Bootheel. Rothstein, who commented to Stryker on newspaper reports of the protest, knew well that the New Madrid crisis had placed the FSA under severe attack by Missouri officials. And Rothstein also knew that the FSA needed *some* state and local cooperation in order to carry out its aid programs. Rather than playing the pushy FSA photographer, and perhaps giving alarmed locals even more reason to associate the FSA with "troublemaking Communists," Rothstein simply turned to other photographic business. This was the pragmatic side of the cameraman—rather different from the persona presented in his letters. To recognize this side is not to dismiss Rothstein's achievements in the Bootheel. It is merely to suggest the boundaries of FSA innovation.

There were also lapses in other FSA coverages of strike and demonstration stories. Vachon's 1938 series on an interracial farmworkers' strike near Morrisville, Pennsylvania, did not follow the event to its denouement, and neither did Delano's 1941 coverage of a textile workers' strike in Greene County, Georgia. A certain discontinuity, perhaps calculated, was par for the FSA course in this particularly controversial realm. The most detailed coverage of a militant labor organization—Lee's 1939–40 views of STFU, Workers' Alliance, and

United Canning, Agricultural, Packing, and Allied Workers of America meetings in Oklahoma—came in a nonstrike, noncrisis situation. For all the brilliance of that coverage—Lee's sensitivity to differences among the neo-Populist, Socialist, and Communist-influenced organizations; his sensitivity to racial experimentation as well as cultural continuities; his incorporation of union members' comments in his captions—there remained the unanswered question of what these meetings actually produced in the way of action.

The Homeless Junction story left out of Rothstein's coverage tended to be downplayed, as well, in some of the agency's published accounts of the demonstration's conclusion. By 1940, one account was even sounding a distinctly boosterish note. "Perhaps only in Missouri," wrote Constance Daniel in the NAACP's *Crisis*, "could the cause [of the protesters] have found open support from members of the planter class itself. . . . Race lines were crossed, class lines were crossed; and the drama of Southeast Missouri's sharecroppers ended around the council table, with all groups represented."[20] Officially, all was well that ended well. Unofficially, Rothstein knew better.

5

The Photo-Series: Russell Lee, Chicago, and the 1940s

"Undoubtedly, a large number of farmers and especially young rural people have been attracted to the city," Russell Lee wrote his photographic chief in January 1937. "I shall investigate some of these houses. It may be that a photographic survey of . . . slums from the angle of farmers moving [in] and from [the angle of] low-income urban families would be important. Do we have anything in files on the subject?"[1]

The "city" in question, the "city" that Lee would proceed to investigate with characteristic thoroughness, hardly ranked as a city at all—Ottawa, Illinois. Such was also the case with the other "cities," the Muskogees and San Augustines and Belle Glades, that FSA photographers examined intensively in the 1930s. As for the real metropolitan focal points of migration, Stryker did not encourage photographic inquiries. Stryker's photographers, finding a plentitude of fresh material in what for many of them was a previously unseen American hinterland, remained slow to challenge official policy. The FSA record of urban black life in these years, like that of urban white life, consisted mainly of scattered glimpses: Evans, passing through Atlanta on his way to sharecropper country, photographing the interior of a black barbershop; Rothstein, passing through Pittsburgh, catching a few portraits of steelworkers; Wolcott, passing through Memphis on a cotton-marketing story, taking a brief look at sidewalk activity on Beale Street. Even the most sustained of the early urban investigations—Mydans's Washington, D.C., slum work, designed to provide material for Suburban Resettlement before-and-after publicity—generally lacked the multidimensional, social-cultural coverage of the small-community studies.

Not until April 1941 was there a major departure from the pattern.

It came in the city, seventy miles northeast of Ottawa, that Lee had passed up in 1937, the black metropolis within a metropolis, south-side Chicago.

Several developments made the massive Chicago series possible. First, increasing FSA attention to the nation's defense buildup in 1940–41 carried with it a general impetus for coverage of industrial and administrative centers; the action was not in Ottawa. While Stryker never "went" urban to the extent justified by demographic realities, he was more inclined to commit staff time to a Detroit or a Chicago in 1941 than two or three years earlier. Second, the well-publicized 1940–41 congressional hearings of the Tolan committee, the Committee on Interstate Migration, beginning with the subject of migrant farmworkers but ultimately expanding to urban migration, further bolstered and legitimated FSA urban interest. Third, there was the black urban focus in the literary sensation of 1940. "There will be attempts to laugh off [*Native Son*] and to shout it down," wrote an aroused *Chicago Daily News* reviewer Sterling North of Richard Wright's novel. "There will be accusations, and wrathful denials. Organized religion may take the attitude it did toward *The Grapes of Wrath*. And then we may get around to the more sensible idea of a complete and objective investigation of Negro housing conditions, rent, food prices, employment, and relief."[2] The novel alone, predicted Peter Munro Jack in *The New York Times*, "will force the Negro issue into our attention."[3] Whether or not Stryker read the best seller, he could hardly have been unaware of its impact. He recognized the picture-publication opportunities opened up by the book's success, as his response to the May 1940 *Look* spread ("244,000 Native Sons") indicated.

The six-page feature used fifteen images from the Photo League's "Harlem Document," beginning with a view of a tenement child sitting down to dinner on a milk bucket and concluding with an arresting closeup of a scrub-woman on her hands and knees. Although the accompanying text tended to be glib and patronizing (for example, under a sensitive portrait of five young boys sitting on a front stoop, the caption blared, "Five social problems . . ."), the *Look* spread nevertheless demonstrated the market potential for serious urban photography; two months later, the "Harlem Document" gained further exposure at the "Pageant of Photography" section of the San Francisco World's Fair.[4] "I was glad to see that *Look* used photographs from the 'Harlem Document,'" Stryker wrote the Photo League. "You folks up there are getting something started for which I heartily congratulate you."[5] That "something" also intrigued FSA photo-editor Edwin Rosskam, a long-distance Photo League member and occasional lecturer. Rosskam's rising influence inside and outside FSA circles was a fourth impetus for the Chicago series. By the end of 1940, Rosskam had won Stryker's confidence through his work on the much-acclaimed *Home Town* and numerous traveling exhibits; Rosskam's involvement with the "Face of America" book series (Alliance Press) had also given him extensive publishing contacts. Much taken with *Native Son* as well as Wright's earlier *Uncle Tom's Children*—and, as a German émigré, particularly sensitive to minority issues at the turn of the 1940s—Rosskam urged a Wright/FSA collaboration focusing in part on *Native Son*'s locale. Stryker, though recognizing the potentially controversial nature of such a project, remained open-minded; what clinched Stryker's support was Rosskam's securing firm backing from Viking Press early in the venture.

Unlike previous FSA urban encounters, this time the deployment of photographers was no casual affair. Rosskam made one of his rare photographic ventures away from the East while Lee drove straight to Chicago from San Diego, returning to the West after the two-week coverage. In selecting Lee as the principal Chicago photographer (80 percent of the printed images), Stryker and Rosskam chose a cameraman who, though inexperienced in cities, had elsewhere proven particularly adept at capturing the fine points of place, process, and structure. Rosskam, talented in photographing street life, was a logical complement. Lee and Rosskam visited many of the Chicago sites together—Rosskam making necessary contacts, Lee doing the bulk of the shooting as he shifted between three-by-four-inch and miniature cameras, Rosskam filling in with 35-millimeter shots. "Ed opened the doors," recalled Rosskam's wife, Louise, "and Russell got in. Ed had definite ideas about what to cover, though you couldn't completely orchestrate Russell."[6] As Stryker wrote Lee after the coverage: "Ed gave me a glowing report of your prowess as a photographer, and informed me that he had certainly learned a tremendous lot about technique. He also said you folks worked like demons on that job. I can well imagine that when I see the volume of the pictures."[7]

The organization of the images also testified to the seriousness of the undertaking. Standard one- or two-line captions for mounted prints were supplemented by Rosskam's unusually detailed "general captions," defining and exploring the stories ("The Face of the Black Belt," "Pattern for Growing Up," "Relief Family," "Day of a Negro Doctor," etc.) within the larger series. "Ideally," Lee advised Stryker, "[Ed's] general captions . . . should be filed with the pictures."[8] Never formally presented in its original form, this Lee-Rosskam collaboration nevertheless itself constituted something of a photo-text, by no means identical to the work (12 Million Black Voices) that Rosskam ultimately fashioned with Wright.

The full course of the Rosskam-Wright collaboration will be discussed in chapter 6. But it is useful to point out here that Wright's manuscript was far from complete at the time the urban pictures were taken and that, while Rosskam conferred with Wright before the coverage, Wright was not part of the FSA team in Chicago. The FSA investigators had another source of general guidance, namely, the late 1930s–early 1940s Black Belt sociological studies directed by Horace Cayton and W. Lloyd Warner. These were among the materials that Rosskam passed along to Wright in the early months of 1941, and it was no coincidence that Rosskam frequently quoted from Cayton's Negro Housing in Chicago in the general captions. In all probability, members of the extensive Cayton-Warner research team assisted Rosskam in setting up some of the Chicago shoots.

The Cayton-Warner group's statistical surveys and interviews portrayed a world only partially explored in Native Son. It was, of course, a black Chicago rent by poverty and oppression: unemployment reaching over 50 percent in the mid 1930s and still as high as 35 percent in 1940; restricted, indecent, overpriced housing, with a population density over twice that of surrounding white neighborhoods; tuberculosis cases five times more common, venereal disease twenty-five times more common, than in white areas. But it was also a black Chicago estab-

lishing its own social, cultural, and political identities. An environment capable of generating the Bigger Thomases, the south side also
produced a different sort of assertiveness. Chicago, no less than New
York or Detroit, was a center of black political and economic agitation, from National Negro Congress Tenants League picketing, to
NAACP legal action against restrictive housing covenants, to the
March on Washington Movement that was building momentum at
the very time of the FSA photographers' visit.

Forcefully separated by its blackness, the south side encompassed its
own intricate social stratifications, of which a businessman or a Pull-
man porter, a longtime urbanite or a recent immigrant from Arkansas,
a Methodist Episcopal churchgoer or a storefront Baptist worshipper, a
light-skinned "striver" or a dark-skinned counterpart were all keenly
aware. If whites were commonly resented, there was also persistent
tension, subtle and sometimes not so subtle, of an intraracial nature,
whether reflected in a black shopowner's complaint that "Negroes have
never learned to patronize their own," or reflected in an Apostolic
Church pastor's adamant defense of religious emotion: "They [elite
blacks] criticize us for shouting and crying Glory to God. Shouting is a
thing expected from a church. Yes, shout. Say Amen. Say, Halleluiah.
Some people might say, 'Oh I don't see no professional people or high-
up people connected with that Church.' But don't mind that saying.
We are the common ordinary people that Jesus dwelt among."[9] Above
all, south-side Chicago was a world that defied sweeping generalizations. "This is a community of stark contrasts," as Cayton and Drake
later put it,

> the facets of its life as varied as the colors of its people's skins. The tiny
> churches in deserted and dilapidated stores, with illiterately scrawled an-
> nouncements on their painted windows, are marked off sharply from the fine
> edifices on boulevards with stained-glass windows and electric bulletin
> boards. The rickety frame dwellings, sprinkled along the railroad tracks,
> bespeak a way of life at an opposite pole from that of the quiet and well-
> groomed orderliness of middle-class neighborhoods. And many of the still
> stately-appearing old mansions, long since abandoned by Chicago's wealthy
> whites, conceal interiors that are foul and decayed.[10]

Given these complexities, how probing *was* the Lee-Rosskam inquiry? Quantitative analysis of the 420-image series provides some initial indications. Clearly, New Deal "solutions" did not figure significantly in the FSA coverage, much in contrast to Chicago black documentation by other federal agencies. Works Progress Administration and National Youth Administration coverages of 1936–40 focused on federally funded nurseries, subway construction projects, and aircraft-construction training centers; U.S. Housing Authority coverages of 1938–41 focused on slum clearance and the erection of the model Ida B. Wells Homes (apart from black work crews, south-side residents rarely shown). And a later, March 1942 coverage for the U.S. Office of the Coordinator of Information concentrated on uplifting community activities at the Wells Homes—a polished environment made to seem even more pristine, south side "transformed" into north side, with memories of the fiery career of Ida B. Wells herself all but erased amid the Wells Homes serenity. Meanwhile, the FSA series incorporated just seven images pertaining to government projects. The safest route, in short, was not the FSA's. As one of Rosskam's general captions suggested, this absence of New Deal touting reflected a conscious recognition of patterns and exceptions: "A few housing projects, privately financed such as the Rosenwald project, or government financed such as the Ida B. Wells Homes, can accommodate too few tenants to affect conditions substantially. The real obstacle is the [racial] restriction, imposed on a growing community, which prevents adequate expansion in space." Accordingly, the largest bloc of FSA photos, amounting to nearly one-third of the series, was devoted to housing and street-environment problems, subject matter, as Lee confided to Stryker, that at times made Chicago "a pretty depressing place" in which to work.[11] Moreover, unlike Housing Authority prerehabilitation coverages, or the occasional slum exposés in the *Chicago Daily News*, FSA documentation ventured beyond exteriors and into more intimate living spaces: of the 112 shots focusing on housing, interior studies (43 percent) were only slightly less numerous than outside views (57 percent).

But, if Lee and Rosskam were unusually persistent in their slum investigation, they also gave more than passing attention to other dimensions of south-side life. "We are concentrating on social and business activities varying from church life to taverns, and from coffin manufacturing to shots in the Negro five-and-dime stores," Lee reported to Stryker, and the numbers would support his account. Religious activity (18 percent), business life (17 percent), recreation off the streets (13 percent), health care and education (9 percent) all constituted important segments of the Chicago documentation.[12] Statistical breakdowns *within* these categories reveal a breadth greater than the *Look* feature and the original "Harlem Document" and "The Most Crowded Block" as well. In religious coverage, for example, the Photo Leaguers concentrated primarily on fundamentalist sects with their emotional, dramatic, and particularly photogenic services; FSA coverage, by contrast, incorporated a substantial high-church segment (40 percent of the religious pictures coming from an Episcopal ceremony) along with Pentecostal (35 percent) and Baptist (20 percent) sequences. So it was in business and recreation as well. The "Harlem Document" and "The Most Crowded Block" passed lightly over the black business elite in favor of street vendors and small-store employees—immediately appealing subjects, given a particularly noble cast by Aaron Siskind and the other photographers; the more inclusive FSA coverage moved from sidewalk stalls to a prominent insurance firm. Photo League documentation of "recreation" centered on musicians, dancers, and an assortment of stage performers (again, the immediately photogenic territory); FSA coverage extended to less energetic locales, including movie theaters (18 percent) and bars (20 percent). These quantitative measures do not tell the entire story, but they do suggest an FSA commitment to exploring the diversity described in the Cayton-Warner studies.

The dual purposes of the FSA coverage—exposing south-side horrors, exploring the workings of a complex community—were evident in both "The Face of the Black Belt" and "Pattern for Growing Up" subseries. On the one side, there were urban wasteland visions, very much in the *Native Son* spirit. "Miles of Lasalle, Dearborn, and Federal streets, a huge area around Maxwell and many other 'sore spots' look as if they had been bombed," Rosskam wrote. "Leaning tenements stare blindly through broken, boarded, or papered windows past sag-

Fig. 5.1. Russell Lee. "Tenements, South Side," Chicago. 1941. FSA. Library of Congress.

ging wooden outside stairways upon empty lots where children play on the bricks and rubble of a decade's collapse and demolition."[13] The corresponding visuals, tracing deterioration from subdivided brownstones on the decline to burned-out ruins, expose jarring juxtapositions (fig. 5.1). In 38720-D, Lee's inclusion of a dilapidated church edifice amid a scene of crumbling apartment buildings and piles of rubble makes the parallel between south-side Chicago and a European war zone particularly acute: views of churches gutted by Nazi bombs were front-page newspaper staples in the early 1940s. In fact, during the very period of the Lee-Rosskam visit, the *Chicago Daily News* ran a front-page AP photo of England's Coventry Cathedral in ruins, piles of stone and shattered glass all but overwhelming the parishioners making Easter prayers.[14] At least parishioners appeared in the Coventry picture; the utter desolation of the south-side scene points to a costlier, albeit less publicized, "war" at home. Rosskam extended the

Fig. 5.2. Russell Lee. "Abandoned Tenements and Steel Mill," Chicago. 1941. FSA.
Library of Congress.

analogy of the ravages of Nazism to the ravages of American poverty
with a portrait of young boys crouched against a wall, pretending to
shoot machine guns at passing aircraft. Despite a measure of self-conscious posing, the gestures and backdrop remain haunting.

An embattled city, south-side Chicago was also a city of shattered
dreams. In 13018-M2, Lee's glimpse of a distant steel mill through a
long, gloomy corridor of abandoned tenements effectively encapsu-
lates the irony of migration (fig. 5.2). Industrial opportunities lured
thousands of blacks from the South during and after World War I.
"I've watched the trains as they disappeared / Behind the clouds of
smoke / Carrying crowds of working men / To the land of Hope,"
intoned poet William Cross in the *Chicago Defender* in 1917. "Go on,
dear brother, you'll never regret / Just trust in God; pray for the best /
And at the end you're sure to find / Happiness will be thine."[15] Tenement squalor, darkness literal and figurative, often proved to be
"thine"; in the darkness of Lee's foreground, stones once part of a

building's foundation come to resemble gravestones. Composition, as much as lighting, underlines the theme: the photo's central diagonal directs us inward and upward toward the smokestack, yet the route to that destination seems endless. The smokestack beckons; the tenements and rubble nevertheless dominate.

In other scenes, wood-frame houses dominate—rotting, collapsing houses painfully reminiscent of the dwellings that Chicago immigrants "left behind" in the South. The sense not only of unfulfilled promise but of a community consuming itself takes on a literal dimension, both in Lee's view of a "Wood for Sale" sign tacked onto one of the wood-frame structures and his subsequent shot (13002-M1) of a youth actually chopping wood on a broken sidewalk (fig. 5.3). Transposed from the rural setting, the axe-wielder image raises connotations of desperation and danger in the urban slum context. The shadow of trouble here—axe being swung too close to a woman who appears to be holding a wood slab over the axe-wielder's head; ill-supervised younger

Fig. 5.3. Russell Lee. "Tenement Houses," Chicago. 1941. FSA. Library of Congress.

Fig. 5.4. Aaron Siskind. From "The Most Crowded Block," New York City. 1939–40. Aaron Siskind Collection, Library of Congress. Reproduced by permission of Aaron Siskind.

children all too close to the action—is almost as evident as the actual shadow cast by the blade. In fact, nascent violence makes this image more troubling than any of the youth-in-the-street studies by the Photo Leaguers. There is elegance in Siskind's portrait of young Harlemites dueling with wooden swords (fig. 5.4), old-fashioned boisterousness in the stick-waving poses adopted by grinning Lower East Side youths in the group portrait taken by young Photo Leaguers David Robbins and

Fig. 5.5. David Robbins/Arnold Eagle. From "One-Third of Nation," New York City. 1938. Works Progress Administration, Federal Arts Project—New York City Section. National Archives.

Arnold Eagle for the WPA's Federal Arts Project (fig. 5.5). The FSA view, unnervingly chaotic, has none of those reassuring features. This, quite clearly, is Bigger Thomas country. The image directly following 13002-M1 presents further decay on another block, a portion of the street itself submerged under water from a backed-up gutter (fig. 5.6). Note Lee's composition: the water stretches endlessly in the foreground, a refuse-strewn lot stretches endlessly in the background and the young children playing with their boats in the gutter water seem stranded on a patch of sidewalk.

The water washes into the viewer's space, reducing the distinction between the investigator and the investigated. Unrepaired streets and, by extension, south-side maladies in general, threaten "us" as well as

Fig. 5.6. Russell Lee. "Children Playing in the Water Backed Up in the Gutter in the South Side," Chicago. 1941. FSA. Library of Congress.

the young denizens. "Do not hold a light attitude toward the slums of Chicago's south side," Wright's warning echoes through these images. "Remember that Hitler came out of such a slum. Remember that Chicago could be the Vienna of American Fascism! Out of these mucky slums can come ideas quickening life or hastening death, giving us peace or carrying us toward . . . war."[16]

The FSA survey, though, was more than a jeremiad. Ambiguities lay behind the menacing face of the Black Belt, as Lee and Rosskam recognized in such images as 38599-D (fig. 5.7). The photograph's most obvious, and disturbing, implication is its association of death with children's play in a barren lot. Rosskam and Wright would entitle one of the chapters in *12 Million Black Voices* "Death on the City Pavements." Yet there is more at work in this shot. As Lee and Rosskam discovered, the funeral business was one of the few corners of

the commercial world controlled largely by blacks. The competition
was intraracial, with established undertakers challenged increasingly
during the 1930s–40s by funeral systems that not only offered low-
premium, easily accessible burial insurance—insurance that did not
have to be claimed as an asset when holders were applying for public
relief—but often operated their own funeral parlors. In this competi-
tive environment, undertakers were eager to show off their handiwork
to the FSA photographers. Lee even photographed one proud under-
taker next to an open coffin displaying an elaborately prepared body.
Nor was it any coincidence that the companies represented in 38599-
D—McGavock most likely an outgrowth of the flourishing Lincoln
network—offered the hard sell.

In fact, the Cayton-Warner researchers discovered that, in at least

Fig. 5.7. Russell Lee. "Sign," Chicago. 1941. FSA. Library of Congress.

Fig. 5.8. Edwin Rosskam. "Negro Boy in an Empty Lot Which Is His Playground," Chicago. 1941. FSA. Library of Congress.

some cases, funeral systems went beyond aggressive advertising to actual chicanery, the promised first-class funerals amounting to cheap
coffins and slick paint jobs. "The way the thing is worked," one infor-
mant charged, the customers "sign over their insurance policy for
maybe a thousand dollars and are promised a big funeral. . . . What
[the association manager] really does costs him probably a hundred
dollars."[17] Con artists or not, these companies played on some of the
deepest anxieties, concerning family shame, held by impoverished Chicagoans. In a world where security of any sort—whether job, home, or
health—was precarious, the promise of security in death (and security,
moreover, bearing a name with historical associations as potent as
"Lincoln") was beguiling. Accordingly, the signs connote a level of
manipulation every bit as high as that shown by white-owned companies pitching to white families. In short, if death is a presence in 38599-
D, so is money—black-controlled, and not necessarily sympathetically
controlled. If racism had created the impoverished south side, there
were blacks flourishing despite the conditions and, in certain respects,
because of them. Finally, Lee's complex image had more positive implications as well. The roots of the funeral system lay with the southern burial society, a source of economic as well as spiritual sustenance.
The foundations of community connectedness extended to the urban
jungle; accompanying an element of intraracial exploitation was a vital element of cultural continuity.

All was not simple in Lee's street and building studies, nor in
Rosskam's individual portraits. Encountering a young boy playing in
yet another rubble-strewn lot, Rosskam offered shifting perspectives.
In 5192-M2, the camera angle creates a nightmarish effect, with the
blurred, tilted world of refuse appearing to careen down upon the lad,
of whom we see mainly the head and shoulders in the lower-right
foreground (fig. 5.8). The boy's gaze matches the downward slope of
the environment, further accenting the sense of a life out of control.
Rosskam might easily have stopped with this carefully constructed vision of chaos and vulnerability, yet in 5192-M3 he reenvisioned the
same scene with a more balanced composition (fig. 5.9). Here the boy,
shown nearly in full, assumes a much stronger presence on "his" turf,
leaning jauntily against a fence, showing rather natty attire, glancing

upward with a finger deposited casually, perhaps a mite irreverently, in his mouth. Although disturbing elements still lurk (for instance, a portion of the fence collapsing just a few feet beyond where the boy stands), this view is more ambiguous. Perhaps hardened by his environment, but certainly not overwhelmed by it, the subject does not fit neatly into "victim" status. "The challenge for Ed, working in the ghetto, was not the fear—not in those days," recalled Louise Rosskam recently. "What he tried to avoid, at all costs, was condescension toward 'poor' subjects. What he liked to do, even in south-side Chicago, was try to melt into the background, photographing the world as it went by."[18] Like many of Shahn's and Rothstein's rural portraits, Rosskam's second view takes the subject seriously without forcing a

Fig. 5.9. Edwin Rosskam. "Negro Boy in an Empty Lot Which Is His Playground," Chicago. 1941. FSA. Library of Congress.

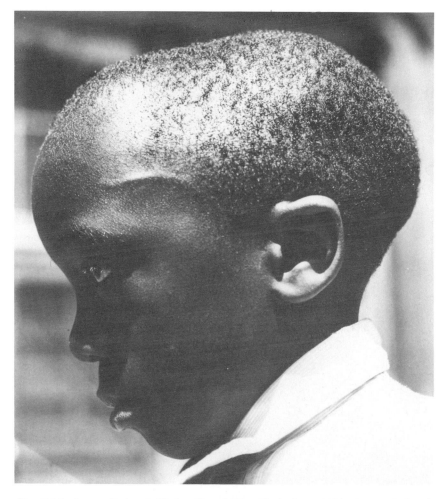

Fig. 5.10. Aaron Siskind. "Schoolboy," New York City. 1932. Aaron Siskind Collection, Library of Congress. Reproduced by permission of Aaron Siskind.

black-youth-equals-social-problem correspondence. At the same time, Rosskam avoids the romantic excesses to which even Photo Leaguers were occasionally given. While one of Siskind's closeups (fig. 5.10) turns the head of a young Harlemite into something out of an African ethnological study (dignity by way of primitive exoticism), Rosskam's depiction keeps the subject very much in his urban context.

Photographs that demanded action and photographs that invited

Fig. 5.11. Russell Lee. "Corner of the Bedroom Where a Negro Housewife is Examining the Bed Clothes Which Were Chewed by the Rats," Chicago. 1941. FSA. Library of Congress.

Fig. 5.12. Russell Lee. "Family on Relief," Chicago. 1941. FSA. Library of Congress.

contemplation were the dual tendencies that also emerged in the FSA investigation of slum interiors. Concentrating on three homes—an unemployed house painter on relief and his family of eleven; an occasional WPA worker with an extended family of eleven, including recent immigrants from Arkansas; a railroad worker's family of six—Lee did his share of muckraking, with textual bolstering from Rosskam. One of the mothers in the extended family exhibits bed sheets chewed by rats, while a young daughter dangles the baby precariously; sheet and baby, associated visually through their alignment on the same compositional diagonal, appear equally vulnerable to attack (fig. 5.11). "Because of the three-year residence requirement," Rosskam extends the indictment, "none of the newcomers have any prospects of any income from public funds for the next two years."[19] The relief family

Fig. 5.13. Russell Lee. "Family on Relief," Chicago. 1941. FSA.
Library of Congress.

crowds into the kitchen for a portrait, with cracked walls forming the backdrop, a near-empty table dominating the foreground, an alarm clock (with its figurative question and warning, "How much longer?") the only decoration (fig. 5.12). And, in a similar vein, one of the relief family's young sons is shown eating biscuits at the table, two sisters without food eyeing him closely, the eater keeping one hand on a hammer as if to guard the biscuit plate. The general caption heightens the sense of emergency: "All of the children suffer from some form of malnutrition, resulting not so much from undernourishment as from the unbalanced diet. Says the mother, 'How am I going to buy meat and green vegetables for 11 on one relief check?' " Lee even borrowed a trick from Jacob Riis's *How the Other Half Lives*, photographing several of the relief children *feigning* sleep in their ramshackle quarters— "an attic," the Rosskam caption elaborates, "under the roof where the plaster has peeled off and the rain pours in."[20]

But, along with the images of overcrowding and dilapidation, there were less predictable turns, certainly out of line with the Riis muckraking tradition. Consider Lee's portrait of a member of the relief family tenderly dangling a young child on his knee (fig. 5.13). The man's fine hat, a badge of respectability, is not the only feature out of the ordinary. The vertical composition emphasizes a set of family pictures lovingly displayed above the sitters. Lee had used a similar juxtaposition in some of his Oklahoma tenant portraits the previous year, but the intact-family theme became especially significant in the urban setting. This shot, 38791-D, underlined a broader trend in the Chicago pictorial coverage. While all three households upon which the FSA investigators concentrated included members who were not strictly part of the nuclear family, none of them conformed to the alleged pattern of absent fathers, shifting partnerships, and disorganized families that E. Franklin Frazier, Ernest W. Burgess, and other sociologists, as well as Wright, were stressing in the 1930s–40s. All three households, in fact, contradicted the formula that Rosskam himself invoked when he was not discussing specific families: "Love or affection are . . . thrown into the pot which contains the rent money and the food, and the family, brought more or less intact from the rural South, may crack in the squalor and overcrowding of the city."

It might be argued here that Lee and Rosskam simply chose the wrong families to photograph and thus obscured the crisis of the black urban home. Certainly the lack of so much as one broken family among the representative three was problematical. But we should not be too quick to accept Frazier's "reality." As Herbert Gutman, Jerold Heiss, Carol Stack, Eleanor Engram, Demitri Shimkin, and other recent scholars have pointed out, the crumbling-family thesis was based on limited, and questionable, quantitative evidence, as well as on a narrow concept of "family" that seriously undervalued the functional importance of extended kin networks. Rural-urban continuities in family structure quite possibly persisted on a considerably larger scale than Frazier recognized.[21] If these continuities did not prevent such problems as rising juvenile delinquency, this may have pointed more to the immensity of urban economic distress than to fundamental family weakness. As Gutman maintained in his massive 1976 quantitative study: "The typical Afro-American household changed its shape in the half-century between 1880 and 1930. But at all times, and in all settings, the typical black household (always a lower-class household) had in it two parents and was not 'unorganized.' . . . The record [of black economic, social, and psychological suffering] is not evidence that the black family crumbled or that a pathological culture thrived. Nor is there reason to believe that the poor black family crumbled in the near half-century that has passed since the onset of the Great Depression."[22] Of course, Lee's photographic work did not constitute a Gutman-style systematic study of black family structures, and it is also possible that Lee's subjects were putting on something of a family show. Still, as an unscientific impression, the pictorial acknowledgment of family ties was an imaginative, and by no means entirely implausible, alternative to then-reigning wisdom.

The sensitivity that prevented "The Face of the Black Belt," "Pattern for Growing Up," "Recent Immigrants," "Relief Family," and "Railroad Worker's Family" from becoming monodimensional horror shows also prevented the subseries dealing with more positive themes from turning into upbeat pap or romantic escapism. For example, "Day of a Negro Doctor" was *in part* a panegyric to the predominantly black-staffed Provident Hospital and to the particular surgical skills of Dr.

Falls—but only in part. Unlike the Provident series taken the following year for the Office of the Coordinator of Information or the Provident photo-features that ran periodically in the *Chicago Defender*, the FSA story moved beyond the confines of the hospital. With opening scenes of the doctor's well-appointed home on the edge of the Black Belt (an area, as Rosskam described it in the general caption, "restricted by its own Negro residents to homes costing a minimum of $5,000"), and with closing scenes of the doctor paying a house call to the aforementioned relief family, the subseries became not simply a depiction of health care but an examination of class distinctions within the black community. When the doctor is photographed knocking at the relief family's door, he knocks as an insider/outsider, a visitor who knows his patients' problems but whose own struggles lie on an entirely different plane. And here is the further twist. That Dr. Falls is making the visit, which will obviously bring him little remuneration, is admirable; but as Lee discloses in other shots, money is hardly a passing concern for this professional. In Lee's portrait of the doctor seated behind his office desk, vying for attention with the authoritative pose and the energetic lighting of the face is the large "Consultations: Cash" sign shown in the immediate foreground. Cash to make up for what he was not receiving from his relief patients, cash to keep his practice going, cash to maintain his elite standing: a sign that proclaims expertise is also a sign that reflects business struggle. Rosskam's caption amplified the point: "Like most Negro doctors he finds himself financially unable to devote himself exclusively to his specialty, general surgery. A great majority of his clients are relief cases. . . . There is a thin sprinkling of upper and middle class Negroes in his clientele and a few white patients. According to him, white doctors in the Negro neighborhood offer intense competition."[23]

Rather than a simple representative of black success and black nobility, the doctor emerged as an individual, not entirely enviable, operating in a tangled web of restraints and conflicting interests. What's more, FSA coverage of the Provident world around Dr. Falls conveyed its own mixed implications. Although the survey did not fully expose the hospital overcrowding that resulted from the immensity of southside needs and the insufficiency of city funding, there were at least

Fig. 5.14. Aaron Siskind. "Revival Meeting, Storefront Church," New York City. Ca. 1936. Photo used in *Look*, 21 May 1940. Reproduced by permission of Aaron Siskind.

hints of the darker side. Played against Rosskam's scenes of a polished surgical team were Lee's views of a tuberculosis clinic's waiting room: cramped quarters, somber faces, an aura of both dreariness and dread. Absent is the bustling quality—action seen almost as a palliative in itself—that would dominate OCI and *Defender* coverages; present is an oppressive silence.

In coverage of south-side religious activity, it was the comparative approach that yielded important insights. Taken alone, Lee's vivid sequence from an Easter service at the Langley Avenue Pentecostal Church presented a view of black religiosity quite similar to the ec-static model used in the *Look* feature, and, for that matter, in a great many media accounts (fig. 5.14). One might note the emphasis, in several Lee shots, on the integration of popular music into fundamentalist practices, with the drummer setting a lively beat while one of the Pentecostal leaders "testifies" to the congregation; or Lee's closeups of the leader caught up in her fervor, thrusting a clenched fist high in the air, bending toward the faithful with light shining dramatically in her face. But the message of the FSA series as a whole was entirely different. In the first place, the series explored multiple dimensions of fundamentalist activity. Not only does Lee show the literate side of Pentecostalism—photographing a letter to congregation members that elucidates church doctrine and, in the process, gives the Easter proceedings a certain logic and integrity—but he juxtaposes the Pentecostal shouting with a contrasting atmosphere of a storefront Baptist church. Rather than the holy rolling with which these establishments were so often associated, contemplative activity is featured (fig. 5.15). Poring over their Bibles, busily taking notes and raising questions, the members of this tiny congregation participate in what more closely resembles a seminar than a holiday service. Amid the old pot-bellied stove and the crude wall decorations, intellectual intimacy, as much as spiritual unity, seems the order of the day. Exciting scenes, with dynamic Photo League–style compositions, these are not, and that is precisely the point. Documentary drama is discarded in favor or a recognition of subtle and, for documentarians, too often undervalued, intellectual searching.

In the second place, the series recognized alternatives to fundamentalism. The middle ground of more conservative Baptist and Methodist churches emerges at least indirectly in the pictures (Hebrew inscriptions, suggesting a more established religion, still evident on the facade of Pilgrim Baptist Church, which was taken over from a stately synagogue) and more clearly in Rosskam's general caption. "With money, no matter how little, comes sophistication, at least in the second generation [of urban immigrants]. High school graduates want a different environment than their transplanted sharecropper parents. . . . In such churches [as Pilgrim Baptist] the service is much more decorous and formal and less inspirational."[24] As for the next step away from fundamentalism, we noted earlier the quantitative extent of Episcopal coverage. Qualitatively, the Pentecostal-Episcopal con-

trast was striking. While FSA camerapeople photographed freely inside the Pentecostal church, they were apparently restricted to outdoor shooting of Episcopal activities; the very location of the coverage
reflected high-church formality, and perhaps high-church exclusive-
ness. What Lee and Rosskam were permitted to photograph was a
"blessing of the bounds" procession. If the literal bounds of the church-
yard were comparatively broad, the ceremony's emotional bounds were
quite the opposite.

   The raw power of the Pentecostals' raised hands gives way, in 13013-
M1, to the ornamental grace of the Episcopal cross and candles, borne
with a quiet, studied reverence (fig. 5.16). Lee's composition, featuring
a triad of foreground worshippers and a triad of holy objects set against
the church's triangular facade, echoes the sense of traditional order.
Serenity, not effusiveness, was the keynote as the photographers followed the male and female choirs around the block. And the processional coverage ended on the same note with which it began. In a tail-
end view (13010-M1) of a dutiful young candle-bearer preceding a
stern-faced priest wearing his ecclesiastical robes, Lee suggests not only
the church's hierarchical structure (Pentecostal robes, by contrast,
were all of one kind) but its socioeconomic base. Beyond the figures,
beyond the series of railings that provide yet another visual metaphor
for order, can be seen parked automobiles and well-kept houses, em-
blems of the black establishment. Appropriately, the class connection
continued in the coverage of congregation members socializing after
the ceremony—with light skin, fashionable clothes, and society-page
poses. "Not only the service and the church," Rosskam observes, "but
the congregation, the minister ('preacher' no longer), the choir in its
vestments, are all exact duplicates of a fashionable white church."[25] In
short, in defining a broad spectrum of religious experiences among
blacks, and in placing that spectrum within a social context, Lee and
Rosskam effectively divorced the analysis of religion from common
myths about inherent black tendencies.

   The Look feature described black urban nightlife in a manner similar to its rendering of black religion—Harlemites engaged in a "fever-
ish pursuit of happiness" (fig. 5.17).[26] Again, the FSA survey dug
deeper. Taken on its own, Lee's view (38609-D) of a broadly grinning

Fig. 5.15. Russell Lee. "Service in a Storefront Baptist Church," Chicago. 1941. FSA. Library of Congress.

Fig. 5.16. Russell Lee. "Start of the Processional from an Episcopal Church on Easter," Chicago. 1941. FSA. Library of Congress.

Fig. 5.17. Aaron Siskind. From "Harlem Document" New York City. 1937. Image at left, "Amateur Night, Apollo Theatre," used in *Look*, 21 May 1940. Photos reproduced by permission of Aaron Siskind.

raconteur holding forth in a crowded bar would seem to sum up the essential spirit of Saturday-night release. Yet the barroom coverage also moved in other directions. In this setting, as in the roller-skating rink featured elsewhere in the recreation subseries, Lee appeared to be sensitive to an informal color code in effect, with light-skinned blacks generally associating most closely with other light-skinned blacks, darker-skinned males at times in the company of light-skinned females, but never the reverse. While the table-by-table group portraits hardly amounted to a systematic investigation, they represented at least rudimentary efforts to acknowledge the findings of Warner's *Color and Human Nature*, which had just been published that spring and was receiving considerable play in the *Chicago Defender* during the FSA visit. All is not social freedom in the bar, nor is it merriment. By incorporating a closeup of a drinker being comforted as she covers her face in apparent distress (fig. 5.18), Lee offers intimations that had been absent from his folksy bar scenes taken in the West—intimations about the problematical impact of a photographer in this very private of public places, intimations about the problematical nature of spiritual escape via the bar.

Fig. 5.18. Russell Lee. "Scene at a Bar on the South Side," Chicago. 1941.
FSA. Library of Congress.

To argue that the FSA's Chicago coverage was innovative and probing is not to argue that it was without its weaknesses. A prime strength
of the survey, its remarkable range, was also a source of limitation, for
individual households, businesses, and institutions did not always receive the sustained attention that would have illuminated *particular*
personalities and relationships. With breadth came, at times, a sacri-
fice of case-by-case depth. In fact, Rosskam made the matter more
problematical by failing to give names in his supporting text. For ex-

ample, as imaginative as was the coverage of the railroad worker's wife, she nevertheless remained simply the "railroad worker's wife." (The same anonymity marked FSA studies of the white community such as Lee's 1939 San Augustine, Texas, survey, though in the case of the black documentation, inclusion of personal names could have been an especially useful tool to combat notions of monolithic black America.) Perhaps an even more extended Lee-Rosskam stay might have produced more complete day-in-the-life-of series within series— perhaps. "I realize," Stryker wrote Lee at the end of April, "you could have gone on for another few months and still wouldn't be through."[27]

Unfleshed-out detail was one matter, wholesale gaps in the coverage quite another. One such gap was the subject of industrial labor. Important to an understanding of black Chicago was an understanding of the often painful adjustment, made by thousands, from agricultural work routines to a new set of skills, pressures, and conflicts in heavy industry. Yet Lee, who had been particularly thorough in his documentation of cotton, rice, and vegetable field laborers in the South, did not pursue the labor story in the North. He photographed a steel mill at a distance but never confronted so much as a single steel-worker. He photographed the railroad worker's home, but nothing of his daily labor. And as for the meatpacking industry, central to the history of black migration, FSA coverage was non-existent.

To be sure, company officials were hardly setting out welcoming mats for the FSA investigators. In at least one instance of a projected meatpacking story, official resistance made documentation all but impossible. At the Swift plant, management knew of the photographer's connection to the Wright project, thanks to a well-intentioned but unstrategic note from one of Rosskam's contacts at the Rosenwald Foundation. Wright, it seemed, was the wrong password. "They did not care to have me going through the plant taking pictures and suggested that they supply me with some," Lee explained to Stryker. "They were quite anxious to state that they did not discriminate between whites and blacks at the plant and that they did not want their pictures to be used in any such way. And they frankly stated that Wright's book would probably be Communistic (in their interpretation)."[28] Still, there is no indication that either of the FSA photographers made any

sustained effort to find an appropriate substitute for the Swift coverage. Nor is there any indication that Lee or Rosskam attempted to
cover one of the principal sources of employment for south-side
women, namely domestic service. Rosskam's account of the same
household made passing mention of members employed as domestics,
but these obvious photographic leads were never pursued. If the closing image and caption in the *Look* feature, depicting a domestic whose
knees were "hard from prayin' and scrubbin'," left the door open for a
more careful, reflective treatment by the FSA investigators, the latter
failed to seize the opportunity. Male workers fared no better.[29] Apart
from a single image of a young shoeshine boy, the legions of service
employees—from waiters and short-order cooks to porters and jani-
tors—were unrepresented, visually and textually.

By not portraying the black presence in the larger fabric of Chicago's
economic life, the FSA series missed the relation between job status
and south-side poverty, between the nature of black roles outside the
ghetto (the "invisible" roles, the roles taken for granted by whites) and
the very existence of the ghetto. The missing relation was a missing
indictment, not just of a set of economic deficiencies but of an entire
social structure. In this regard, Lee and Rosskam fell considerably short
of *Native Son*'s reach. In fact, the absence of labor coverage, along
with the absence of any attention to courts, prisons, and the administration of justice, reduced the chances for photographing blacks and
whites together in situations that might have revealed hierarchies and
tensions. While there were a few such scenes in the business and recreation series, these did not constitute a thorough investigation of
urban racial realities. Missing from the business series, for example,
were any views of white managers and black employees; the only such
view in the recreation sequence, Lee's tavern shot of a white owner
and black bartender standing side by side beneath a "God Bless
America—We Are Proud to Be Americans" sign, has the insipid flavor
of Office of War Information pap. Moreover, suggestions of black-
white business *competition* within the ghetto were muted. No clear
indication emerged, for instance, of the pattern of white-owned firms
situated in more favorable spots than their black-owned competitors.
There were only hints: while the contrast between a deserted sidewalk

outside a black-owned grocery and a busy scene outside an A&P sug-gested a white edge, the focus of the A&P shot—black youths clown-ing for the camera as they wait to cart customers' bags—obscured the more serious theme.

"I don't want any of the black bastards hanging around here," one tavern owner on the edge of the Black Belt told the Cayton-Warner researchers. "All they can do is to cheapen the tavern's name."[30] Obvi-ously, translating such extreme passions into visual terms was not easy. The segregation signs that Lee had photographed so trenchantly in Oklahoma City did not exist in Chicago. And we cannot expect Lee or Rosskam to have waited for a racial incident to occur, whether in a tavern or on the street. Still, the FSAers *could* have gone beyond Rosskam's brief description of whites resenting middle-class blacks who were moving out of the ghetto; photographs might have emphasized the all-white and all-black residential blocks on the "frontier." A simi-lar approach might have been taken with stores, parks, schools, or, for that matter, taverns—interracial comparisons as a logical extension of the intraracial comparisons that appeared frequently in the FSA se-ries.

But such did not occur. Timidity, rather than the imaginativeness that Lee and Rosskam showed elsewhere in the Chicago coverage, marked the FSA approach to racial division, as it marked the ap-proach to the crucial subject of black activism. Again we find promis-ing leads never followed up. Despite the intimate involvement of the railroad laborer and his wife in union activities, documentation of such matters never went beyond the home and into the meeting hall, where the full force of collective organization could have been ex-posed. Similarly, Rosskam's view of a "Know Your Country" store-window display included several books concerning CIO organizing (*Labor's Civil War, As Steel Goes*), but coverage of the major CIO black story in Chicago—a story profoundly affecting the lives of meatpacking workers, among others—never moved beyond this indi-rect reflection. Portraying CIO-related books next to flying manuals and other military guides only obliquely hinted at the tension between new streams of social activism and old conventions of military and governmental organization. CIO voices were among those raised against armed-forces segregation and defense-plant discrimination; in fact, the specific issue of whether blacks should volunteer for a segregated *air corps* loomed prominently at the time of the Lee-Rosskam survey. "It is to be regretted," a *Chicago Defender* editorial declared, "that so harmful and indefensible a view [that blacks should volunteer] should be given public hearing precisely at the time when the black masses everywhere are struggling for the extension of democratic procedure."[31]

Lee's "coverage" of the South Side Action Committee headquarters exemplified the FSA limitations. Amounting to just three images, the coverage was all but lost amid a sea of tenement shots in the "Face of the Black Belt" subseries. Limited to exterior views that showed a deserted sidewalk and a rather grimy facade, the coverage produced the impression of an organization as decrepit as the surrounding housing. Rosskam's text provided no corrective evidence about the committee and, in fact, made no mention at all of black protest. The *untold* story, by contrast, found a South Side Action Committee very much alive, leading rent strikes and demonstrations, contributing to a protest culture that in June produced some of the largest civil rights rallies in the country. If the Action Committee received misleading coverage in the FSA study, such pivotal organizations as the NAACP and the Negro Labor Relations League received not even a glance. And so it was that—a year after Chicago's NAACP branch had taken the fight against restrictive housing covenants to the U.S. Supreme Court, a week after Chicago's black congressman, Arthur Mitchell, had won his legal battle against Jim Crow accommodations on interstate railroads, and in the same week that the Negro Labor Relations League was launching a boycott campaign against discriminatory firms as well as sponsoring rally appearances by the Rev. Adam Clayton Powell, Jr., on behalf of the Harlem bus boycott—Lee and Rosskam were implicitly portraying black Chicagoans as politically quiescent, politically nonthreatening. To the extent that black migration *liberated* political energies, that liberation could not be found in Lee and Rosskam's urban vision. Indeed, given Lee's careful attention to radical agrarian protest in Oklahoma in 1939–40, the implication almost seemed to be that blacks were *less* assertive in the North.

The only real photographic suggestion of Chicago militancy oc-
curred fortuitously three months later when John Vachon, visiting the
city on another assignment, happened upon a group of predominantly
black picketers protesting high rents and low wages outside the Mid-
City Realty offices. Vachon's brief sequence proved adventurous, emphasizing the female presence on the picket line, suggesting the interracial character of the CIO–United Office and Professional Workers,
and juxtaposing black picketers ("Slavery Was Abolished—Yet We
Work for $8 a Week") with an uninterested white government em-
ployee. But the rich photographic possibilities of a situation such as
the Mid-City battle called for an extended series which a community
study was supposed to foster. Vachon did not have the time for a major
"Face of Black Protest" sequence, as Lee and Rosskam had; that the
protest coverage came only as an afterthought, rather than a genuine
part of the Chicago study, underlined the problem.

Was it left to a *black* FSA photographer to transcend the limitations
evident in the Lee-Rosskam urban coverage? Was Gordon Parks's
Washington, D.C., work, the following summer, significantly bolder?
Certainly the experience of Washington held a painful immediacy for
the young black intern that Chicago had not held for Lee or Rosskam.
Accustomed to the relatively benign racial environments of Fort Scott,
Kansas, and Minneapolis, Parks found the essential southernness of
the nation's capital a shock. "Suddenly," he explained later, "you were
down to the level of the drug stores on the corner, where I went to
take my son for a hot dog or a malted milk, and suddenly they're
saying, 'We don't serve negroes,' or 'niggers' in some sections, and
'You can't go to a picture show.' "[32] At least initially, Parks harbored
grand visions of fighting back, via the camera. After an introductory,
nonphotographic tour of the city—including a visit to a department
store where he was refused service—Parks returned to the FSA office
"roaring mad, and I wanted my camera, and [Stryker] said, 'for what?'
and I said I wanted to expose some of this corruption down here, this
discrimination. And [Stryker] says, 'how you gonna do it?' Well with
my camera. So he says, 'Well, you sit down and write a little paper on
how you intend to do this.' I said fine. He kept after me until he got
me down to one simple little project."[33] Parks took some scattered

slum shots in June and July (extending, for example, exposure of the rat-infestation problem from Lee's view of gnawed bed sheets to a closeup of a young girl lying ill from a rat bite), then settled on the story of Ella Watson, a twenty-five-year government charwoman. Ironically, it was Stryker who provided the tip, though Stryker's guidance ended at that point. "I came to find out a very significant thing," Parks recalled from his conversations with Watson. "She had moved into the [office] building at the same time, she said, as the [white] woman who was now a notary public. They came there with the same education, the same mental facilities and equipment, and she was now scrubbing this woman's room every evening."[34]

The series produced at least one image with which Parks would long be associated: the image of a grim-faced, mop-wielding Watson against the background of the stars and stripes blended some of the compositional features of "American Gothic" with the bitterness of *Native Son* (fig. 5.19). But more important was his sustained narrative that followed the charwoman from her workplace to her home to her church. The series gave quantitative weight (eighty-five images) to a domestic-worker theme notably absent from the Chicago documentation. Moreover, the series came at a time when the federal government, making headlines with its Fair Employment Practices Committee investigations of black employment in private industry, needed to be reminded of its own black employees' situation. A great many blacks shared Watson's status. At the end of the 1930s, 90 percent of the 9,700 Washington blacks regularly employed by the federal government held custodial positions, and it would take much more than the war to change that. While the Lee-Rosskam series worked around these sorts of issues, and while OWI photography stressed new black economic opportunities, Parks confronted a persistent tradition.

The "invisible" presence of the after-hours cleaner was made visible, and identifiable; Parks's repeated mention of Watson's name in the captions (as well as the names of other members of her church and of blacks with whom she dealt in her neighborhood) underscored his intentions. Interplays between images, interplays between captions and pictures, gave this visibility a critical edge. We see Watson cleaning the carpeted stairs near the Office of the Registrar of Treasury; we also

Fig. 5.19. Gordon Parks. "Mrs. Ella Watson, Government Charwoman,"
Washington, D.C. 1942. FSA. Library of Congress.

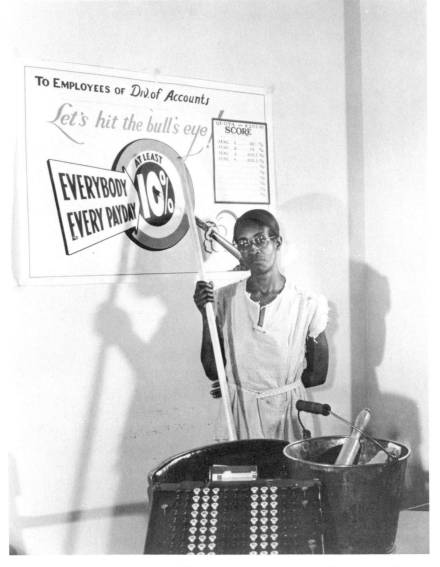

Fig. 5.20. Gordon Parks. "Mrs. Ella Watson, Government Charwoman," Washington, D.C. 1942. FSA. Library of Congress.

see Watson descending the decidedly cruder stairs of her apartment building, bidding farewell to her grandchildren as she departs for work at a time (5:30 P.M.) when higher-level employees are doing precisely the opposite. Watson's descent carries literal as well as symbolic significance. Heading for her job, she moves from her status as household head (sole provider for three grandchildren and an adopted daughter) to that of a bottom-level functionary in a white world. We see Watson sweeping near a door marked "Division of Security Files"; we also see two of the young grandchildren sitting on the floor at home next to a badly cracked wall that suggests the precariousness of "security" for those dependent on a custodial salary. We see Watson juxtaposed not only with the American flag but with an office sign exhorting government employees to devote 10 percent of their monthly salaries to war-bond purchases (fig. 5.20); while the caption notes Watson's contributions on this score, it also makes clear just how small Watson's paycheck is to begin with ($1,080 a year for a family of five). Surrounded by symbols of secular authority in her workplace, including a certificate on the wall bearing FDR's signature, Watson does not choose to extend the nationalist spirit to her home—not a miniature flag or a presidential portrait in sight. Instead, the cramped apartment is adorned with religious pictures and statuettes, as Parks emphasizes with several closeups of an improvised altar on Watson's bedroom bureau. This is "her" realm, limited but at least free of the contradictions of the workplace.

The full significance of Watson's participation in the St. Martin's Spiritualist Church services also emerges through the contrast with her custodial labor. After evenings spent cleaning white people's environs, the charwoman walks, barefoot, on what the congregation calls "holy ground"; after long hours of bending over sinks and toilets at the government offices, Watson is anointed by a long line of church members, and blessed by the minister who invokes a very different sense of "cleansing" during the church's annual flower bowl demonstration. As in Lee's coverage of the Baptist storefront services, Parks avoids an emphasis simply on the picturesque. But what the larger connectedness of the Parks series drives home, more powerfully than the Lee photography, is the importance of religious activity as a source of pride.

Fig. 5.21. Gordon Parks. "Mrs. Ella Watson, a Government Charwoman, and her Grandchildren," Washington, D.C. 1942. FSA. Library of Congress.

If the series effectively conveys the charwoman's multiple roles, it also conveys something of the multiple moods within the Watson household. In a sequence showing Watson feeding her grandchildren (e.g., fig. 5.21), Parks also incorporates the reflection of her older daughter in the bedroom mirror—the young woman pensive, seemingly detached from the rest of the household, and juxtaposed hauntingly with Watson's wedding portrait on the bureau. The busy scenes become studies of urban generations: the innocence of the toddlers, the persistent coping of the grandmother, the uncertainty of a young adult for whom Washington may or may not hold more opportunities than it has held for the elder Watson.

In short, Parks ventured into what for the FSA was new territory. But even the black photographer's work was not without its limitations. Certain problems arose indirectly from strengths. On the positive side, Parks, consistently able to gain his subjects' cooperation for close-in, low-angle shooting, achieved a considerable degree of immediacy in indoor as well as outdoor documentation. Parks appears to have gained sufficient trust to take a free hand with arrangement of people and objects. The most famous shot of Ella Watson, as the photographer acknowledged later, was hardly unplanned: "So out of her I got a charming story but in the heat of all this I took her into this white woman's office and there was the American flag and I stood her up with her mop hanging down . . . and did this marvelous portrait, which Stryker thought was just about the end."[35] Close inspection of the sequence inside Watson's home reveals that Parks moved a Bible on and off the dresser (13411-G, 13445-C) and shifted the portrait of Watson and husband to various points around the bedroom mirror (13412-C, 13437-C, 13436-C) in order to intensify the juxtaposition with Watson's daughter reflected in the mirror. Whether such tinkering takes away from the quality of the final product is an unresolvable question; clearly, if Parks is to be indicted on this count, so must Rothstein, Lee, Delano, and other FSA photographers who did their share of photographic "constructing."

Full-length, extreme-foreground human figures draw us into Parks's scenes. Slum children stand at a dimly lit kitchen table in 13302-C (fig. 5.22), leaving an obvious spot at the table's head for the *viewer* (the composition more dynamic, more engaging, and with the little girl seen by us and not necessarily by her family to be holding a toy gun under the table, more intimate than Lee's family-at-the-kitchen-table portrait); the Rev. Vondell Gassaway, in 13463-C, is utterly absorbed in, and absorbs us in, communion with a Jesus figurine at the St. Martin's Church altar. But the other side of Parks's immediacy was a certain repetitiveness. Rendered with increasing frequency in the late summer and autumn of 1942, and continuing all the more prominently during the cameraman's OWI period, the monumentalizing effect of Parks's upturned camera extended from children at play to the elderly in rockers, from civil defense volunteers to peanut vendors to a machine-shop worker posing on the street corner, from a woman

Fig. 5.22. Gordon Parks, Slum kitchen, Washington, D.C. 1942. FSA.
Library of Congress.

Fig. 5.23. Gordon Parks. "Mr. J. Benjamin, Owner of the Grocery Store Patronized by Mrs. Ella Watson," Washington, D.C. 1942. FSA. Library of Congress.

pumping water in her tenement backyard to the owner of a grocery toting a huge watermelon on his shoulder (fig. 5.23). After a while, the subjects verged on a Parksian stock figure, powerful, statuesque, imposingly noninvisible, but a bit predictable. Eschewing any "pathetic victim" vision, Parks turned increasingly in the wake of the Watson series to the opposite extreme, creating a procession of black working-class heroes. The latter were as visually dazzling as the elite heroes, the "Race leaders" pictured in black newspapers—and, at times, just as one-dimensional. The monumentalizing effect, combined with progressively more upbeat settings, ultimately fit in well with the government need for visions of American strength.

What's more, for all of Parks's stylistic aggressiveness, certain controversial themes were as notably absent from his coverage as from the Lee-Rosskam survey. While Parks experienced discrimination directly, the reality of segregated theaters, restaurants, bus stations, and street-car stands, as well as public bathrooms, parks, playgrounds, and schools was not to be found in Parks's Washington documentation. "Did you know," a 1942 *Baltimore Afro-American* article warned young blacks planning to move to Washington for war work, "that there are only four movie theatres to which colored can go, and that you will never be able to attend a legitimate play or a concert in Washington?"[36] Parks knew; he did not record. This was the period when even staid *Harper's* ran a story entitled, "Washington: Blight on Democracy," that concluded in part: "Negroes who have lived in many parts of the country say that nowhere else in America is there such bitter mutual race hatred."[37] And this was the summer when the mere appearance of a black foursome on the Fairlawn Golf Course, a mile from the Capitol, produced a near race riot, with "40 white children, adults, and soldiers using sticks, stones, clubs, and abusive language" (according to the *Afro-American*) to drive off the minority party.[38] Parks turned his photographic energies elsewhere. He did not turn them to the subject of black activism. While his subjects had an impressive physical presence, they appeared to have little more political presence than the Lee-Rosskam subjects. To be sure, Washington was not the capital of black protest in 1942. Yet there were signs of change that Parks might have investigated, whether organized campaigns connected to events on Capitol Hill (the fight for the Geyer Anti–Poll Tax Bill in July–August), the long-standing battle against employment discrimination by the Capital Transit Company (involving, at various junctures, boycotts, rallies, and FEPC pressure), or the smaller rebellions that were no less important—the refusal, in July, of several black postal employees to eat in the "Colored" section of the city's largest post office cafeteria, under the rationale that "if we are good enough to be called for the draft, we are good enough to eat with any other post office employees."[39] Only at the very end of 1942 did Parks offer any suggestion that Washington blacks were not suppressing their grievances for the sake of the war effort, and even that coverage, showing Adam Clayton Powell addressing an anti–poll tax meeting, was one of the briefest of Parks's FSA-OWI career.

Gordon Parks fell short of a full documentary encounter with urban conflict and change, as had Lee and Rosskam the year before. To some extent, these shortcomings reflected a long-standing weakness in FSA documentation of the deepest class and race divisions in American society, the fissures that could not be healed with New Deal initiatives. FSA photographers had always made their share of compromises, as we saw with Rothstein's coverage of the New Madrid troubles. But particularly strong reasons encouraged compromise in the later years of the project. For if there were 1940s forces that prompted increased documentary attention to cities, other equally important forces not only tended to discourage concentration on the touchiest urban topics (the color line, and efforts to change it) but produced more striking compromises in rural photography. The 1940s gave, and the 1940s took away. Stryker, the photographers, and the agency did not, and probably could not, remain isolated from the powerful nationalist currents of these years. *Look* and Viking Press experiments aside, the publishing market increasingly demanded upbeat photography, as did FSA exhibits (see chapter 6); FSA camerapeople found themselves spending more time on straight-promotion contract work for the OCI, OWI, and other war-related agencies; and with the Farm Security Administration as a whole under increasing congressional attack as a "non-essential" domestic agency, Stryker had reason to be concerned with providing visual evidence of FSA successes—and, in a broader sense, with guaranteeing the Historical Section an administrative home and a future. "It is very important," Stryker wrote Jack Delano in April 1941, "that we keep our finger in defense activities the way the whole world is moving now; and particularly the way things happen around [Washington], we may have to do much more for defense than we are now doing. Of course, there are various phases of defense and a great variety of things to be done, and I am determined that we are not going to find ourselves liquidated because we got on the wrong wagon."[40] Not coincidentally, Stryker advised Delano in the same letter to keep his knowledge of the FSA-Wright project as quiet as possible. Or, as Stryker described priorities even more bluntly in another letter to Delano: "Emphasize the idea of abundance [in New England]—the 'horn of plenty,' and pour maple syrup over it; you know, mix well with white clouds, and put on a sky-blue platter. I know your damned photographer's soul writhes, but to Hell with it. Do you think I give a damn about a photographer's soul with Hitler at our doorstep?"[41]

Stryker's pragmatism made itself felt: photographers' letters from this period show a combination of hard-edged descriptions of rural conditions, including racism, and reports of dutiful, soft-edged photographing. Rosier images of white and black life on the American countryside grew more prominent after 1940, and more prominent still after Pearl Harbor. Virtually all of Stryker's 1940s staffers contributed to the trend; one can trace the changes in the work of the veterans Lee and Vachon, or in the work of the later arrivals Wolcott, Delano, and Collier. A comparative look at a Delano turn-of-the-decade coverage (documentation of black migrant workers following the crops in North Carolina, Maryland, and Virginia) and a Delano story from a year later (a day-in-the-life chronicle of a young black farm lad in Greene County, Georgia) provides one of the many possible examples in this regard.

"The whole background against which the seasonal migration of large numbers of Negroes takes place," noted a 1940 FSA economic report, "is in the general impoverishment of agriculture in the South, and a long-time trend in certain areas of the South Atlantic states leading to the displacement of Negroes on the farm. This is creating a large group of foot-loose people whose background in agricultural work leads them to seek seasonal agricultural labor, which they often obtain through acceptance of a lower wage scale." And later in the same report: "Overcrowding [in migrant quarters] is typical, 12 to 15 people often being housed in a shack measuring about 12 by 15 feet. . . . In most cases, toilets, when they exist, are so filthy and unsanitary that the migrants refuse to use them and seek the nearest patch of woods instead."[42] In part, Delano's July 1940 migrant coverage was an attempt to give visual expression to the textual exposés being developed by FSA economists, by the House of Representatives' Tolan Committee on Interstate Migration, and by the Senate's LaFollette Civil Liberties Committee. Visual exposés could counter the common public impression, conveyed in *Fortune* and elsewhere, that while the predominantly white West Coast migrants were displaced farmers deserving federal attention and assistance, the predominantly black East Coast migrants were essentially gypsies by their own choosing. "Social maladjustment, wanderlust, the curious satisfactions of personal liberty without economic freedom," noted an April 1939 *Fortune* account, were among the factors that kept the "habitual" migrant on the road. "It is even possible to think of him romantically."[43] What's more, visual exposés could help loosen FSA purse strings for an extension of the migrant shelter program, already in place in California (and even saluted in *The Grapes of Wrath*), to the East.

In that spirit, Delano shot a number of scenes every bit as damning as the FSA migrant visions that had inspired Steinbeck: barefoot children toiling, on their knees, in the Maryland vegetable fields; barbed-wire fences surrounding migrant barracks; a single, primitive water faucet serving as the sole water source for a large work crew at a North Carolina potato-grading station; wretched living quarters in shacks, barns, warehouses, and box cars. "Tomorrow," Delano wrote Stryker from Bellcross, North Carolina, "I am going out to a house occupied by some transients about 11 miles from here. They're lucky to have a house but there are 37 of them staying in three rooms and an attic! I gave one of them a lift the other day to get talking to him and went up to the house. They think I'm a 'pretty right guy' and I ought to be able to get some pictures there."[44] Camera angles accented Delano's protest objectives: the over-the-head view of a youthful potato-harvester, heightening the sense of the lad's vulnerability; the frames-within-frames view, through a doorway, of a migrant woman sitting in the gloom of a shack, underscoring the impression of imprisonment; the nighttime juxtaposition of a railroad crossing sign with a young boy eating dinner on the tracks, serving quite literally to flag the viewer's attention to labor conditions too often passed over (fig. 5.24). On at least one occasion, Delano's muckraking interests led him to hit-and-run documentary extremes in the style of Margaret Bourke-White. "Last night," he reported to Stryker from Belcross on 2 July, "I tried to get some pictures of the box car sleepers. If you had been here at 2 A.M., you would have seen three scared figures in the darkness (myself and two boys carrying flash-bulbs), quietly opening the door of a box car, seeing exactly (pitch blackness), pointing the camera in the general direction of loud snoring, setting off the flash, then running like Hell!"[45]

But if Delano delivered shots designed to awaken consciences, and occasionally awakened literal sleepers in the process, such did not constitute the sum total of his migrant coverage. As in the Shahn and Rothstein rural series described in previous chapters, the FSA photographer pursued more intimate and textured dimensions as well. Without any guidance from government reports, without any guidance from Stryker (who would take much more interest in Delano's work that autumn among *white* ethnic groups), Delano was attentive to the undramatic details comprising a life. At the same time, Delano avoided the happy-go-lucky tack that characterized a 1940s Department of Agriculture series on Jamaican migrant farm laborers in Michigan. Contrasting with the USDA portraits of grinning enthusiasts, Delano's photograph of migrant men, dressed in their Sunday best and playing cards outside their barracks, has an almost Cézanne-like gravity, emphasizing thoughtfulness over merriment. His numerous images of workers eating lunch on the porch of a camp store, of migrants carefully packing suitcases and loading them into trucks, of groups chatting on the roadside while several of their members attend to a flat tire, of drivers consulting road maps at filling stations (travelers showing a certain precision and purposefulness, countering the impression of footloose gypsies), reveal routines that are neither particularly colorful nor pitiful (fig. 5.25). The very pacing of the series, with its drawn-out sequence on the rituals of preparation for travel, conveyed an essential rhythm of migrant existence without minimizing or exaggerating its burdens.

To be sure, some of these mundane themes were not without their political implications, as suggested in the noble-endurer tone of the field notes kept by Delano's wife, Irene. "They were bitter about their housing here and hoped they would be able to get something better in Virginia," she reported from Belcross. "In spite of difficulties, they did their best to keep clean and keep their house orderly. By the time the truck arrived, they had swept the house, burned the rubbish, washed as best they could at the pump, and put on their best clothes for the

Fig. 5.24. Jack Delano. "Migrant Agricultural Worker Harvesting Potatoes," Camden, N.C. 1940. FSA. Library of Congress.

journey."[46] These are strivers, not overt protesters; survivors, not troublemakers. Still, within limits, there was a freshness in the photographer's approach. In closeups such as that of a young migrant aboard the Norfolk–Cape Charles ferry writing a post card to his parents, Delano overcame a number of conventions and barriers. The image in 40871-D (fig. 5.26) jars the conventional conception of the black migratory laborer as utterly rootless, at home on the road. It jars the conventional notion of the migrant as a physical rather than mental presence, needing a documentarian to convey his or her experiences. In its angle—the writer seeming to lean down into our space, rather than the opposite—the image gives the migrant what is quite literally the upper hand, and, in the process, balances the over-the-head victim shots found elsewhere in the series. In its seriousness, the image demands the sort of contemplation—about the possible content

Fig. 5.25. Jack Delano. "Migrant Agricultural Workers Consulting a Roadmap at a Filling Station," Camden, N.C. 1940. FSA. Library of Congress.

of the note, about the impact of the work and travel routine on the individual spirit, about the writer's future—that the USDA shot of Jamaican migrants writing home, with their broad, self-conscious grins, their writers-as-entertainers aura, does not (fig. 5.27). Finally, inasmuch as the Delano shot seems relatively unposed, the photo suggests that the appearance of spontaneity in a close-range black subject was an accomplishment within a white FSA photographer's capacity. At least on this occasion, Delano managed to overcome what, in other shooting contexts, he later described as

> a reticence [on the part of black subjects] toward us, a kind of distance that made us feel a bit like we were intruding, but that they couldn't tell us to go.

Fig. 5.26. Jack Delano. "A Migratory Agricultural Worker on the Ferry, Writing a Postal Card to His Parents," Norfolk–Cape Charles Ferry, Va. 1940. FSA. Library of Congress.

Fig. 5.27. Unidentified U.S. Department of Agriculture photographer. "Two Jamaicans Write Home from Michigan." 1943. Office of the Secretary of Agriculture. National Archives.

... I remember one Sunday morning [in Georgia, 1941], Irene and I drove by a black church; we stopped and asked the deacon if we could take some pictures inside. There was a long pause. I think he would have been happy if a huge hole had opened up and we had just disappeared. He wanted us to go, but he probably felt he couldn't say no. We ended up making a mess of the place, flashbulbs all over the place. When I asked Irene to hold a flash near the altar, she didn't want to continue; we argued. We felt pretty horrible. Several years later, we felt a little better when we saw several of the church pictures published in *12 Million Black Voices*.[47]

The balance, toughness, and imaginativeness that marked Delano's migrant coverage also extended to certain of his later 1940s series. But these qualities appeared less regularly. More typical of the later photography was the series on a young Boyd Jones, part of Delano's larger Greene County documentation (June and November 1941) with an unmistakable accent on government-induced rural progress. Greene had long been considered a "test case" by FSA officials and other reformers. It was in 1927 that future FSA administrator Will Alexander, intrigued by reports of a mass exodus from depressed counties in central Georgia, persuaded sociologist Arthur Raper to investigate Greene and neighboring Macon County; the investigation ultimately led to Raper's 1931 doctoral thesis, A Study of Two Black-Belt Counties. In 1936, again at Alexander's urging, Raper returned to the area, and wrote the jarring report on economic and racial injustice, A Preface to Peasantry.

With these studies in mind, Alexander and his FSA staff developed a "United Farm Program" for Greene, with an unusually expansive network of grants and loans (FSA client families increasing from 146 to 530 in 1939) coordinated with a variety of WPA, NYA, CCC, and USDA ventures. Three years into the program, Raper made his final visit, during a portion of which he worked with Delano gathering materials for Tenants of the Almighty, one part Greene County history and two parts New Deal celebration. "While in Greene County," Stryker advised Delano before the photographer joined Raper, "think about doing a series of 'after' shots we can use to contrast with 'before' pictures taken a few years ago."[48] As if to underline the request for upbeat photography, Stryker also sent Delano a Pare Lorentz article on the greatness of the American land, "What We Are About to Defend." Delano understood the message: "We showed some of the Greene County pictures to a group of the people down here and they were tickled," he reported back to Stryker. "Arthur [Raper] keeps talking of the [photo] of the man-plowing-in-cotton-field-with-lottsa-sky-and-white-clouds-in-a-row as the frontispiece [for the book]."[49] And, as Delano recalled later: "I respected Stryker for what he was trying to do; if he felt he needed some positive pictures, I didn't feel uncomfortable about doing it. . . . I certainly liked some of the people I met in Greene County, and there were some beautiful things to be found there."[50] If Raper and FSA administrators wanted to emphasize a

Greene County, black as well as white, on the forward march, Delano's Boyd Jones story certainly fit the bill.

It was no coincidence that the subject of Delano's only black day-in-the-life chronicle in Greene was a youth who attended one of the county's newest, best-equipped black schools, the pointedly named Alexander Community School outside Greensboro. Nor was it any coincidence that over 60 percent of the images followed Boyd's school day. The emphasis on the building of a bright future obscured what were still immense gaps between black and white socioeconomic circumstances, including education. Statistics showed Greene's black schools receiving less than a tenth the funding of white schools, black teachers receiving salaries that averaged half those of their white coun-

Fig. 5.28. Jack Delano. "Boyd Jones Doing His Arithmetic Lesson at the Blackboard in the Alexander Community School," Greene County, Ga. 1941. FSA. Library of Congress.

terparts, black pupils attaining an average of a low third-grade education while whites attained an average of an eighth-grade education,
and the county's blacks being turned away from the military for reasons of illiteracy seven times more frequently than whites—but these
conditions seemed a world away in Delano's classroom rendering. That
the photographer was at least aware of a more stark reality was suggested in Delano's description of some experimental color photography: "I have taken a few shots in color of the red eroded land and a
Negro shack of a schoolhouse with the bright American and Georgia
flags hanging out the window, as required by Georgia law."[51] In the
course of his Greene County coverage, Delano also took a handful of
noncolor shots of the dilapidated Veasey School for Colored Chil-

Fig. 5.29. Jack Delano. "Boyd Jones Playing Tug-of-War with Class Mates During Play
Period at Alexander Community School," Greene County, Ga. 1941. FSA. Library of
Congress.

dren; still, the lion's share of the black education shots went to the sparkling Alexander Community School.

Delano took every opportunity to depict a well-supplied facility. Hence the repeated closeups of Jones arriving at school with multiple schoolbooks under his arm. Hence the pointed angle in a view of Jones helping his teacher reshelve classroom texts—an open picture-book being read avidly in the foreground, Jones standing beside what appears to be a well-stocked bookcase, and the caption offering no hint that, as even Raper conceded, except for bare beginnings "the Negro schools and the Negro population remain without library books or library service."[52] And hence the closeup of several female pupils being trained on sewing machines, with "technology," skilled hands, and a devoted instructor all pushing into the viewer's space. If there were vague hints, in one or two classroom shots, that there may not have been enough desks to go around, such a possibility was never explored in the captions or in further images. Instead, Delano swept on to an inspirational view of Jones, pointer in hand, demonstrating his mathematical skills at the blackboard (fig. 5.28). As if the star pupil's pose was not reassuring enough, the photographer made sure to include the Pilgrim ship drawings (along with the Thanksgiving-season saying, "All is safely gathered in") atop the blackboard, with the resulting juxtaposition suggesting a connection between black progress and American heritage, between the fruits of the Alexander School and those of the original white American communities. The vision of an energetic Boyd carried over to a lengthy sequence of recess images. Not only was the lad featured in statuesque ball-throwing poses, but he was shown linked with his friends in a tug-of-war game, bearing implications of military as well as athletic teamwork (fig. 5.29). Boyd's self-conscious glance together with the broad grins of his teammates, produced a not altogether convincing impression of ebullience, the sort that would grow even more artificial in OCI and OWI shots of 1942–43 (for example, the "cheesecake" smiles of another set of black Joneses, the Feggan Jones farm family of Zebulon, North Carolina, photographed for the OCI by Rothstein in March 1942). Just as Delano's schoolyard views pointed forward to war-agency work, so did his shot of Boyd Jones and classmates walking home from school and just "happening" to pass a prominent building under construction—perhaps another new school.

After the largely celebratory rendering of Boyd's educational life, Delano might have sought at least a measure of balance with a more probing inquiry into the youth's home life. He might have explored the nature of Boyd's work role, relationships within the family, routines and conditions around the house and farm. He might have endeavored to push beyond the immediate FSA photographic needs, as he had done the year before in the migrant series. Delano certainly had the time for a more careful second look at Jones: the photographer did some weekend shooting as well as the school-day photography. But the home-life documentation proved to be as one-dimensional as the coverage of Boyd at school. The foundation of mundane detail that had made the migrant series particularly innovative was absent here; in striking contrast to the migrants, Boyd Jones was seen in what amounted to a socioeconomic void. Delano showed little of the Jones farm, and, in fact, the family's land tenure status was never identified. (The vaguer the better from the government angle: for all the changes that the FSA claimed to have wrought in Greene, nine out of ten black farmers were still sharecroppers or tenants in 1941, with incomes averaging one-third those of their white counterparts.) The series showed little of the family other than Boyd, and the few family shots were tinged with rustic sweetness.

In one sequence showing the family riding a horse-drawn wagon into town, Delano depicts Boyd's smiling father turning over the reins to his even more broadly smiling son, Boyd's glowing face photographed against a backdrop of bright sky and fleecy clouds (fig. 5.30). If Boyd appears commanding, the white horses, photographed from below, are also made to look as majestic as possible. There seems little need for automobiles or improved country roads in a scene such as 46593-E, where equine beauty and power (and, implicitly, black success displayed through a creature of *white* grandeur) fill the foreground. Rural strength takes on a pioneer flavor in Delano's view of the family at home: the Joneses, all looking industrious, seated around the fireplace. Inasmuch as the scene holds a less positive implication (that the Joneses were huddled around the fire because, like the rest of the

Fig. 5.30. Jack Delano. "Boyd Jones Driving into Greensboro for Saturday
Afternoon," Greene County, Ga. 1941. FSA. Library of Congress.

94 percent of black farm families without electricity in Greene County,
they lacked a better source of light), that implication is never bolstered with further photographic or textual exploration. Views inside
the house remained effectively unrevealing. Coverage of Boyd at the
breakfast table, a subject that might have yielded insights into the
Jones kitchen circumstances, was limited to a single shot dominated
by cheerful motifs: Boyd's upraised glass of milk, a splash of sunlight
on Boyd's forehead, and the window through which we see only soft
shapes and the morning glow (fig. 5.31).

To be sure, Delano's treatment of Boyd Jones was no more saccha-
rine than his renderings of Greene County *white* youths. And to be

Fig. 5.31. Jack Delano. "Boyd Jones Eating His Breakfast," Greene County, Ga. 1941. FSA. Library of Congress.

sure, Delano's presentation of black well-being, for all its shortcomings, avoided some of the most demeaning typecasting. It was a bright, able, generally dignified Boyd, more than an entertaining Boyd, who took center stage here, as would be the case with the many Boyd equivalents rendered by Gordon Parks for the OWI. The assumption, implicit in the Jones series, that blacks formed part of the nation's rural backbone was not without its progressive implications in 1941: strength deserved cultivation, in economic terms and perhaps beyond. Still, these implications remained distant. In its essential circularity, the Jones series ultimately affirmed precisely what the migrant series had questioned: the convenient notion, for whites, not only of the contented rural black but the *easily classifiable* rural black. As if shots

of young Jones poring over his Bible at Moses Chapel were not sufficient to establish his religious faith, the boy was shown with his sister
saying bedside prayers, the two figures looking distinctly angelic with
their bowed heads and nightgowns. As if the school scenes were not
sufficient to establish Boyd as an earnest learner, Delano added a view
of the boy stretched out in front of the hearth, doing his homework by
the firelight—necessity turned into Lincolnesque virtue. The hammering went on, and Boyd, the rural foil for Bigger Thomas, the Will
Alexander-esque alternative to Richard Wright's nightmare, ceased to
be believable. "I won't be especially proud of some of the shots we've
been getting," Delano confided to Stryker about the Greene coverage
in general.[53] It was not the last time that Delano or other FSA photographers would put photographic pride, and documentary innovation,
on the back burner.

6

The FSA Black Image in the Marketplace

By early 1937, the Historical Section photographic file amounted to nearly seven thousand mounted images. A few—a Lange "Migrant Mother" here, a Rothstein "Dust Storm" there—had gained considerable exposure in the print media. Publication and exhibition momentum was building, but it was not yet clear that, as a commentator would confidently assert of the FSA photographers in 1940, "You have seen their pictures."[1] Roy Stryker was still knocking on doors, and doors were not always opening. "[It wasn't easy] finding places where they would use the pictures, finding outlets," Lange remembered of the early years, "and the pictures piled up and they piled up, and Roy used to disappear and not come to the office. He made the rounds."[2] Stryker wanted the files put to work for political and artistic reasons. He *needed* the file put to work—and not just the project shots most useful for official agency productions—in order to justify his budget. And so it was that, when Archibald MacLeish launched plans for a visual and poetic collaboration using pictures from the Historical Section file, Stryker was eager to cooperate.

The MacLeish book, an excited Stryker informed Lee in April 1937, will present "a series of pictures which will portray the people left behind after the empire builders have taken the forests, the ore, and the top soil. From now on, you should keep this general theme very much in the back of your head when you are taking pictures." As the manuscript took shape over the summer, MacLeish, consulting frequently with Stryker, made cuts from Stryker's initial selection of five-hundred photographs, meanwhile developing ideas for images not already in the Historical Section file. By autumn of 1937, picture possibilities to be kept "in the back" of photographers' minds had become immediate

priorities. "Stop everything and work on the MacLeish pictures,"
Stryker ordered Lee in October. "There are a few things we still need
. . . photo of a great sweep of land, the widest possible open country,
the best grass picture possible . . . kitchen in the dust area with windows sealed with towels . . . and a typical Midwestern four corners,
with church falling down, store caving in, fences failing."[3]

No casual collaboration was "the MacLeish book." No small opportunity, from Stryker's standpoint, was *Land of the Free*. MacLeish was a
figure of national stature, a Pulitzer Prize-winning poet and editor at
Fortune, with connections in the Roosevelt administration (MacLeish
would become Librarian of Congress in 1939). MacLeish had the backing
of a major publisher, Harcourt Brace, and there were plans to publish
the book in Britain through Boriswood, Ltd. While two books had
already made some use of Historical Section photographs (Rupert
Vance's *How the Other Half Is Housed: A Pictorial Record of Sub-mar-
ginal Farm Housing in the South* and Charles Morrow Wilson's *Roots of
America: A Travelogue of American Personalities*), the MacLeish volume promised to use a greater quantity, displayed much more prominently. "The foreword to *Land of the Free* . . . says that it is photographs illustrated by a poem, which was not an attempt to be funny
but to tell the truth," as MacLeish described the broad strategy later.
"The poem is an illustration of [the photos] in the sense that it tries to
give them a theme, a running, continuing sort of choral voice."[4]
What's more, Stryker knew, at least by the end of the summer, that
MacLeish's "choral voice" would not fundamentally deviate from the
American political-cultural mainstream: an angry voice, yes, but not
one whose screeching indictment of capitalism would alienate important reviewers and take attention away from the photographs.

Some of the written material that MacLeish removed in the course
of summer revisions was the very sort that could have provoked controversy. "Sections Two and Four, the *exploiters* and man against waste,
have been dropped," Stryker reported to Lee in August (emphasis
mine).[5] MacLeish's final text, laced with a populist bitterness, nevertheless proposed no clear alternative to New Deal reform; even the
question at poem's end, "if there is a liberty a man can mean that's /
Men; not land," was cast in language sufficiently vague to accommo-

date Rooseveltian ideas of reform. MacLeish's refrain, "We wonder /
We don't know / We're asking," softened whatever militant inferences
could be drawn from the "Men; not land" duality. Even stodgy *Time*
would call the conclusion "soft-boiled" and "limpid."[6] Emphatic as the
poem was about the gap between America's bountiful promise and her
Great Depression reality, MacLeish did not arraign any specific group
or institution for creating the gap. The shackling of the land of the
free was generally without overseers. In fact, MacLeish's indignation
led to no fundamental reexamination of American history. The hero-
ism of the pioneers, the grandeur of their original conquest, remained
essentially intact. "It was two hundred years from the smell of the
tidewater," sang MacLeish, respectfully. "Up through the Piedmont:
on through the piney woods: Till we came out / With our led calves
and our lean women / In the oak openings of Illinois."[7] Pained as
MacLeish's modern "we" often were, "we" retained a national identity.
A touch of nationalism, a touch of agrarianism; a dose of Lincoln and
Whitman, a particularly heavy dose of the Turner frontier thesis—in
its appeal to the American conscience, MacLeish appealed to some
strikingly traditional sensitivities, many of them shared by Stryker.

Stryker saw in the collaborative venture the possibility of presenting the Historical Section file in terms not only more quantitatively
sweeping than before but more spiritually sweeping—the agony of the
American spirit, the reaffirmation of the American spirit. Sweeping
new attention the Historical Section most certainly received. While
the book, published in April 1938, was not a best-seller, it received
heavy play in the media, from *Time* to the *San Francisco Chronicle*.
Reviews in most of the prominent centrist publications, as well as in at
least one more liberal journal (*The New Republic*), hailed *Land of the
Free* as a majestic achievement: "a grim and beautiful book, a masterpiece of collaborations," raved Peter Monro Jack in *The New York
Times*; a book, predicted Ruth Lechlitner in *The New York Herald-
Tribune*, that "will be remembered, not only as an admirable technical
experiment, but as a document of real social significance."[8] Enthusiasm about MacLeish's "choral voice" was not always unqualified, but,
significantly, even those who had reservations about the text were sold
on the photographs. The Rothstein "skull" controversy apparently for-

gotten, reviewers of varied political orientations remarked on the power of the Historical Section's photographic truth, the power, as Eugene Davidson wrote in the Yale Review, of "our faces."[9] This was an important moment for Stryker. Rather than being viewed simply as government picture-taking for government purposes, FSA camera work was invoked as central to a shared national experience: *our* faces. Not only did commentators devote considerable space to the book's visuals, but reviews often reprinted sample photo spreads. A New York Herald-Tribune reader, for example, who might not have been persuaded to buy Land of the Free, was nevertheless exposed to Lee's "Farmer On Cutover Land Near Iron River, Michigan." "Our faces"— the notion appealed even to FSA publicists oriented toward project shots. "I have now one damned good stock argument when they [other FSA, Department of Agriculture officials] lay out one of these broad campaigns of photographing rehabilitation clients, etc.," Stryker explained to Lange in October 1938, "and that is to ask them how in the hell we would have had a MacLeish book . . . if their type of photography had been pursued consistently. That always wins the argument."[10]

Were these, in fact, our faces? While a few reviewers recognized the presumption of MacLeish's "group" voice—presumptuous for any writer dealing with American experience, doubly presumptuous for a writer who had had very little direct contact with the dispossessed groups for which he presumed to speak, and triply presumptuous for such a writer appropriating the often complex visions of multiple photographers— only one touched on the question of picture selection.[11] "MacLeish," noted John Holmes in the Boston Transcript, "excludes immense areas of American life by excluding pictures of them."[12] For Holmes, the important images excluded were those of better-off Americans. But there was more to the exclusion problem. When measured against demographic realities, "our" faces in Land of the Free were disproportionately rural, disproportionately native-born American, and disproportionately *white*. The first two distortions reflected the nature of the principal photo-file from which the book's images were drawn. The third, however, did not. Of the total of eighty-eight photographs used in Land of the Free (sixty-two from Stryker's file, along with a scattering from other government agencies, news-picture services, and independent photographers), only five incorporated black subject-matter (4.5 percent). Of the FSA batch, only two (3.2 percent) included blacks. In neither did blacks appear in the foreground.

For its depiction of the landless, the homeless, the wandering, *Land of the Free* could have made use of such black-related work as Shahn's Arkansas sharecropper/day-laborer series, the Evans-Locke Arkansas flood refugee material, Rothstein's Florida and New Jersey migrant scenes, Mydans's Mississippi Delta cotton-chopper coverage, Lange's Georgia orchard-worker series. It did not. The only image of black agricultural laborers included was a pre-1930 Department of Agriculture shot of Georgia peach-pickers, with figures stiffly posed, faces all but hidden under the trees, individuals merging into an anonymous mass. Compared with the Lange shot of white farm workers on the preceding page, or with the many Lange and Rothstein black fruit-picker portraits that could have been tapped, the USDA image was notably static. "We've got the fruit tramps' road from Florida northward," sang MacLeish; the accompanying image failed to make the black "tramps" a convincing part of the human "we."[13]

Land of the Free did make use of Lange's Clarksdale, Mississippi, work, but it was a questionable use. The original "A Plantation Owner" had much to say about caste and class in Mississippi—the blacks adopting postures as tight and protective as the landowner's was aggressive and commanding (fig. 6.1). The version appearing in the MacLeish book did not. Cropping removed four of the five blacks (those whose body language figured most decisively in the photograph's message), leaving a portrait not, as Lange described the original, of "a man as he was tied up with his fellow," but of a sturdy white individual (fig. 6.2). The cropped view was not entirely unfamiliar to Lange, who had included a landowner closeup (along with the group shot) in the Clarksdale coverage. But while a case might be made for a note of ambiguity in the original series—more likely, Lange intended to have the landowner closeup played off against the group shot, suggesting a commentary on Southern white surfaces and interracial depths—*Land of the Free* made of Lange's work an unambiguous tribute to the old-fashioned American spunk. Opposite the cropped shot, MacLeish defined the American heritage: "We told ourselves we were free because

Fig. 6.1. Dorothea Lange. A Plantation Owner, Clarksdale, Miss. 1936. FSA.
Library of Congress.

we were free . . . We were Americans / All you needed for freedom was
being American / All you needed for freedom was grit in your craw /
And the gall to get out on a limb and crow before sunup."[14] It is
extremely doubtful that MacLeish intended an ironic contrast between
words and image here, for such an interpretation would make this
word-image pairing unique in the book. Irony in *Land of the Free* flowed
not from an implied tension between poem and photographs but from
an implied tension between two ideas (America's historic meaning,
America's present crisis), each expressed through word-image alliances.

As for the book's other black-related FSA photo, Vachon's 1937
shot of Arkansas sharecroppers lining the road after being evicted for
membership in the Southern Tenant Farmers Union, there was no

Fig. 6.2. Dorothea Lange. Mississippi plantation owner, as used in *Land of the Free*, 1938.

cropping. But with blacks shown amid a heap of possessions in the distance, the selection (from several Vachon possibilities that included pictures of evictees at closer range) did little to bring black sharecroppers into the viewer's world; in both the preceding and succeeding published images, homeless *whites* (Lee's Missouri flood refugees, Lange's Missouri migrants) approached us face to face. The matching of MacLeish's text to the evicted-sharecropper image produced a distancing of a different variety. While the story behind the eviction involved socialist-sponsored black economic militancy, MacLeish's commentary cast the sharecroppers not as rebels but as simply another set of victims: "Shot-gunned off in Arkansas—the cotton—."[15] Reference to the cause of the eviction was left to the picture credits following the poem. Even in the credits, there was a peculiarity. The eviction shot was the only FSA photo listed without a specific photographer credit. Was the attempt here to shield Vachon from potential reprisals by Arkansas authorities who did not want photographers digging up dirt on anti-STFU activities? Unfortunately, what documentation exists for the making of *Land of the Free* reveals nothing on this point. But, whatever the justification, the effect of omitting the name was to suggest that this photo, unlike the Langes and the Rothsteins and the Lees, was merely a Historical Section throw-in.

To be sure, blacks were not completely absent from MacLeish's "Men; not land" finale. Two of the closing photos, from Acme Newspictures and Pictures, Inc., included blacks among crowds of labor demonstrators. Yet faces in the crowd remained just that; the closing images did not remedy the problem of distancing, literal and psychological, affecting what little black portrayal existed in *Land of the Free*. Faces not seen well, faces not seen at all: through selection, cropping, and, in effect, recaptioning, *Land of the Free* left shadowy the group whose past and present formed such a central, and such a controversial, part of "our" American experience. The history buried under the *Land of the Free* formulation of freedom—"We were free because of the Battle of Bunker Hill / And the constitution adopted at Philadelphia / Now we don't know"—was the history dealt with so crudely and exploitively in the previous year's *You Have Seen Their Faces*. In the wake of the photographic exploitation came photographic invisibility.

If Stryker was at all displeased with the use of images in *Land of the Free*, his letters did not indicate it. Nor did the photographers'; the pleasure of seeing their work emerge from the files into the sunlight of publication seemed to outweigh considerations of selection. From Stryker's standpoint, criticism of the book would have been, in part, self-criticism. Chances are that, quite beyond the initial picture selection, Stryker had a hand in any number of pictorial decisions. Other FSAers were probably involved as well—Locke, whose varied Historical Section roles included publications work, and Shahn, who spent considerable time in the Washington office in 1937 as an unofficial photo-editing advisor. Who, in particular, was responsible for the cropping of Lange's "A Plantation Owner," or who decided to use the USDA orchard shot instead of an FSA alternative, is impossible to determine; in general, however, responsibility for the problematical treatment of black America in *Land of the Free* cannot be placed solely with a Massachusetts poet playing, as *Time* put it, "poetographer." MacLeish's safe (i.e., white) vision of American community, the "team playing" of Stryker and possibly other FSA insiders, the apparent lack of interest on the part of reviewers in the book's ethnic omissions— the case of *Land of the Free* does not throw any of these parties into a particularly favorable racial light. But, as in previous chapters, we face the question of typicality. Was the case part of a broader pattern of FSA photo-utilization that underexposed, or, in instances where quantity was not a problem, misexposed the black file during the depression and war years? If the FSA black file was innovative in important quantitative and qualitative respects, was this innovation hopelessly obscured in the public arena? Was the black file prevented from making a cultural impact?

In exploring these questions, we must cast the investigative net widely. The effect of the tremendous publicity accorded *Land of the Free*, combined with other contemporaneous factors—the activism of a photo-minded John Fischer at the top of the FSA Information Division, the continued willingness of Stryker to devote as much time and energy to FSA photo dissemination as FSA photo accumulation, the dramatic success of *Life* and attendant expansion of market interest in documentary photos of all sorts—was to increase the flow of FSA images into a variety of publication and exhibition channels. *Land of the Free* was one of the more than a dozen photo-books, published between 1936 and 1943, making use of FSA images. The list spanned the scholarly (Herman Clarence Nixon's *Forty Acres and Steel Mules*) and the popular (Sherwood Anderson and Edwin Rosskam's *Home Town*), the photo-dominant (Walker Evans's *American Photographs*) and the textually dominant (Arthur Raper and Ira Reid's *Sharecroppers All*), the passionate (Dorothea Lange and Paul Taylor's *An American Exodus* or Richard Wright and Edwin Rosskam's *12 Million Black Voices*) and the utterly innocuous (Samuel Chamberlain's *Fair Is Our Land*).

The FSA section at the 1938 International Photography Exposition in New York City was one of dozens of such shows mounted in galleries and museums, not only those in traditional East Coast artistic and cultural centers (New York's Museum of Modern Art or Philadelphia's Franklin Institute) but those in the "hinterland"—the Cleveland Museum, the Kansas City Institute of Sciences, and the Tucson Center for the Arts and Crafts. For the multitudes of Americans who did not consume photo-books or visit galleries, there were other sources of potential exposure to FSA photography. *Land of the Free* may not have sold as well in Greenwood, Indiana, as it did in New York City, but Greenwood Presbyterian Church parishioners viewed an FSA traveling exhibit in the church lobby in October 1940.

And so the story went in hundreds of locales across the country. Agency exhibits, either sets of photo-panels designed for wide circulation or displays designed for specific settings, appeared in schools, churches, and libraries, at fairs, expositions, and conferences, in department store windows and even, from December 1941 through much of 1942, above the main lobby of New York's Grand Central Station. "Traffic experts," announced the *New York Herald-Tribune* in a feature on the Grand Central photo-mural, "estimate that during 1942 the mural will be seen 242,500 times."[16] Press coverage of the Grand Central mural was extensive; but if FSA images found their way into newspaper pages through such reports, they were also tapped, with increasing frequency in the late 1930s and 1940s, for story illustrations and picture pages. By the end of the 1930s, it was clear that the Historical Section had become a veritable picture service for newspapers and magazines. It was a service diverse in resources, reasonably efficient (with some allowances made for the less-than-orderly condition of the Washington file), and, of prime importance for the media, free.

"Keep the following things in mind when planning," Stryker once advised an FSA staffer on preparing agency traveling exhibits. "Simple layout. Some text. Emphasize what has been *accomplished*."[17] The instructions came in 1939, but they might just as easily have been written in 1936 or 1941. Traveling exhibits were generally purveyors of agency hard sell, intended to elicit the sort of comments reportedly heard around an FSA display at the Franklin County, Nebraska, Fair in September 1936: "This is the first real program that has actually helped the poor farmers"; "Could see nothing wrong with that kind of a program"; "Thought it was just an Alaska plan, did not know they were carrying it on in Kansas."[18] A single, forty-picture prototype exhibit sufficed in 1936; by 1941, there were over fifteen standard shows, each addressing a different angle. "New Start on the Land," "From . . . Toward," "Design for Living," "Rural Rehabilitation," "Farm Security Is National Security," "Farm Security through Better Sanitation," "Live-at-Home Farming," "Food for Victory"—such assemblages provided the daily working tools for John Fischer in the national information office, for Harold Ballou, O. B. Dryden, Jonathan Garst, and other officials in the regional information offices.

General ideas for these shows came from an agency-wide Exhibits Committee, of which Stryker and Fischer were members, while responsibility for practical planning and execution, originally shared by the Historical Section and the RA's Special Skills Division, devolved increasingly on Stryker's office. Beginning in 1939, it was the particular responsibility of Stryker's "visual information specialist," Edwin Rosskam, who was joined the following year by a design artist, Milton Tinsley. Stryker wanted all phases of the work coordinated: "Rosskam has been able to demonstrate this year something of the potentialities of a visual information program," as Stryker reported to Fischer prior to the hiring of Tinsley. "We do not feel, however, that his efforts were entirely justified mainly because of the lack of a person on our

FARM SECURITY ADMINISTRATION AIDS THE NEGRO FARMER

THE NEGRO FARMER'S PROBLEM IS THE SOUTHERN FARMER'S PROBLEM

95 PERCENT OF NEGRO FARMERS ARE IN THE SOUTH. 47 PERCENT OF THESE ARE SHARECROPPERS. 32 PERCENT ARE TENANTS. —

ONLY 21 PERCENT ARE OWNERS.

Toward

From

FARM SECURITY HELPS THROUGH ...

1. REHABILITATION LOANS FOR EQUIPMENT, LIVESTOCK, SEED, FERTILIZER.

2. TENANT PURCHASE LOANS TO MAKE OWNERS OUT OF CROPPERS AND TENANTS.

3. DEBT ADJUSTMENT TO REDUCE INTEREST, RE-SCALE PAYMENTS TO THE FARMER'S CAPACITY.

4. CO-OPERATIVE COMMUNITIES TO ENABLE SMALL FARMERS TO COMPETE WITH LARGE, MECHANIZED FARMS.

Fig. 6.3. Farm Security Administration Exhibit: "Farm Security Administration Aids the Negro Farmer." 1939. FSA. Library of Congress.

staff who is qualified through skill and experience to develop the designs worked out by Rosskam."[19]

We have previously noted Rosskam's subtle touch as a photographer, but Rosskam was one who shifted mind-sets as he shifted roles.
Rosskam the exhibits creator was as slick as any PR man in Washington. No exception to the rule was a traveling exhibit prepared in late
1939 to bolster the "Negro program" publicity efforts of Joseph Evans,
Constance Daniel, Jerome Robinson, Giles Hubert, Frank Pinder, and
their race advisor equivalents on the regional level. (Robinson assisted
Daniel after she took over from Evans as chief racial advisor in the
national office, while Hubert and Pinder were black assistants in the
national rural rehab division and settlement division, respectively.
Other black assistants in Washington after 1940 included James
Peterson, Ivie Foster, Maggie Young, and Elvie Crenshaw.) As Arkan-
sas-based regional information chief George Wolf described the exhibit needs of one black advisor: "As you probably know, we have on
the staff of our Tenant Purchase Division Joseph H. Dean, who is
working closely with Negro educational institutions. He has been extremely successful in his contacts both with educators and other leaders of his race. . . . I made up for him a collection of Negro pictures
which he has now practically worn out. The photos I used were mostly
of Lakeview [Project] and both he and I would prefer to have a
Southwide story portrayed by his material."[20]

Rosskam's exhibit, "Farm Security Administration Aids the Negro
Farmer," presented a story of industrious blacks across the South making the most of government assistance (fig. 6.3). Of the thirty-six photos spread across seven panels, thirty were of the project variety, drawn
principally from Lee's coverage of the Sabine Farms (Texas) and
Lakeview (Arkansas) projects, Wolcott's coverage of the Flint River
(Georgia) and Gee's Bend projects. The reminders of black poverty
were carefully matched with upbeat shots, creating before-and-after
suggestions that were somewhat deceptive. Atop the fifth panel, for
example, was Lee's shot of makeshift home education in a Louisiana
tenant shack. "To Avoid This," declared the panel caption, with no
reference to Louisiana—and the focus shifted to a spanking new classroom in an entirely different locale, Lakeview. (In fact, the area pho-

tographed by Lee in Louisiana was soon to be cleared for an all-white project, much to the distress of local black residents, who gained concessions from the FSA—an all-black project in the district—only after vehement protests taken up in the black press).

Along with the contrived before-and-after connections, the exhibit made exaggerated claims. While blacks had undoubtedly made progress through resettlement, there was no basis for the claim, printed opposite photos of cooperative farming activities on the third panel, that "small farmers [were] thus able to compete with big mechanized farm corporations." And while food consumption statistics, cited on the seventh panel opposite Lee's picture of a beaming Texas farm woman holding newly canned vegetables, were technically correct ("Negro clients now consume 20 times as much milk as they did two years ago, eat 10 times as much meat, can 10 times as much home-grown fruit and vegetables"), there was no indication of the actual food consumption levels that would have placed comparisons such as "20 times" in proper perspective. Agency hard sell was distinctly quiet on the more troublesome issues. The opening panel, declaring that the "Negro farmer's problem is the Southern farmer's problem," quoted statistics on black landlessness without any suggestion, by way of comparison with white land-tenure statistics, of the special black burden in this regard. The nonproject shots used in the exhibit suggested health, housing, educational deficiencies; omitted was the child labor subject—less given to standard FSA solutions—that, in fact, appeared frequently in the original photo-file. None of Shahn's cotton hands, none of Lee's young strawberry pickers or Wolcott's vegetable pullers made it into this exhibit; certainly none of Rothstein's evicted sharecroppers or Lange's plantation hands with plantation owner.

Determinedly upbeat, determinedly safe, "Farm Security Administration Aids the Negro Farmer" was probably no more propagandistic than other FSA traveling shows. The exhibit made the rounds of black colleges, conferences, and expositions: "Many favorable comments have been passed on this exhibit, such as 'The government is helping the forgotten man' [and] 'I wonder why we can't get some of these services in our community,' " as Princess Ann College (Maryland) Professor J.A. Oliver wrote Stryker in 1939.[21] But a further question is whether black images were included along with white images in the general FSA traveling shows. Was there, in effect, a segregated exhibits approach?

The agency's first traveling exhibit of 1936, hailing the march from rural slums to "new frontiers of farm independence," left black frontiers all but invisible, with only one black image among the exhibit's forty. Blacks were completely absent from a majority of the later shows, including the big nationalist pitches in 1941 ("Farm Security Is National Security" and "Food For Victory"). Where black images *were* included, representation tended to be quantitatively slight, qualitatively problematical, or both. Note, for example, the use that the 1940 "New Start on the Land" exhibit made of Lange's coverage of an ex-

Fig. 6.4. Farm Security Administration Exhibit: "New Start on the Land." 1940. FSA. Library of Congress.

Fig. 6.5. Dorothea Lange. "Ex-Slaves Who Occupy an Old Plantation House," Greene County, Ga. 1937. FSA. Library of Congress.

slave couple occupying a decaying antebellum mansion in Greene County, Georgia (fig. 6.4). Of several images showing the couple seated on the mansion steps, Rosskam selected the one in which the background was least evident; cropping removed all remaining traces of the mansion (critical to the historical irony of the original series), leaving only the two figures with their grizzled faces (figs. 6.5 and 6.6). Above the altered image, Rosskam placed a caption extolling the benefits of the FSA program: "In the last five years, FSA borrowers have almost doubled their net income, have greatly increased their production of vegetables, milk and eggs for home use. Already they have repaid $130,000,000 on their loans." The message was a far cry, indeed, from Lange's original story of an *unaided* old couple scratching out a living amid the literal ruins of civilization that had marked them: "I remember when the Yankees came through," one of the subjects had told

Lange, "a whole passel of 'em hollerin', and told the Negroes, you're free. But they didn't get nothin' cause we had carried the best horses and mules over to the gully." Protecting the livestock—one suspects more for themselves than for their erstwhile masters—these doughty souls had now inherited the Big House, such as it was.

With this complex history, this strange legacy "erased" by Rosskam, the image was enlarged to fill the exhibit's final panel, which was matched, in turn, with an opening panel showing an elderly white couple. It was the whites who bore the "before FSA" message in this arrangement ("Millions of American farmers lack the tools, land, and training they need to make a decent living"), and Rosskam's manipulations were complete. While the white figures were plucked out of

Fig. 6.6. Dorothea Lange. "Ex-Slaves Who Occupy an Old Plantation House," Greene County, Ga. 1937. FSA. Library of Congress.

their surroundings (a ramshackle midwestern farmhouse) as well, the distance between original series and exhibit utilization was not nearly so great as it was for the black subjects: the whites *were* two of the millions of American farmers in need. The one aspect of the black image that Rosskam could not alter was the suspicion in their facial expressions. And perhaps this was the final irony. The Yankees did not get the mules; Rosskam did not quite get the faces that conformed to the spirit of "New Start on the Land."

Rosskam's perspective, of course, was not the only one that counted here. From the standpoint of some FSA regional officials, the problem with "New Start on the Land" was not that it misused a black image but that it used a black image at all, that the very inclusion might be interpreted as an agency commitment to a new sense of American community. "Knowing the people in this region as I do, I doubt the wisdom of using a panel showing a Negro farmer beside a panel showing a white farm woman," complained key Texas operative Garford Wilkinson to the national office about an exhibit ("Live-at-Home Farming") that, like "New Start on the Land," incorporated a single black image. "Was it necessary to use a picture of a Negro farmer on the fourth panel? Surely [you have] photos of German farmers, Russian farmers, Italian farmers, Irish farmers, etc. . . . Rex B. Baxter, Texas state rehabilitation supervisor, shares my lack of enthusiasm for this set of panels; . . . he suggests that we keep them in the warehouse unless we can obtain a substitute. He said even a Spanish-American farmer's picture would not be popular in West Texas."[22] Arkansas FSA official George Wolf feared the same negative response to the exhibit: "The use of a Negro farmer [on panel #4] will limit [the exhibit's] use in much of the region."[23] What's more, objections to the black presence also came from administrators outside the South. As one Wisconsin FSA official advised: "As for Panel No. 4 . . . a plow or harrow operated by a white man would be much better."[24] Given these widespread trepidations about including faces that were, at best, unfamiliar and, at worst, reminders of troublesome issues, one can understand why only a minority of general traveling shows used black images.

Pragmatism in the national office and in the regional offices reduced black-photo exposure in the traveling shows. Limitations existed, as well, in exhibits of a more stationary sort. Outside of museum and gallery, university, or progressive-conference settings, exhibits with an appreciable factor of racial mixing were rare. Consider the 1941–42 Grand Central Station display. Designed as a promotion for defense bonds, the mega-mural was a *Land of the Free* without the growl, a showcase for the scenes that Stryker was urging his photographers to keep "ever in your mind: Lots of food, strong, husky Americans, machinery . . . big and powerful, good highways, spaciousness." Passersby gazing up at the enlarged figures would have seen, among other subjects, happy children from an FSA migrant camp nursery in California, a smiling Idaho farmwife, a hardy Nevada construction worker, picturesque Vermont sky and Montana mountains, and a proud American soldier. What they would *not* have seen was a black face. This was no problem for *Time*, which showed the mural on the cover of its final 1941 issue—"The perfect 20 [photos] made a giant picture puzzle."[25] And there was no distress for Rosskam or Stryker, who, amid the FSA's most ballyhooed exhibits project, stayed within cultural bounds that were conservative even by wartime standards. In the immediate post–Pearl Harbor period, the Historical Section probably could have gotten away with an unobtrusive black face somewhere in the depths of the mural. But the Rosskam-designed "perfect 20" was a risk-free formula. The ironies here were several. Not only were there more than a few potential black viewers passing through Grand Central every day, not only was the all-white mural planned in the same month that the Rosskam-edited *12 Million Black Voices* appeared, but one of the FSA staffers who played a key role in the physical mounting of the mural (a monumental task in itself) was none other than the young man out of Howard University, Walter Payton.

The greater the likely percentage of well-educated or reform-minded viewers in an exhibit audience, the greater the tendency for FSA exhibit designers to incorporate black content. For example, the University of Oklahoma Union Lounge in Norman was hardly a place that would have attracted the average Oklahoman in March 1940; the FSA exhibit there, sponsored by an old Stryker friend (Willard Z. Park) in the university's anthropology department and drawn principally from Lee's summer 1939 work in the Sooner State, included among its 49 images a 10 percent black representation. This was not quite up to the 16 percent in Lee's original series, but it was not a bad sprinkling for an exhibit appearing at the time of peak state and national interest in Steinbeck's *white* Oakies. Similarly, tickets to the Midwest Conference on Tomorrow's Children were hardly hot items in Chicago in March 1941; the social workers, educators, and political officials who did turn up at the Palmer House saw an FSA exhibit that included among its 28 images a 14 percent black representation. In museum and gallery displays of FSA photography, black representation generally matched or exceeded the black presence in the original file: 23 percent of the 104 photos at the 1936 College Art Association exhibition in Philadelphia; 16 percent of the 50 photos comprising the "Documents of America" show that originated at the Museum of Modern Art (August 1938) and later reached galleries across the country; 13 percent of the 75 images at the International Photography Exposition in New York; 13 percent of the 80 images appearing at the Cleveland Museum in 1939 and the Cincinnati Museum in 1940; 8 percent of the 185 images constituting "In the Image of America" at the New York Museum of Science and Industry and Philadelphia's Franklin Institute. In the case of some of the art shows, museum officials or guest curators played an important role in the image selection, but many vital decisions were still made in Washington.[26]

Making an exhibit racially integrated was one matter; incorporating the more imaginative black images was quite another. Such 1930s shows as the International Photography Exposition did represent steps forward. The international exhibit juxtaposed, for example, Lange's "A Plantation Owner"—blacks in tightly constricted poses, in back of the white authority figure—with Shahn's portrait of an Arkansas sharecropper's sons seated on their front porch, manifesting the full spectrum of reactions amid the freer atmosphere. It was also the case, however, that blacks generally fared badly in the American boosterism shows of post 1940. The summer 1941 "In the Image of America" exhibit was a case in point. Black representation declined slightly from a quantitative standpoint, and qualitatively, the fall-off was even greater.

"[This exhibit]," declared Rosskam in the opening caption, "presents, in most abbreviated form, a panoramic sketch of country—this vast, rich continent—and our country's people, strong in their variety." As applied to blacks, this celebration of ethnic heterogeneity involved the reemergence of some conventional associations. In the ethnic portraits on the opening panels ("We all . . . are Americans"), most of the white faces were allowed to stand on their own; the black face was not. The "representative" black American was a Missouri sharecropper absorbed in the Bible, following the lines with his finger. It is difficult to avoid the inference that the worthy black was the religious one—patient, faithful, reliant on the Good Book. The irony here is that the image derived from Rothstein's follow-up series on the participants in the 1939 highway demonstration. The old man depicted may have been religious, but not in a way that kept him from economic militancy.

Rosskam also played it safe in other respects. The panel on democratic processes included, among its scenes of citizen gatherings, a shot from Vachon's coverage of court day in Rustburg, Virginia. One photo after another in the original series had focused on the encounters between a white judge, seated on high and backed by the "eye of God" symbol on the wall, and black defendants (figs. 6.7 and 6.8). The shot chosen for the exhibit, however, was the only one in which the defendant's racial identity was obscured (back to the camera; hat, shawl, collar covering the back of the head) (fig. 6.9). Lost was the provocative undercurrent in Vachon's investigation of judicial proceedings. As the exhibit had it, the defendants could have been any Americans on trial, and the image became as prosaic as that of the Pie Town, New Mexico, community meeting placed beside it. Blacks were not a great deal more visible in the fields. Eschewing the wealth of labor closeups available, the exhibit featured several Wolcott scenes that emphasized the lay of the land—a distant view of a farmer plowing in picturesque curves (further accented by the photograph's placement next to an image of a racetrack curve), a distant view of a black-driven wagon rolling through the cotton fields, a mid-distance view of a sharecropper couple picking cotton, the figures all but blending into the harvest. White working men, such as the coal miner shown in the exhibit's "Underground Wealth" panel, cut striking figures; black work-

Fig. 6.7. John Vachon. "A Day in Court," Rustburg, Va. 1941. FSA. Library of Congress.

ers were part of the scenery. Such an imbalance was not characteristic of the original FSA file, 1930s or 1940s. In this regard, "In the Image of America" presented an "FSA" view very much in line with other U.S. Department of Agriculture agency views.

Newspaper reviewers did nothing to direct prospective viewers' attention to the black images that were included in FSA exhibits; and what little evidence we have of audience reactions to the shows (the 539 comment cards returned by viewers at the International Photography Exposition, with only three mentioning black-related images) suggests that exhibit-goers needed prodding in this regard. "Subjects very sordid and dull for an exhibition—[Need] more nudes," complained one 1938 respondent. "The U.S. as a whole," declared another, "ought to be ashamed to have such conditions existing. Instead of sending money to help Jews and other foreigners, they should stop [groups]

Fig. 6.8. John Vachon. "A Court Room with the Judge Presiding. The Eye of God Surrounded by a Glory on the Wall behind the Judge's Seat," Rustburg, Va. 1941. FSA. Library of Congress.

Fig. 6.9. Farm Security Administration Exhibit: "In the Image of America," at Museum of Science and Industry, New York City. 1941. FSA. Library of Congress.

from sending money out of the country. I say help America first."[27] But, apart from exhibit reviews, what sort of play did newspapers and magazines give the FSA black file?

In many respects, we find a familiar pattern: omissions, questionable selections, and captioning in general newspapers and wide-circulation magazines. Particularly in the early years, the press had a tendency to play up stories that, by their very nature, offered few black-picture angles. But even as late as 1940, omissions could be glaring. A *Washington Daily News* feature on eastern migrant agricultural laborers ("Oakies at Our Door") was illustrated with six photos, all from noneastern sites, and all of whites. No sign of either the Wolcott and Rothstein Florida work or Rothstein's Maryland vegetable-field series could be found in this spread. While the article stated flatly that "most of the migrants are Negroes," the latter were apparently to be imagined, not seen. "When we dealt with newspapers," recalls Ed Trapnell, the regional information chief for North Carolina, Virginia, West Virginia, Kentucky, and Tennessee, "our basic concern was getting space, getting attention for FSA programs. We'd send out regular releases, we'd suggest feature stories, we'd provide selections of pictures. But in most cases, the editors did the picking."[28]

Of the FSA black faces that *were* seen in the general press, the image most frequently tabbed in the early years was the very one lending itself most readily to conventional racial associations: Shahn's Plaquemines Parish, Louisiana, portrait of an unemployed trapper lying full-length on his cabin porch, head propped casually by a hand, face no more energetic than the rest of his body. Viewed within its original series, the portrait was the least imaginative of a number of shots of the trapper family, whose overall characterization did not emerge as languishing or apathetic. However, when taken out of its series context, and when used as the "representative" black image in an FSA poverty spread, the portrait appeared to support traditional notions of a black laziness-and-poverty nexus (fig. 6.10). Such an effect prevailed in a May 1937 *Look* feature on "Caravans of Hunger," which in addition to misidentifying the subject as a "wandering . . . farmer," explicitly linked him to government relief (not mentioned in the original Shahn caption). Such was the effect in a March 1936 *Washington Post* feature on "Truly Rural America That Faces Resettlement" (the more rural the black, the more hopeless), as well as in a contemporaneous *Washington Star* photo-spread that connected the image with a bit of ungrammatical verbal color, to wit, "Trappin' ain't what it was!"[29]

Black images more probing than the Plaquemines portrait or the project shots made very occasional appearances in wide-circulation newspapers and magazines. More often than not, however, these photos were accompanied by captions or other text that softened their impact. One nationally syndicated picture spread of July 1936, addressing the South's "Knotty Land Tenure Problem," included a Shahn closeup of young black cotton pickers but sought, at the same time, to dispel any implication of a black disadvantage. The caption exuded defensiveness: "The race problem has been exaggerated, according to students of Southern conditions who met in Chapel Hill. These young Negroes have 698,000 fellow tenants in the cotton lands, but they have 1,091,000 white neighbors who are tenants."[30] Such hard numbers, of course, were misleading, since the percentage of tenants out of total agrarians was much higher for blacks than it was for whites, and the black disproportion among day laborers (in which class Shahn's subjects fell) remained even greater. The "students of Southern conditions" (participants in the Conference of the Institute of Regional Development at the University of North Carolina) in fact recognized this black disadvantage, as did, at least implicitly, Shahn's original series. Captions for the other five Historical Section pictures on the page were not exactly paragons of sensitivity (above a Rothstein photo of a plaintive-faced white sharecropper tot, the pointless description, "He doesn't like the outlook. . . . This sack-garbed youngster may grow up to be lacking in ambition"), but the attempts to suppress particularly disturbing implications were not as strenuous.[31]

Very few photo-spreads devoted primarily to blacks showed up in mass-circulation publications. In fact, the two most prominent instances in which editors ran "black" stories revealed more about the strength of popular culture conventions—cutting across the middlebrow/lowbrow lines distinguishing *The New York Times Magazine* from *The Saturday Evening Post*—than they did about FSA photographic innovation. Black primitives made the *Times* (an August 1937 feature on Gee's Bend—a "picturesque community of Negroes in Alabama," as the story emphasized); rollicking blacks made *The Saturday Evening Post*.[32]

"Along 30 miles of highway across the northeast corner of Palm Beach County, Florida, there are more than 100 jooks, three out of four of them Negro. At some of them it is slow week without several knifings or shootings," began Theodore Pratt's "Land of the Jook" (April 1941), illustrated with eight photos (six with black subject-matter) from Wolcott's Belle Glade series. Moving breezily from accounts of "Negro tales" in the vegetable fields to brief glimpses of migrant living conditions, the *Post* story swung into high gear with the adventures of John Kirk, Belle Glade constable and juke-patroller. According to Pratt, Kirk knew his Negroes as being troublesome in a childish sort of way. " 'Mister John' is there," Pratt described the constable confronting a nervous crowd outside one joint. "Mister John walks among them, his eyes catching every gesture. He sees one man holding his hand below his sleeve in a peculiar way [a long blade dropping out; Kirk reprimanding the holder]. The man and the crowd know what Kirk means. There are sheepish grins. The people file back into the jook. Another nickel goes into the organ, . . . and the jooking starts again merrily, as if there had been no interruption at all."[33]

Such happy-go-lucky characterizations, along with such unqualified endorsement of white paternalism, made it difficult for readers to view the better Wolcott samples with the seriousness that these images deserved. Taken in its original context, Wolcott's image juxtaposing two grim young men seated at a juke-joint booth with an advertisement, above them on the wall, for Cobb's Creek Whiskey ("Judged Mild 43 Million Times!" declares the old judge, pounding his gavel), had an ironic bite with its suggestion that all was not well in the relationship

Fig. 6.10. Ben Shahn. Unemployed trapper. Plaquemines Parish, La. 1935. Library of Congress.

of the judge and the judged. In the context of the Pratt article, however, the white authority symbol took on some of Constable Kirk's
benevolence. Further weakening the original effect was the placement
of the Cobb's Creek photo next to a picture of a black woman grinning and clapping her hands as she converses with a white policeman
outside a juke door. The image was a rare exception in the Wolcott
coverage, but unfortunately useful for *The Saturday Evening Post* story.
Captioning made matters worse, with a quotation that appeared to be
coming from the woman ("I've been dealing with the devil") but actually came from the title of a juke song. The photo-spread also appeared
to establish a contrast between white juke and black juke that worked
to the disadvantage of the latter. The image that opened the spread
showed a rather polite, all-American, mixed male-female crowd at the
white "Silver Dollar"; the final image depicted black men hunched
intently over a poker table at a joint across town. Good-time whites,
skin-game blacks: the contrast was the *Post*'s, not Wolcott's.[34]

For an alternative to these manipulations, one might think logically
of FSA photo utilization in black-edited publications. Predictably, such
publications were free of the "I've been dealing with the devil" captioning. At the same time, however, black-edited journals proved even
less apt than mass circulation publications to run hard-nosed FSA
black images. Pictures published were those indistinguishable in tone
from the many NYA, WPA, CCC, and USHA photos also used in
black weeklies—Lee's beaming vegetable canner from Sabine Farms or
Wolcott's portrait of the Frederick Oliver family, first black tenant-
purchase participants in South Carolina. It was not just the dearth of
problem shots that was important here; absent was any hint of FSA
photographic complexity. Such absence characterized the *New York
Amsterdam News*, the *Atlanta Daily World*, and other moderate black
journals. And such proved to be the case, as well, with the *Chicago
Defender*, the *Baltimore Afro-American*, the NAACP's *Crisis*, and other
militant publications.

What's more, black-published photo-spreads incorporated some
tricks of their own. When, for example, the *Pittsburgh Courier* ran
Joseph Evans' RA promo piece, "Race Has Major Part in Resettle-

ment Drive" (October 1936), the accompanying photographic montage had Shahn's smiling sharecropper wife superimposed on views of model homes under construction. "Note the smiling countenance," directed the captions, clearly suggesting that the smile had something to do with the project starts. In fact, no connection existed; Shahn's Arkansas subject was an unaided agrarian.[35] Selections were simplified and sanitized. In the case of the *Atlanta World*'s August 1941 front-page spread on the FSA relocation of Georgia blacks residing in defense-construction areas, the strength of the original Delano series—closeups of older residents for whom the move was a profound, and disturbing, upheaval—gave way to a routine series of before-and-after housing shots, with human figures distant or turned away from the camera.[36]

Adventurousness was not totally absent on the newspaper and magazine front. In some of the smaller-circulation progressive journals (*Ken, Friday*, Baptist *Missions, Coronet*, and *Survey Graphic*), and in at least one prominent photographic journal (*U.S. Camera*), we find bolder picture choices, less intrusive texts and captions. Black representation in *U.S. Camera*'s major FSA spread of 1939 was impressive both quantitatively (14 percent of the forty-two selections) and qualitatively. Lange's "A Plantation Owner" was included here, one of the very few times it was published anywhere in uncropped form. So was Shahn's view of a sharecropper wife and child peering suspiciously out of their cabin window. The image revealed much more than sharecropper poverty; in implicating the photographer as the target of suspicion, the image suggested the not-always-favorable ramifications of FSA investigation. One of Evans's poster studies was included, as well, its juxtaposition of myths (minstrel imagery in one fading poster, Hollywood Western imagery in another, sharing the same Southern small-town wall) offering penetrating commentary on the status of Southern "truth."[37] To be sure, publishing images of this quality did not prevent *U.S. Camera*'s editors from taking steps backward in other issues. But the very fact that the more progressive images were presented at all gave these photographic currents some respectability in professional circles. While the powers-that-be did not read *U.S. Camera*, nor did the average citizen, young documentary photographers coming of age in the 1930s and early 1940s certainly did.

"It seems to me," mused Sherwood Anderson in the opening pages of *Home Town*, his 1940 collaboration with the FSA, "that [Abraham Lincoln] grew out of a house, a street, a shabby little country lawyer's office; out of his touch with the common men he met in little country courtrooms; and that all this made him the man he became."[38] The rhythm of the seasons, the rhythm of the people presumably still in touch with nature caught Anderson's fancy, and the romanticism—a far cry from his *Winesburg, Ohio* broodings of an earlier era—grew particularly blinding when he turned to small-town blacks. "In the cotton country," as he described the arrival of summer, "young Negro men and women are now out in the streets at night. In the Negro section of Southern towns you hear the soft voices and the laughter of Negroes. . . ."[39]

Anderson's formulations probably could have been altered by photo-editor Rosskam, who, in addition to selecting and arranging pictures for *Home Town*, cut the original manuscript by more than a half. That Rosskam did not temper Anderson's tone suggests a level of complicity beyond matching pictures to text. As for the photographic layout, the pictorial "honesty" was hardly of the tough variety. In general Rosskam either selected the blander scenes (heavily using, for example, one of Lee's least penetrating series, taken in San Augustine, Texas), or, what's worse, created them, as in his use of an Evans study of a deserted Alabama train station to illustrate Anderson's nostalgic croonings, "Do you remember when you, now for so long a city man, your hair graying, were a small-town boy and what the railroad meant to you? Did you dream of some day being a railroad engineer?"[40] Rosskam should have known better; Evans, intrigued by the elusiveness of the taken-for-granted, was no more a photographer of the nostalgic than he was a photographer of the pathetic. A generally mediocre sampling of the FSA file, the pictorial *Home Town* was particularly weak when it came to blacks. The problem was not so much quantitative (out of 122 pictures, black content was discernible in 8 percent) as qualitative.

It was one thing to distort an Evans image essentially devoid of

Fig. 6.11. Walker Evans. "A View of the Negro Quarter," Vicksburg, Miss. 1936. FSA. Used in *Home Town*, 1940. Library of Congress.

human content. It was another to give his human content a racist cast, nostalgic constructions turning into more pernicious impositions. "Soft voices and laughter" was the Rosskam caption opposite an Evans view of blacks in the Vicksburg slums—that, despite the somber mood, as well as the lack of visibility of the faces, in the Evans photograph (fig. 6.11). Among the other black selections, there was a preponderance of images that, with a little help from the surrounding text, fit traditional assumptions. Hence the black workman asleep on his bundles in the warehouse, à la *You Have Seen Their Faces*; or the black child with a winning smile, from a cropped Shahn image that originally showed several children with a mixture of expressions; or the black man kneeling to shine a white man's boots—an image far less probing than Shahn's Natchez shoeshine scene.[41] While the book's final chapter provided at least some passing references, textual and visual, to the less rosy side of small-town civilization, there was no inclusion of tougher black material. Rosskam had an opening here for a presentation that might have balanced the "soft voices and laughter" material; he elected not to take it. The result was an implicit message that black problems were of considerably less account than white problems. And, sure enough, at least one major reviewer, the *New York Times*'s R. L. Duffus, made it explicit with his jaunty remarks about the ever-sunny personality of the impoverished black.[42]

Our *Home Town?* The book's affirmation of American stability and continuity had a broad appeal in a year of decreasing attention to

Fig. 6.12. Marion Post Wolcott. Tobacco auction, Durham, N.C. 1939. FSA. Used in *Home Town* and reprinted in *Des Moines Sunday Register*. 1940. Library of Congress.

domestic maladies, mounting anxiety over the international crisis, a year when even many progressives were beginning to believe, with *Commonweal* reviewer John Cort, that "perhaps America is worth blessing after all."[43] Without the anger of *Land of the Free*, *Home Town* carried on the earlier work's quest of American identity—keyed, as before, to the scent of the past, to a belief in common sense, to an assumption that the authentic was the nonurban.[44] If, unlike the thrust of *Land of the Free*, blacks were now to be incorporated in that identity, they were to be incorporated in what, for the majority of readers, was the simplest and least challenging fashion. Soft voices and laughter, soft consent to an American destiny governed by others. "If we wished to show a foreigner what an American small town was most generally like," as the *Saturday Review* summed up the pictures, "we should certainly give him this book."[45] Newspapers, liberal and conservative, "gave" their readers the book in visual as well as text-review form: a front-page spread in the *New York Times Book Review* (an honor not even bestowed upon *Land of the Free*), a nine-photo spread in *PM* (complete with nostalgic statements by the much-respected photo-editor, Ralph Steiner), a thirteen-photo spread in the *Des Moines Register*—including, as the representative black entry, the snoozing farmer at the warehouse (fig. 6.12), accompanied by a caption emphasizing the general hustle and bustle of such places—and much the same across the country.[46] Whatever the book's eventual sales, the media hoopla helped cement the Historical Section's reputation as a photo-agency very much in tune with the times. Success, whatever the racial cost, was sweet for Stryker, who had been thinking along *Home Town* lines long before the book was written. And success was sweet for Rosskam, who, though no small-towner at heart, absorbed the spirit of the project. Even twenty-five years after the fact, there were no regrets: "Of all these [photo-books]," Rosskam would say of *Home Town*, "it's by far the best."[47]

Of course, there were also FSA photo-books less concerned with national identity, books whose authors were not major literary figures. In most of these works, racial presentation was somewhat stronger. Quantitatively, in fact, it was extremely strong. H. C. Nixon's *Forty Acres and Steel Mules*, lost in the shadows of *Land of the Free* in the late spring of 1938, included among its 148 FSA selections (all southern) 53 black shots. This was a proportion (36 percent) higher than both that of blacks in the southern population and that of black images in the FSA southern file. Walker Evans's *American Photographs*, appearing both as a Museum of Modern Art exhibition and a book in late autumn 1938, had 13 percent black representation among its 87 selections, which were a mixture of Evans contributions to the RA/FSA file, photos taken under government auspices but kept by the photographer, and images that Evans took prior to his government employment. The Paul Taylor–Dorothea Lange collaboration of the following year, *An American Exodus*, gave strong play to black images in the relevant southern chapters. A full quarter of these 60 photos from Dixie, a mixture of Lange's FSA and independent work, concerned blacks; for the book as a whole, black representation was 13 percent. Rosskam's first book-editing venture, *Washington, D.C.: Nerve Center* (part of the Alliance Press "Face of America" series that would present, a year later, *Home Town*), included no great mass of FSA images to begin with, but gave blacks reasonable exposure (11 percent of 27 selections). Black images figured prominently in *Sharecroppers All* (26 percent of the 38 pictures) cowritten by Arthur Raper and the Atlanta University black sociologist Ira Reid, with layout assistance from Rosskam. *Tenants of the Almighty*, the finale in Raper's socioeconomic trilogy on Greene and Macon counties, Georgia, made considerable use of the black material that Delano took expressly for the book project: 39 percent of the 101 selections. Again, the pictorial design was by Rosskam. In the cases of the very divergent photo-books whose black images were sparser, *Fair Is Our Land* and *Let Us Now Praise Famous Men*, there were special circumstances. *Fair Is Our Land* amounted to a compilation of pure landscape shots, mixed FSA and non-FSA. And the pictures for the *original* edition of the Evans-Agee work showed relatively little of the world, white or black, not immediately connected to Agee's principal tenant families.

Qualitatively, many of these works did more justice to the FSA black file than did *Home Town*. While the text for *Forty Acres* was as earnest and plodding as one might have expected from a Tulane University political scientist assessing the causes of and solutions for southern poverty, and while Nixon's tone as a reformed Agrarian frequently turned leaden ("The south has known slavery," he declared in his pitch for regional revitalization, "Why should it not know and appreciate mechanical slaves?"), the photographic side turned out to be a livelier affair. On the same page that included a Mydans primitive housing shot from the Gee's Bend–like community on St. Helena Island, South Carolina, was Mydans's shot of an unaided black landowner's substantial house only a few miles away. On the same page that included Rothstein's white landowner's daughter weighing the cotton for tense-looking black pickers was Shahn's attentive *black* cotton-checker with clipboard in hand. In short, there was a broad sociological sweep. The book's few project shots were chosen with some imagination: Rothstein's view of a resettled North Carolina family's living room had not only the usual keynote of material improvement but, with its picture within the picture (portrait of family relations on the wall), suggested an experiential level that rehabilitators too often forgot. The pictorial *Forty Acres*, a non-Rosskam creation, surveyed the towns as well as the countryside, with Shahn's street-musician and medicine-show scenes, Evans's minstrel-poster and segregated theater scenes all receiving exposure. This representation of diverse currents, tapping the work of multiple photographers, was quite pioneering; *Survey Graphic*'s similar exposure of the FSA black file came several years later.[48]

Pioneering of a different sort came in *An American Exodus*, where Lange and Taylor made a very conscious effort to avoid the presumptuous "we" voice of MacLeish and the fictional quotations of Caldwell and Bourke-White. In her work in the field, Lange, often assisted by Taylor, was as intrepid a verbal recorder as she was a visual recorder, and the fruits were evident in her letters to Stryker, her field notes, and her often lengthy captions for the FSA file shots. The same spirit extended to the photo-book. Quotations from picture-subjects, blacks no less than whites, appeared in a number of instances directly beneath the pictures. The effect, as in the case of Lange's photograph of ex-slaves sitting on the steps of a Greene County, Georgia, mansion, was to restore layers of meaning chopped out in other contexts. The survivor's distrust, not the humble victim's openness to assistance, marked the comments of these ex-slaves, who, as we saw earlier, were rendered voiceless (and punchless) in one of the FSA traveling shows. Of course, *An American Exodus* was not without its heavy-handed touches. But the book was nevertheless significant for simultaneously affirming that (1) black economic problems were an integral part of the rural crisis that most Americans associated with the Joads, and (2) black testimony, whether the memory of the ex-slaves or the complaint of the woman camped along U.S. 80 ("Do you reckon I'd be out on the highway if I had it good at home?"), was to be taken as seriously as white testimony.[49]

Raper and Reid's text for *Sharecroppers All* included discussion of issues from which Lange and Taylor had steered clear in *An American Exodus*: segregation, disenfranchisement, racial violence, the double burden of black womanhood. "The South's bogeys! What have they made us do to ourselves?" lamented the authors in a description of disinherited whites and their scapegoats. Picture selections were not quite so bold, but they did include several of Rothstein's Missouri sharecropper demonstration scenes and a striking Wolcott closeup of a ramshackle black schoolhouse. "Separate and equal says the state constitution," noted an uncompromising caption, "but this schoolhouse for Negro children says otherwise." Were sharecroppers all in the same boat?[50] Visual and textual content often transcended the implications of the book's title. Finally, even one of the most upbeat books in this batch, *Washington, D.C.: Nerve Center*, celebrated the New Deal while incorporating a haunting glimpse of the "other" Washington, namely, Vachon's portrait of a troubled black man standing in front of a historical marker recording the site of Lincoln's death.

Achievements these were, but there were also notable limitations on the quality of some of these more imaginative photo-books, their level of exposure, or both. Some of the problems we have seen before. The most potentially controversial photos in *Forty Acres and Steel Mules* were accompanied by captions designed to temper their impact. Evans's view of the "Rex Theatre for Colored People," for example, drew the purposefully irrelevant description, "A small-town amusement denied to isolated farm tenants and sharecroppers." Geographical denial was a great deal more comfortable subject than racial denial, just as, in the text, Nixon found it easier to justify wage increases with recourse to stereotypes than to moral arguments. "Negro laborers are good spenders," wrote Nixon, advocating massive priming of the Southern pump. "A colored worker once gave me his pay-day philosophy by saying, 'The eagle on the dollar means to let 'er fly, and I lets 'er fly.' "[51] Books by former Agrarians were not the only ones employing questionable captions. *Sharecroppers All* gave with one hand and took with the other, presenting a discerning caption for Wolcott's black schoolhouse and a decidedly cheap caption for Lange's barefoot Georgia plowboy. "The New Deal?" the young black laborer was made to say. "Yas, sir, it's done been by here." The words, in fact, did not belong to this photographic subject. Lange's field notes had emphasized the isolation of the boy's world, and her caption for the file had emphasized the subject's youth. The quotation in question was based on one from an older black farmer appearing in the Raper-Reid text. And note the change. As it appeared in the text, the quotation included more than "typical" black English: "'Oh, the New Deal? Yes, sir, I know,' Sam replied, 'it's pretty good, I guess, pretty good. It's done been by here.'" Transferred to the picture realm, the "yes" turned into a "yas," and the "done been" gained added weight. While the overall message, that of New Deal deficiencies, remained the same, the captioning trick came at the expense of black dignity.[52] Significantly, it was blacks, not whites, who had words put in their mouths in *Sharecroppers All*; in another instance, one of Rothstein's Missouri roadside demonstrators was "given" the voice of a more casual wanderer: "I looked at my cotton receipts and my debts, so me and my ole lady just tied up our stuff and lef'" (fig. 6.13).[53] Again, this was a familiar voice for an unfamiliar photograph; so it was that Rosskam's photo-editing glitz extended even to a book that, originally published by an academic press (the University of North Carolina Press), was not designed for a mass audience. Inasmuch as Raper, as chief author, approved the picture layouts, the latter revealed the limits of vision for one of the South's most respected liberals, who was once arrested in Greene County, Georgia, for addressing a black man as "Sir."

Captions, and photo selections in key places, also marred *Tenants of the Almighty*. The textual side of this concluding Greene County in-

Fig. 6.13. Arthur Rothstein. "An Evicted Sharecropper along U.S. Highway 60," New Madrid, Mo. 1939. FSA. Used in *Sharecroppers All*, 1941. Library of Congress.

vestigation reflected a more moderate Raper, interested in highlighting FSA successes at a time when Congress was in a mood to do away with the tenant program and interested in highlighting American strength at a time of peak international danger. "Dr. Raper seems to have become more sympathetic to the problems of the southern plantation owners than he was when he published *Preface to Peasantry* in

1936," observed the southern moderate Virginius Dabney in *The New York Times*. "That book left the impression that southern landlords are a pretty ornery lot, who swindle their tenants with distressing frequency. But in his current discussion of the United Farm Program, which involves many of the same problems, he does not reiterate these excessively caustic opinions."[54] The pictorial *Tenants of the Almighty* played heavily on Delano's rehabilitation shots—no surprise here. What was particularly unfortunate, however, was the manner in which the book used one of the few remarkable aspects of Delano's original coverage, namely, his photography in the predominantly black convict camp.

While Delano did not present a Spivakian horror show, he also managed to avoid a whitewash, despite working under extremely unfavorable conditions (Delano's closeup of convicts' hands reaching through the top of a cage was one of a number of evocative angles). However, of the two prison pictures reproduced in *Tenants of the Almighty*, one was decidedly a Delano exception, a photo of tap-dancing convicts that was more akin to *Life* material. Captioning hammered the happy-go-lucky stereotype harder: "Colored convicts sleep and eat behind bars and will dance like the dickens for your dime."[55] Such characterizations were not found in Raper's main text, which was reasonably hard-nosed in its brief prison passage. This revisualization of the prison coverage was a Rosskam "contribution," worked out in consultation with Raper. "Rosskam will have to take off a couple days and sit down with you [in Washington] and work out complete plans," Stryker had explained to Raper. "Then he will have to be left alone for the next move. . . . It is really too bad he can't come down [to Georgia]. It would have done him a world of good and would give him a feeling for the country, but we have little choice these days."[56] Among other editing excesses was the imposition of Raper's cheery "we" on a Delano farm scene with very mixed implications. The image of a white farm woman, apron tied neatly and bucket in hand, supervising a stooping black laborer in the garden, hinted of social structures less inspiring than those hailed in the accompanying caption: "We know the land and the pines stand back of our homes, back of our churches and schools, cotton mills and sawmills. We know, too, now we are in

war, that this land of ours is called upon to feed us at home, feed our
fighting men wherever they are, and a portion of the hungry world."[57]
A visit to Greene would have been enlightening for Rosskam, but,
direct experience or no direct experience, the bottom line here was
Rosskam's habit of catering to popular taste, political and artistic, when
he worked with images and words. Interestingly, Delano's involvement in picture selection and editing for *Tenants of the Almighty* appears to have been nil. "I never saw that book until long after it was
published," he reflected recently. "I was busy, on the road; maybe no-
body ever bothered to send me a copy."[58]

Where photo-editing decisions were not as much of a problem, reviewing decisions were. *An American Exodus*, appearing in the wake of
The Grapes of Wrath, was presented almost exclusively in the Stein-
beckian light. It was not the Greenville, Mississippi, plantation hand,
complaining to Lange and Taylor about tractors "being against the
black man" ("Every time you kill a mule, you kill a black man"), who
caught the reviewers' attention; it was the voice and image of the real-
life Joads, "starting from Joplin, Missouri with $5, . . . bound for Cali-
fornia if we can make it in time for grape picking."[59] A book dealing
with the broad economic context of migration, a book that at least
suggested multiple migrations (blacks to the cities, whites to the West),
"became" a much simpler book, a much safer book (the Oakies had
been receiving heavy press for four years), a book charged with mythic
significance—westward, ho! "They were bound for California," pro-
nounced the *New York Herald-Tribune* review headline, identifying
the book as an "album that illustrates *The Grapes of Wrath*."[60] Obviously, readers of such reviews who also read *An American Exodus* were
not prevented from appreciating the true nature of the book, but to
the extent that many newspaper readers substituted reviews for book
reading, review content was pivotal. Only readers of Paul Strand's
review in the Photo League's *Photo Notes* received the full flavor of
Lange and Taylor's investigations, and they constituted a highly select
group. As for the photo-books concerned exclusively with the Deep
South (*Forty Acres, Sharecroppers All*, and *Tenants of the Almighty*),
reviews tended to be short (albeit complimentary), low-profile, and
focused away from whatever racial issues were raised in these works. In

the case of the Raper books, the subject of tenants, white or black, was often considered yesterday's news by 1941. "The sharecropper," Jonathan Daniels observed in *The Saturday Review*, "is emotionally a long way off in these days. Albania often seems a good deal closer than Arkansas."[61] In the case of all three southern books, pictorial strengths that *did* exist, white or black, did not receive detailed treatment. One sentence devoted to the pictures constituted the norm. "The photographs," as the *Survey Graphic*'s Leon Whipple reported about *Forty Acres*, "are strong enough to arouse a tempered determination: 'The U.S. cannot waste such people.' "[62]

Where images did not gain the physical prominence that they did in *Land of the Free* or *Home Town* (relatively small reproductions in *Forty Acres*, relatively few pictures in *Sharecroppers All*, a picture section followed by a much larger textual section in *Tenants of the Almighty*), reviewers rarely took the initiative to do much careful looking. With *American Photographs*, of course, images had to be treated as primary items, but even here we find the familiar reviewing pattern. Featured picture subjects were Evans's Cape Cod houses and not his South Carolina black churches, his Pennsylvania auto junkyard and not his Tupelo slums, his Italian-American bench-sitters in the Bronx and not his fur-coated black woman on Forty-second Street. Reviewers generally hailed Evans's aesthetic sensitivity, lamented a fallen America, and passed over racial messages. Perhaps *The New York Times*'s Edward Alden Jewell was conscious of racial typecasting when he observed: "[Evans] never pictures for us a person or an object as a 'type.' Each lives a life of his or of its own."[63] And perhaps *New Republic* guest reviewer William Carlos Williams was conscious of Evans's black subjects when he wrote: "We see what we realized, ourselves made worthy in our anonymity."[64] Perhaps. Troubling is the realization that William Carlos Williams could perceive the worthiness of Evans's subjects one day and then return to romantic racist themes in his own poetry the next.

Given factors of publication timing, low-profile reviews, or, in some cases, small academic/art press runs, it is doubtful that any of these photo-books gained the readership levels of *Land of the Free* and *Home Town*. Timing was a major market handicap for the book that made the greatest quantitative use of the FSA black file, Wright and Rosskam's *12 Million Black Voices,* which appeared shortly before the cataclysm of Pearl Harbor. But sales aside, was *12 Million Black Voices* the publishing milestone for the black file, the purest representation of the multi-photographer achievements we have discussed in earlier chapters? Was this the finest hour for Rosskam, the tour de force that we should keep in mind when surveying his other photo-editing performances? Rosskam certainly showed ample initiative during the course of this project. As we saw in chapter 5, it was the FSA photo-editor who first approached the editors at Viking Press in 1940 with the idea of a picture-book on black America.

While Rosskam's "baby" was not the first visual-textual production inspired, directly or indirectly, by *Native Son,* it was by far the most ambitious. Rosskam, who had never met Wright before December 1940, raised the author's interest with a sampling of some of the touchier FSA pictorial possibilities: "Lord of the Land," as Wright described Lange's plantation owner in his notes, which also indicated immediate interest in images of chain gangs, Jim Crow signs, cotton-chopper gangs, and what he called a "monument to race prejudice" (Lange's photo of a New Orleans monument inscription celebrating the 1876 return of white supremacy).[65] Rosskam sent a stream of research materials Wright's way while the author was preparing his text. Rosskam helped coordinate the Chicago coverage, arranged meetings with Wright in the summer of 1941 to coordinate an evolving pictorial layout with Wright's evolving text. "I remember Wright coming down to Washington to talk to Ed," recalled Louise Rosskam, "and having to deal with what was a very segregated city in those days. It wasn't easy."[66] After the book went to press that autumn, Edwin Rosskam pushed hard for proper media accounting of the black author–white editor partnership. When, for example, the *New York Post*'s Leonard Lyons suggested in a "forthcoming books" column that Wright's role was secondary, Rosskam sent the newspaper a passionate rebuttal: "The quality of my association with this young Negro writer was just about the opposite of what it appears in the story. I learned a vast amount from an enormously talented, informed specialist about the problem of the Negro in the U.S. I was the pupil, he the teacher."[67]

Rosskam's enthusiasm was not feigned. Nor was he out to make Wright more palatable to white audiences. Rosskam sensed an opportunity, in a Wright-connected, black-devoted project, to satisfy his liberal conscience. Besides, once Rosskam received the first draft of Wright's text and began working on the picture layout, it was not difficult for the photo-editor to adopt the color of the turf on which he was working. That, for better or for worse, was Edwin Rosskam's style. Wright, for his part, pulled few punches in 12 Million Black Voices. Beginning with a wrenching description of the horrors of the Middle Passage, Wright's self-styled "folk history" of American blacks proceeded grimly and relentlessly through the trials of slavery, post-bellum southern repression, migration, and life in the northern ghettoes. "Even when," as Wright described 1930s Dixie, "the sprawling fields are drenched in peaceful sunshine, it is war. When we grab at the clay with our hoes, it is war. When we sleep, it is war. When we awake, it is war. When one of us is born, he enters one of the warring regiments of the South." There was hell in Mississippi, there was a different hell in Chicago. "The kitchenette is the funnel through which our pulverized lives flow to ruin and death on the city pavements, at a profit [for the white owners]."

Wright avoided the standard conclusions about a new black-white unity in perilous times; if in the final chapter, there was a brief note of optimism in his reference to a "common road of hope which we all [black and white] have travelled," this fell considerably short of confident nationalism. Also absent, more unfortunately, was coverage of the higher echelons of black society—omitted, the author openly declared in his foreword, "in an effort to simplify a depiction of a complex movement of a debased feudal folk toward a 20th Century urbanization." Wright would have no part of the multi-tiered black reality presented by sociologists (including the black scholar Horace Cayton) whom, ironically, he credited in the foreword. Wright wanted his reality in strictly black and white terms. Or, one might add, black, white, and red. While avoiding ideological verbiage, while taking a more sympathetic view of religion and a more mystical view of womanhood than he probably would have taken in his Communist party days, Wright nevertheless employed what he called, in his working notes, a "guiding Marxist concept." The machinations of the Lords of the Land, the Bosses of the Buildings lurked at every turn, from the deadly Triangle Trade to the sharecropping system, from Jim Crow to employment discrimination. To the extent that racism was explained, it was more an economic phenomenon than a political or psychological one in 12 Million Black Voices. The text extended the anger of Native Son, but certainly not the philosophic meditations of the earlier work's final chapter.[68]

Philosophy aside, Wright's folk history had its moments of remarkable power. But the author's fondness for sweeping generalizations produced serious flaws. Intent, in his Marxist mood, on portraying blacks as both the ultimate victims of capitalist exploitation and the possessors of a superior proletarian culture, Wright lurched wildly, and often illogically, between extremes. Black culture had been "blasted," "pulverized" by slavery's "long shocks" over 250 years, yet, Wright maintained, blacks were spiritually one-up on whites: "Because our eyes are not blinded by the hunger for possessions, we are a tolerant folk." Black families, held together by "love, sympathy, pity, and the goading knowledge that we must work together," represented uniquely humane values: "our gold is in the hearts of the people we love, in the veins that carry our blood, upon those faces where we can catch furtive glimpses of the shape of our humble souls." Yet in urban slums, there was utter disaster: "desperate and unhappy people . . . thrown into unbearable closeness of association . . . giving birth to never-ending quarrels of recrimination, accusation, and vindictiveness, producing warped personalities." Saints and Biggers were here, with too little attention to the vast continent between. Other problems of credibility marred the text. In excluding the black uppercrust, Wright was doing more than merely excluding a few black success stories. The result was the implicit suggestion that black political, economic, and cultural leaders had only insignificant contact with, and impact upon, the lives and consciousness of the masses; the suggestion flew in the face not only of scholarly studies but of common sense. Only in the religious realm did Wright allow some hints about the effect of leaders on the common folk, and the very existence of these hints begged a flurry of questions that Wright refused to answer.[69]

Most problematical, however, was Wright's adoption of the "we" voice for the masses, past and present, northern and southern. It was a flawed "we" in practice. In the course of his narrative, Wright shifted, without acknowledging the implications of the shift, between an all-encompassing voice and an obviously male voice, between a cross-generational voice and an obviously parental voice. It was a flawed "we" in principle as well. Granted, Richard Wright had made the northern migration himself, had suffered the blows of poverty and discrimination, had lived the experiences of which he wrote to a much greater degree than that other cultivator of the "we," Archibald MacLeish. But Wright's "we" presumption remained a fundamental act of cultural suppression: 10.8 million "ordinary" black voices were no more blendable than 12 million total black voices, and no more blendable than 108 million white voices. Wright himself had acknowledged as much in *Native Son*, even with its limited cast of black characters. Ironically, the white tendency that had proven so stultifying over the years, that of treating the black millions as a monolithic mass, was repeated in 1941 by a black author who knew much better. "The book is described in the subtitle as a folk history of the Negro in the United States," *The Nation*'s Charles Curtis Munz would point out correctly, "but beyond a little doggerel verse from a few Negro folk songs, and an occasional sharp interpretation of the Negro's mind at work, it is not a folk history at all."[70]

Textually, *12 Million Black Voices* raged and roared, at a cost in sensitivity. Pictorially, the dominant accent was one of muckraking. Among Rosskam's selections (eighty-three from the FSA file and a handful from other sources) were Lange's image of plantation owner and field hands, uncropped and appearing on the same page as Wright's discussion of the term "Negro" and the slavery legacy. A few pages later, there appeared the International News photo of Georgia lynch victim Lint Shaw and his executioners, enlarged to nearly full-page size and juxtaposed, menacingly, with one of Vachon's Virginia courtroom scenes. And still later a left-right combination dripping with

irony: Lee's view of a mother and son in a dilapidated Chicago kitchenette apartment, Wolcott's view of a black maid tending a white
toddler in a kitchen a caste apart.[71] Curiously, the segregation sign,
chain gang, and white supremacy monument images upon which
Wright had commented when he was first introduced to the FSA file
did not appear in *12 Million Black Voices*; in this respect, Rosskam may
have shown some government caution, leaving to private sources the
burden of the *most* controversial photographs in the book. (Along
with the International News shocker, a photograph by Wright himself
appeared later in the book, showing a "Just Opened to Colored" sign
on a Brooklyn apartment house.)

Fig. 6.14. Jack Delano. "Tenant Woman," Heard County, Ga. 1941. FSA.
Used in *12 Million Black Voices*, with commentary, "There are times when we
doubt our songs." 1941. Library of Congress.

Fig. 6.15. Russell Lee. "Son of Sharecropper," New Madrid, Mo. 1938. FSA. Used in *12 Million Black Voices*, with commentary, "There are times when we doubt our songs." 1941. Library of Congress.

But the essential difficulty with the pictorial *12 Million Black Voices* was not the downplaying of harsh imagery. To fault Rosskam on this now-familiar count would be to miss the broad significance of the book, with its steady stream of hard-labor and bad-housing images, its fair number of black-white interaction shots. The difficulty lay in the opposite direction. If anything, Rosskam was too single-minded in fitting—or bending—FSA pictures to the textual message. Within the urban section of *12 Million Black Voices*, for example, Rosskam sacrificed much of the richness, the illumination of multiple worlds within a world, available in the original Chicago coverage. Discarded, ironically enough, were many of Rosskam's own probing individual portraits; included for publication was one crowded tenement scene and one dangerous street-corner view after another. Even the religious shots used in this pivotal section were principally from the same church, suggesting a uniformity that contrasted notably with the original Easter Sunday survey by Lee and Rosskam. Fundamentalist services, with their supreme emotional release, served Wright's argument ("Lord in Heaven! Good God Almighty! Great Day in the Morning! It's here! Our time has come! We are leaving!" as Wright applied standard revivalist lingo to the migration theme), and fundamentalist images became the be-all and end-all of black religion in *12 Million Black Voices*.[72]

Throughout the book, Rosskam's manipulations were also crucial, with old tricks involving captioning and visual-textual juxtaposition turned to new purposes. Images respectful of profoundly private thoughts were yoked to melodramatic Wright laments: hence, Delano's portrait of a young Greene County farmwoman pausing, meditatively, in the open doorway of her cabin (the image playing on the idea of physical interiors opened, mental interiors closed), and Lee's shot of a Missouri sharecropper's son lying reflectively on his bed, "became" illustrations for the generalization, "There are times when we doubt our songs" (figs. 6.14 and 6.15). Whose doubts? And whose songs? The yoking was a bit less offensive than the "soft voices and laughter" inferences in *Home Town*, but no less presumptuous. Vachon's photo of a gesturing Maryland steelworker "became" an illustration for Wright's description of divide-and-conquer strategies employed by the Bosses of the Buildings; in fact, Vachon's subject was no more a "straw-boss" than any other black laborer pictured in the book. So much for just treatment of the individual. Or consider the book's utilization of family scenes. Lee's shot of a tenement mother and children, from a series that indicated the presence of a father figure in this Chicago home, became an illustration for Wright's bemoaning of the broken family: "The kitchenette creates thousands of one-room houses where our black mothers sit, deserted, with their children about their knees."[73]

An even more glaring instance of creating victims came in the book's use of another Lee mother-and-children shot from Chicago. In the original photo, one of the children was shown reacting to the camera as any child, black or white, south-side or north-side, might have reacted—tongue clearly stuck out (fig. 6.16). It was a feisty touch, reminding the viewer that, among other things, subjects were not necessarily under the photographer's thumb. A bit of irreverence, it enriched what would otherwise have been a standard slum exposé. It did not fit the desperate mood of *12 Million Black Voices*, but instead of simply using an alternative image, Rosskam did something worse (fig. 6.17). Careful retouching erased the girl's tongue, and the cleaned-up image became the illustration for Wright's thundering indictment: "The kitchenette blights the personalities of our growing children, disorganizes them, blinds them to hope, creates problems whose effects can be traced in the characters of its child victims for years afterwards." Altered photos produced altered personalities. Rosskam's tricks, as photo-historian William Stott has pointed out, even extended to the use of a nonblack photograph for a vital black reference early in the book. Beneath the chapter heading that introduced an account of slave origins, "Our Strange Birth," appeared Lange's closeup of a sharecropper's hands gripping a hoe. At first glance, the word-image combination provided a perfect integration of past and present—blacks brought to America for laboring purposes, blacks remaining the humble toilers in "freedom." Only when one consults the FSA file does one realize that the Lange subject was, in fact, a tanned *white* sharecropper.[74]

But did Wright and Rosskam's ends—grabbing the attention of white readers apt to overlook blacks, countering the weight of traditional portrayal—justify some of their questionable textual and captioning means? George Streater, reviewing the book in *Commonweal*, thought so. A self-described "light-skinned" black who had qualms about Wright's dismissal of mulatto leadership, Streater nevertheless endorsed *12 Million Black Voices*. "There is no need to say that this book is propaganda, for it is. . . . Why should we not have a good propaganda, after four centuries of vicious propaganda to make life easy for white folks who have bled and exploited black folk?"[75] The same reasoning was adopted by *The Nation*'s Charles Munz and other liberal white reviewers who raised specific criticisms of Wright's distortions. Columnists for such black weeklies as the *New York Age*,

Fig. 6.16. Russell Lee. "Kitchenette Apartment," Chicago. 1941. FSA. Library of Congress.

Fig. 6.17. Russell Lee. Chicago kitchenette apartment, as used in *12 Million Black Voices*. 1941.

Atlanta World, and *Pittsburgh Courier* gave even heartier assent—despite the obvious preference of their editors for pictorial portrayal very different from the book's, and despite the consideration, offered by one of the few dissenters, the *Baltimore Afro-American*'s Beatrice Murphy, that blacks might be "hopelessly discouraged" by the long lament. Said the *Courier*'s J. A. Schuyler: "I don't see how any white person reading the book can help feeling guilty."[76]

At least outside the South, the book received some play in the general-circulation press. To be sure, the coverage was nothing like the splashes given *Land of the Free* or *Home Town*, but there were modest one- or two-photo spreads in *The New York Times*, *New York Herald-Tribune*, *Saturday Review*, and *PM*. (The Wright-Rosskam book received considerably more play than Claude McKay's *Harlem: Negro Metropolis*, which, appearing the previous year, was textually both quieter in tone and far more insightful about the political, religious, and economic dynamics of urban black society. FSA pictures deserved a text as sensitive as McKay's. Illustrations for *Harlem: Negro Metropolis*, drawn from non-FSA sources—news-photo services, black studios, and, in a few cases, the Photo League—were generally unremarkable but at least not imposed upon with captioning tricks.) And, sure enough, white guilt echoes through one of the longer *12 Million Black Voices* reviews (Richard Crandell, *Herald-Tribune*), as it did through some of the letters Wright received from white readers. "As a member of the white race, I know that I am as responsible as any one else for these conditions," confided one correspondent. Declared another: "This is the first time the story has been brought home to me, and frankly, it gave me quite a jolt."[77]

There were jolts here, jolts there, but, for all the Wright-Rosskam ploys, *12 Million Black Voices* hardly amounted to the shocker that *Native Son* had been. Heightened war consciousness obviously played a part here, with shocks from a very different source flowing in daily. Although certain visual parallels between urban decay and the war front existed, as we noted in chapter 5, the media views of European or Pacific battlegrounds seized American hearts and minds as no other pictures could. Even some of the black newspaper reviews reflected tempering war concerns. "Not only are all the vital gains that the

Negroes have made in America in danger," noted Ben Davis, Jr., in the *Atlanta Daily World*, "but the right to continue the fight against the terrible evils which Wright so eloquently describes are now being fought out before Moscow, Rostov, and Chunking."[78] Slick defenses also limited the controversy that Stryker, among others, feared the book would arouse. For example, William Shands Meacham, a politically moderate Virginian newspaper editor reviewing the book in *The New York Times*, avoided direct criticism while adding a happy ending to *12 Million Black Voices*. The very existence of the FSA black poverty photographs, Meacham asserted, proved that the Roosevelt administration was acting decisively to ameliorate conditions: "The Administration has done more to further the second emancipation of the Negro than any since the Civil War."[79] Even aside from such defenses, the simplification of the black world that presumably lent punch to *12 Million Black Voices* could backfire. The Wright-Rosskam translation of black history into a more-or-less single experience did not make it difficult for whites to turn on the condescension. "This is what a Southern Negro sings," observed *PM*'s David Lindsay, quoting a black folk rhyme, "when he feels blue."[80] Understand the song, understand the Negro: this sort of confident typecasting was less possible in response to the more complex *Native Son*. Running roughshod over individual black voices, and individual black faces, *12 Million Black Voices* sometimes wound up accomplishing precisely the opposite of what it sought. Hence the dangers of "good" propaganda.

"We are not," Wright advised early in *12 Million Black Voices*, "what we seem."[81] The truth extended further than Wright thought. Racially, the FSA vision was not what it was made to seem. Amid Wright's thrusts and Meacham's parries, the innovative quality of the FSA black file was hardly given its due. Such was a familiar story—and worse, as we have seen, on other fronts. FSA innovation, involving not only recognition of black realities deeper than "soft voices and laughter" and "Yas, sir," but recognition of black individuality and diversity, tended to be lost in the various currents of the 1930s and 1940s: populism and romanticism, New Deal boosterism and wartime nationalism, not to mention outright racism.

The revisualization, or suppression, of the black file was no accidental occurrence, no mysterious process. It depended on specific choices made for specific photo-presentation situations—some very pragmatic choices at times, some understandable choices in the racial climate of the times, but choices nevertheless. Whites contributed to the process, but so, on occasions, did blacks. Political mainstreamers were at work here, but so, at times, were self-styled progressives. Authors and editors chipped away, but so, as we have seen, did reviewers, mediating between product and public. Individuals with a fairly limited knowledge of the FSA files were responsible, but so, in a great many instances, were individuals who knew the file better than anyone in the country—Stryker and, particularly, that man for all too many seasons, Rosskam. Editing manipulations were seldom as crude as the cropping out of blacks in a *Land of the Free* photograph, but subtler moves, designed (with the exception of *12 Million Black Voices*) to refamiliarize the unfamiliar, wrought their share of damage. To some extent, of course, the FSA file as a whole suffered in the public arena. The removal of any photo, whether black related or not, from its original series context, the separation of any image from its original caption, was bound to produce changes. A usable resource was also readily abusable. As one FSA enthusiast complained to Stryker in July 1941: "Do you know that FSA photos are being used by the America First Committee to show 'want in America' as a propaganda tune to keep out of the European business? I saw the unmistakable FSA prints plastered all over a window in the midtown [New York] area—without credits!"[82] Noted Delano recently: "You never knew what was going to happen to our photos once they were in the file. Years later, one of my [OWI] photos—of two or three nice young women on a lunch break at a munitions factory—was used in an advertisement for a jeans company."[83] But the black sector suffered more, not only because of the *absence* of black images from some of the important settings noted in this chapter, but because the conventional associations often imposed on FSA images tended, by the very nature of convention, to be more demeaning for blacks.

Still, the record of the utilization of the black file was not without its bright notes, as we have seen. The very fact that a publisher as prominent as Viking was willing to reproduce as many serious, non-leering, nonproject black photos as were presented in *12 Million Black Voices* was a sign of progress. There were photo-books (or aspects thereof), museum shows, exceptional magazine spreads that tapped some of the file's creative ventures. The audiences for most of these productions may have been specialized, and many members of these audiences may have been inattentive to racial subjects. Still, a chapter from *An American Exodus* or a feature in *Survey Graphic* or an exhibit at the Museum of Modern Art may have offered some quiet encouragement—to forward-looking scholars and activists investigating black America, to the more imaginative New Deal agency and war information agency camerapeople, to young photographers—black and white, inside and outside the government—who would build on FSA accomplishments in the 1940s and 1950s. Innovation was carried on, though sometimes amid distinctly difficult circumstances.

At the Office of War Information, Stryker and the photographers with whom he was associated—Delano, Vachon, Lee, Collier, Collins, Parks, Esther Bubley, Ann Rosener, Paula Ehrlich, and, to some extent, Roger Smith—faced heightened pressure from agency administrators for upbeat documentation. What's more, by early 1943, Stryker's unit lost its status as a distinct administrative entity, merging with what had been the OEM/OWI News Bureau photographic staff in a newly unified OWI Domestic Branch Division of Photography. If Stryker's liberalism had its limits, he now encountered veteran photographers whose notion of photographic mission made Stryker's own viewpoint look wildly radical. Remembered Alfred Palmer, who had been chief photographer for the News Bureau: "When Stryker and I began to work together, he'd be so proud to show me the [FSA] pictures that had been reproduced in newspapers all over the country and abroad—gruesome pictures of poor sharecroppers, shacks, trash all over the floor. My reaction was, 'Look, Roy, those pictures aren't helpful to us, they're not going to contribute to what we're trying to accomplish here.' He considered me a 'glamour photographer' who had to be taught the facts of life, but I felt that what he did at the FSA was manipulation—encouraging the photographers to show the worst conditions. I didn't carry a skull on the back of my car to plant in the foreground of

a picture to make a point. I didn't light a sharecropper's shack in such
a way as to make it look as stark as possible. I believed in looking at
things in a helpful and encouraging manner."[84] Disagreement even
extended to the matter of photo-stories: Palmer, Howard Liberman,
Howard Hollem, and the other ex–News Bureau photographers were
much more oriented toward single images that could be tapped easily
by the media. There were further tensions: "As time went on, we saw
less and less of Stryker," remembers Paul Vanderbilt, brought on in
1943 to begin organizing the FSA/OWI file. "He was holed up in his
office, on the phone, in meetings, trying to hang on to the kind of
photography he believed in. By the end [Stryker's resignation], we had
become basically just a picture supplier for the New York [Overseas]
office." While Stryker fought administrative battles, Parks and Smith
faced other kinds of obstacles. "Roger [Smith] would request that his
material be sent to my lab to be processed," recalls Steve Wright, the
black photographer who ran the Federal Works Agency photo lab in
the early 1940s, "because he felt that people were sabotaging him at
the OWI lab. There were some whites, mostly at the lower-level positions, who felt that a black man shouldn't be holding a photographer's
job—they were looking to take his job away."[85]

The typical OWI black images—accenting minority contributions
in "safe" contexts ranging from civilian defense meetings and scrap
drives in Washington, D.C., to shipyards in Oakland, from classrooms
at Bethune-Cookman College to defense factory assembly lines in New
Britain, Connecticut—we have noted before. But amid the celebratory images, a scattering of less predictable views filtered into the OWI
file. Parks, visiting Bethune-Cookman for a series that presented an
idyllic view of the all-black college, also ventured into the surrounding community and came up with a few more probing views of life for
the majority of blacks in Daytona Beach: the buses operated by the
city "which," the caption noted, "are used only by Negroes"; shacks in
the black quarter, across the street from a movie poster beckoning
customers "Across the Pacific." And Parks, visiting New York City for
a glittering piece on Duke Ellington, also managed to record a politically intriguing scene, on a Harlem street corner, of a Marcus Garvey
follower reading the OWI publication, "Negroes and the War."

Similarly, Smith, while producing hundreds of photos of black defense workers, also managed to do some Harlem street shooting; moreover, Smith raised the touchy question of whether an OWI black photographer would be limited to covering only "black" stories, and, in the course of doing a nonexclusively black story at a Coast Guard training center, made a point of documenting an integrated mess hall. But the more daring coverage came from Bubley, whose September 1943 story on a long-distance bus trip (Washington, D.C., to Columbus, Ohio, to Louisville to Memphis) captured both the special subculture of the bus world—that curious mixture of communality and alienation—and the larger Jim Crow culture of the South: segregated waiting-room and rest-stop signs. Recalled Bubley recently: "I didn't get the sense that Roy [Stryker] was extremely interested in these [racial] issues. It was never put to me that I should look out for segregation signs. But I was free to take what impressed me as odd, interesting, horrifying. I was twenty-one years old at that time, I had grown up in an area where very few blacks lived. Those segregation signs were awful. I didn't know how anyone could overlook them."[86]

In the immediate postwar years, the best-known documentary project involving Stryker and some of his former FSA/OWI camerapeople—the Standard Oil of New Jersey Picture Library (followed in the 1950s by the Pittsburgh Photographic Library and the Jones and Laughlin Steel Corporation Picture Library)—was hardly a more promising context than the OWI had been for a frank exploration of black America. But, as photo-historians fond of berating 1930s–40s documentarians for selling out to the corporate establishment have tended to forget, the postwar years saw other documentary undertakings of a more penetrating nature.

Lee's extensive 1946–47 work for the U.S. Coal Mines Administration documenting coal miners' lives in the South (part of the Medical Survey of the Bituminous Coal Industry, sponsored jointly by the Department of the Interior and the United Mine Workers) extended many of his FSA achievements. While series focusing on particular families—including such black families as the Curringtons of Kenvir, Kentucky; the Howards of Gilliam, West Virginia; the Davises of Welch, West Virginia; the Cains of Adamsville, Alabama—served to counter conventional images of a faceless coal-mining mass, Lee's carefully constructed image-text combinations produced messages both biting and haunting. At Welch, a seemingly innocuous image of a black miner being examined by a white doctor was accompanied by a caption that spoke volumes about the level of company interest in miner health: "Dr. Rucker takes pulse of miner who has come in for a back-to-work slip. Patient complained of aches and pains all over; the doctor said he might have rheumatic fever, prescribed a mild pain-relieving drug and signed a back-to-work slip. There was no examination other than the pulse-taking." At Gilliam, another seemingly innocent view of Mrs. James Robert Howard washing the supper dishes was accompanied by the pointed reminder that the sink and running water

Fig. 6.18. Russell Lee. "Miners in the Community Building," Bishop, Va. 1946. U.S. Solid Fuels Administration. National Archives.

had been installed by Mr. Howard at "no expense to the company. . . . Such improvements become the property of the company." And again at Gilliam, Lee used a seemingly routine view, of James Howard picking up his lunch pail as he leaves for work, to explore a miner's grasp of a precarious future: "I grab my lunch and go on," as Howard is quoted in the caption. "I never look back." In the course of the coverage, Lee also managed to suggest the divisions in coal country that went beyond class. Although black and white miners are shown working together, waiting together in pay lines, shopping at the same company stores, and attending the same union meetings, the force of racial convention appears as strong as ever in Lee's views of a bifurcated pool hall in Bishop, Virginia (figs. 6.18 and 6.19).

Fig. 6.19. Russell Lee. "Miners in the Community Building," Bishop, Va. 1946. U.S. Solid Fuels Administration. National Archives.

Outside the government realm, the presence of ex-FSAers (Mydans, Rothstein, Vachon, Evans, Parks) on the staffs of *Life*, *Look*, and *Fortune* may have contributed to the trend—albeit very gradual—of increasing seriousness in mass-media treatment of black life during the postwar years. Certainly W. Eugene Smith's extended *Life* photo-story on a black nurse midwife in rural South Carolina ("Nurse Midwife: Maude Callen Eases Pain of Birth, Life, and Death," 3 December 1951) was a far cry from *Life*'s 1938 spread on America's "Negroes": replacing the colorful primitives were rural citizens struggling, often courageously, with immense health, housing, and educational needs. The theme of the persevering black medic, developed in a sustained visual narrative, recalled an important dimension of the Lee/Rosskam "Day of a Negro Doctor." The intimacy of the Callen-and-patient shots recalled aspects of Parks's Ella Watson story. The drama reached beyond even FSA capabilities.[87]

If there were echoes of the FSA in W. Eugene Smith's passionate contributions to *Life*, there were echoes as well in Robert Frank's decidedly cooler contribution to photo-documentary publishing. One does not usually think of *The Americans* as a work exploring the black situation, yet there are striking glances. The intensely private gesture of the black man, fingers held over mouth, standing near a car during a funeral procession in St. Helena, South Carolina, is strongly reminiscent of a gesture captured by Delano in his Heard County, Georgia, black funeral story; and Frank's portrait of a black maid holding a white baby in Charleston, South Carolina, bears some of the same tensions that Wolcott had conveyed in a black maid–white toddler photo published in *12 Million Black Voices*.[88] The FSA connection to other pioneering photographers of the 1940s–50s is more direct: Helen Levitt, who knew Shahn through the Photo League and other contexts, was undoubtedly exposed to Shahn's photos of the scrawlings of black sharecropper children on the walls of their shacks; her own studies of New York City children's sidewalk drawings expand upon this sensitivity to youthful creativity amid apparent deprivation, art amid the ruins.[89]

Or take the case of Rondal Partridge, the young assistant to Lange in the late 1930s, creator of a brilliant photo-series on California youth problems for the National Youth Administration in 1940 (the special project including a direct swipe at racial discrimination in the armed forces), and a documentarian who would explore black life in contexts ranging from 1940s Baton Rouge to 1970s Roxbury. "Dorothea's work has influenced me throughout my career," observed Partridge recently:

> She taught me I could go anywhere, photograph anyone. She had this way of incorporating people into her "conspiracy." . . . "We'll show the government what is going on, we'll cooperate here and make a difference." She'd hang around, listen to people, take notes, go back to the car, talk a bit. . . . That's how her pictures would evolve. Letting people talk to you—therein lies the secret. I'd be in a black area of Oakland, or Roxbury during the busing troubles, and people might be suspicious at first: "Hey, what are you doing?" "Well, I'm photographing." "Trying to show us in a worse light?" So I'd start photographing signs, street architecture, and gradually I'd get people interested.[90]

For black photographers, the very presence of Parks at the FSA, and of Parks, Smith, and the free-lancer E. F. Joseph at the OWI, helped open the government door a crack. Steve Wright, the black photographer who worked his way up from an assistantship at the Public Works Administration to direction of the Federal Works Agency photo-lab and ultimately leadership of the Photographic Section of the State Department in the late 1940s and 1950s, widened the opening. "At the State Department, I was in a position to help get black photographers appointed, and appointed at higher levels than they otherwise would have been," observed Wright later. "So I was able to help [Robert] McNeill, [DeWitt] Keith, and others. But when it came to assignments, I didn't discriminate between whites and blacks on the staff; whoever was in line for the project did it. I didn't want the situation that Roger [Smith] had faced at the OWI, where he was pretty much assigned the black stories because he was black. No, we photographed them all. . . . I can remember doing an assignment that took me into the office of Theodore Bilbo. We couldn't stand Bilbo, with all his racial hatred; but in private, amazingly enough, he was perfectly cooperative, just a human being."[91]

The FSA precedent had its impact for black photographers working outside the government as well: the line that extends from the sponta-

neous street shooting of Shahn, Delano, Rosskam, and Wolcott to the
well-known street work of the later Parks also extends to the urban
explorations—the striking juxtapositions of beauty and blight—of Roy
DeCarava, Moneta Sleet, Austin Hansen, and others. Hence, in
DeCarava's 1949 "Graduation, New York," one finds the charged interplays among advertisements, figures, and urban rubble, reminiscent
of the Lee-Rosskam Chicago series; or, in DeCarava's 1949 "Two Boys
in Vacant Lot, New York," one finds the distinctly Shahnesque meditation on urban space and precarious urban identities.[92] Reflections of
FSA interest in assembling the mundane pieces of a "day in the life"
chronicle (the whole amounting to much more than the sum of the
parts) can also be found in a few of the more imaginative *Ebony* features of the 1940s and 1950s: Griffith Davis following black truck
drivers from Kansas City to Chicago, Richard Saunders documenting
black coal miners in Wheeling, West Virginia, David Jackson looking
at black steelworkers in Gary, Indiana.[93] "You couldn't help but be
guided by what they [FSA photographers] had done," notes Robert
Williams, the black FSA exhibits assistant who later photographed
black troops in World War II Italy and went on to establish his own
photography and graphic arts business in New York. "By developing
those photo-stories, they were able to catch the essence of things they
were shooting, the mood of a scene."[94]

Of course Davis, Sleet, DeCarava, Jackson, Hansen, Parks, as well
as white photographers in the postwar years, departed from the FSA
model in some important respects. There was a much greater concentration on the big-city setting. There was a heightened sensitivity to
the relationship between, on the one hand, technical advances in photography and, on the other, the quest for photographic intimacy, the
effort to convey psychological drama, the effort to capture the surreal
along with the real. Perhaps most important, there was intense investigation of the realm in which the Lee-Rosskam Chicago coverage had
been so notably lacking, the realm left unexplored even by Parks in his
FSA days, the realm that Rothstein touched upon only in an exceptional series: the realm of social and political activism. With coverage
of the events—and, just as important, the culture—of the civil rights
movement, what had been hints of assertiveness (in Shahn's shoe-

shiner, or Delano's migrants, or Parks's charwoman) became more explicit affirmations of an individual and a collective will for change. Amid the new documentary directions, however, tensions that had been evident during the depression and war years continued: tensions between individual photographic inclinations and organizational (or market) needs, tensions between the interest in exposing black problems and the interest in promoting positive black role-models, tensions between the desire to avoid victimology and the desire to avoid what Robert McNeill would call "sugar-coating." As McNeill, the black photographer who worked inside and outside of government through five decades, observed in 1989:

> *Ebony* was so intent on showing blacks in a complimentary light in the 1940s and 1950s, [the editors] tended to sugar-coat everything. All those brilliant success stories. . . . I couldn't believe that a lot of those people had actually accomplished what the articles and the pictures claimed. I couldn't stand some of those features. But on the other side, for years you didn't see many black faces in the [white-edited] mass media, except of course the advertising stereotypes—the Aunt Jemimahs, or the smiling Pullman porters. Slowly, things improved. The impact of the FSA had something to do with it; and Gordon [Parks], with his success as a photographer and a poet and a filmmaker; and photographers like [the *Washington Post's*] Ellsworth Davis, whom I always admired, made a difference. The war opened things up for some black photographers who were in the right place at the right time. And of course the civil rights movement. . . . Remember when we were always getting pictures of the "first"—first black policeman, first black fireman, first black bus driver, etc.? Now we take all those things for granted.
>
> When I was starting out in the 1930s, I was a real student of photography, looking at every photo magazine and photo book I could get my hands on. The FSA work was a definite influence. I remember being taken with the [Rothstein] photo of the [black] girl doing the Lindy-Hop in front of the jukebox, a sort of slice of life from the dance hall; and the contrasts in the [Vachon] photo of the Capitol dome, all glittering, set against all that litter and trash in the foreground; and the dignity of the "Migrant Mother." Even though they were white, the FSA photographers seemed to be able to overcome a lot of the distrust that blacks had [inherited] from the days when the "pony" photographers would come through their areas and make a fast buck. I think [the FSA camerapeople] really

touched the earth, really listened to the Mrs. Joneses telling the anecdotes about the tree that the storm had thrown across the street, and really got to know the sights and sounds and smells of places. I admired Gordon's parody of American Gothic, though I've seen other things by him that I've admired more. Gordon was doing so many things that were different [in 1942–43]. I remember seeing him covering a Howard University commencement, and even the other black photographers who were there were saying, "Who is that crazy [guy]?" I mean, Gordon would use four flashbulbs for a single shot, outdoors where he could have gotten away without using any. He wasn't content just to stand up and take shots from a position that was comfortable for him—he lay on the ground, he shot up, he shot down. He was more like a movie director, trying to capture the whole academic atmosphere.

I wanted to get away from the black stereotypes, and I wanted to get away from the studio posing. In 1938, I did an FSA kind of story in New York—through a contact at the N.Y. Institute of Photography, I got *Fortune* to send me on an assignment to cover the Bronx "slave market." You know, these black domestics would stand on a particular street corner in the Bronx, and rich old white widows would dicker with them on the terms of a day's employment, usually something like twenty cents an hour. So I followed one [domestic] from the street corner to the [white] home, showed her washing, sewing, ironing, fixing food, washing windows. Well, I sent in the pictures, and I guess *Fortune* thought they were too hot to handle, and never published them. Years later, a few were published in *Flash*, which was like a mini-*Life*.

I've always thought of photography as a sort of chiseling from a moment in time. Spontaneity, humor, irony—that's what I was after when I did the *Negro in Virginia* assignment [WPA Writers Project], where I had the FSA type of freedom. So I'd photograph a woman fishing from the Norfolk pier. . . . Yes, she was poor, but she didn't think of herself as poor; this was her recreation. She was coping, she had her own vision. Or the group in South Richmond admiring the new car [fig. 1.17]. . . . Yes, it was a poor neighborhood, but at least there were some jobs, and they had pride in the fact that one of them was able to get a car. I knew what he felt like. Or that guard at the gatepost, with the sign, "No Loafers Allowed." That guard just stared at me the whole time I was there, defying me to intrude on his domain. There he was, the biggest loafer of them all.

I never considered myself a protest photographer. Maybe I was always more interested in artistic depth than shaking things up. Once I began at the State Department [1956], of course, I had to be careful not to be associated too closely with the civil rights movement—I would have lost my job. Still, when I was running the McNeill News Photo Service, I took my share of pickets and demonstrations. Someone like Edgar Brown, the D.C. activist, would call me with a tip, and I'd hop in the car and race down to photograph "Don't Buy Where You Can't Work" pickets in front of People's Drugs or Safeway, pickets in front of Senator Bilbo's home, demonstrations for the anti-lynching bills. I saw my role as trying to be objective, even at those congressional hearings where Senator Tom Connally would always refer to blacks as "nigrahs." I was a conduit, supplying photos to the [Washington] *Afro-American*, [Pittsburgh] *Courier*, and other black newspapers that were running more of those sorts of pictures in the late 1940s and 1950s.

Most of my News Service clientele was black, but not all. I got a call once from a company that needed pictures of a new plane it was trying to get the military interested in. So I showed up, carrying my camera gear, and a company official asks me, "Where's the photographer?" I said, "I'm the photographer." They couldn't believe a black man was running a photo service. I did the job, sent them the pictures, and never heard from them again. I also faced that kind of prejudice when I worked for the Army photo lab; at first they didn't want to hire me at the advertised grade, and then once I was hired they didn't want to send a black photographer on any assignment out of the lab. When Steve [Wright] called me to the State Department, he was able to protect me from that kind of thing. I did all the assignments that everyone else did. I can remember, one assignment, racing across the White House lawn to get some pictures of a diplomat who had just been named ambassador to Russia, as he was about to take off in the presidential helicopter. You can imagine what the Secret [Service] people must have been thinking.

One of the mandates I had felt when I started out, looking at those FSA pictures, was [to pursue] the idea of the photo-story. Unfortunately, constraints of time, and money, and job over the years prevented me from doing as many photo-stories as I would have liked. When I had the chance, I tried to be inventive . . . doing a story, pictures and text, on an integrated Army unit in Virginia; or turning a routine portrait coverage for State into more of a symbolic thing, sort of my own version of American Gothic. But you never knew how these great things you'd see in your mind's eye would turn out. I had the hot idea once of doing a picture-story on what goes on at a typical men's smoker. So I took shots of girls dancing with the G-strings, the reactions of the men. I went all out. Well, when I developed those "great" pictures, I found something interesting. All I had ended up illustrating was the smoke.[95]

Notes

1. Politics and Culture

1. Wolcott to Stryker, Jan. 1939, Roy E. Stryker Papers, microfilm reel
    NDA 30, Archives of American Art, Washington, D.C. See also Wolcott
    to Stryker, Dec. 1938, 15 May 1940, 28 July 1940, 21 Sept. 1940, 25 Oct.
    1939, Roy E. Stryker Papers (Washington) microfilm reel NDA 30, Ar-
    chives of American Art.
2. "Feud of the Range," *Variety*, 19 July 1939, included in *Variety Film Re-
    views: 1907–1980*, vol. 6 (New York: Garland Publishing, 1983).
3. Roy Stryker's photography operation, initiated in July 1935 as the docu-
    mentary wing of the Resettlement Administration, became part of the
    newly constituted Farm Security Administration in September 1937.
    With the termination of the Farm Security Administration in October
    1942, the photo unit was transferred to the Office of War Information,
    where in functioned in various administrative forms (Division of Photog-
    raphy, Bureau of Publications and Graphics, Domestic Branch—Fall,
    1942 to Winter 1943; part of the Division of Photography, Domestic
    Branch—Winter 1943 to Fall 1943; Washington Office, Picture Divi-
    sion, Overseas Branch) until Stryker's resignation in Oct. 1943. This
    study will concern itself primarily with the RA/FSA phase, partly be-
    cause the OWI year presented an entirely different set of administrative
    pressures (worthy of a separate study), and partly because of the difficulty
    of determining what material from the OWI year was connected to
    Stryker. The 60,000-print figure refers to the RA/FSA phase. The overall
    RA/FSA/OWI collection, as it currently exists at the Library of Con-
    gress, includes (by the author's recent systematic survey) some 110,000
    black-and-white prints, 182,000 negatives, and 1,600 color transparen-
    cies. The 110,000-print figure includes material taken for the OWI be-
    fore and after Stryker's involvement, material taken for OWI-predeces-
    sor agencies (the Office of Emergency Management and the Office of the
    Coordinator of Information, both of which used Stryker's photographers

for contract work), material taken for U.S. military branches, industrial public relations departments, foreign information agencies, and miscellaneous organizations. This author's best estimate of the total RA/FSA/OWI black-and-white prints connected to Stryker's leadership is 75,000.

4. Edwin Rosskam, editor's note, in Sherwood Anderson, *Home Town* (1940; rev. ed. Mamaroneck, N.Y.: Paul Appel, 1975), 144.

5. Roy Stryker to Dorothea Lange, 18 June 1937, Roy E. Stryker Papers, microfilm reel NDA 30, Archives of American Art.

6. Stryker to Russell Lee, 26 June 1941, Roy E. Stryker Papers, microfilm reel NDA 31, Archives of American Art.

7. See William Stott, *Documentary Expression and Thirties America* (New York: Oxford Univ. Press, 1973); Pete Daniel, et al., eds., *Official Images: New Deal Photography* (Washington, D.C.: Smithsonian Institution Press, 1987); Carl Fleischhauer and Beverly Brannan, eds., *Documenting America* (Berkeley: Univ. of California Press, 1988); Maren Stange, *Symbols of Ideal Life: Social Documentary Photography in America, 1890–1950* (New York: Cambridge Univ. Press, 1989); James Curtis, *Mind's Eye, Mind's Truth: FSA Photography Reconsidered* (Philadelphia: Temple Univ. Press, 1989). For more traditional studies, see F. Jack Hurley, *Portrait of a Decade: Roy Stryker and the Development of Documentary Photography in the Thirties* (Baton Rouge: Louisiana State Univ. Press, 1972); Thomas Garver, ed., *Just Before the War* (New York: October House, 1968); and the three massive FSA photo samplers: Edward Steichen, ed., *The Bitter Years, 1935–1941: Rural America as Seen by the Photographers of the Farm Security Administration* (New York: Museum of Modern Art, 1962); Roy Stryker and Nancy Wood, eds., *In This Proud Land: America, 1935–1942, As Seen in the FSA Photographs* (Greenwich, Ct.: New York Graphic Society, 1973); and Hank O'Neal, ed., *A Vision Shared: A Classic Portrait of America and Its People, 1935–1943* (New York: St. Martin's Press, 1976).

8. See especially Sally Stein, *Marion Post Wolcott: FSA Photographs* (Carmel, Ca.: Friends of Photography, 1983); F. Jack Hurley, *Marion Post Wolcott: A Photographic Journey* (Albuquerque: Univ. of New Mexico Press, 1989); Andrea Fisher, *Let Us Now Praise Famous Women: Women Photographers for the U.S. Government, 1935–1944* (New York: Pandora Press, 1987); and the Evans chapter in James Curtis, *Mind's Eye, Mind's Truth: FSA Photography Reconsidered.* Curtis's effort to debunk one of Evans's better-known images, taken on a sidewalk in the black district of Vicksburg, Mississippi, is provocative but flawed: while failing to take into proper account the various degrees of "posing"—actual arrangement of figures by the photographer, versus a more dynamic cooperation between Evans and subjects—Curtis appears to make the questionable assumption that

photographs must be perfectly spontaneous to be significant explorations of racial nuance. Curtis misses the larger point of the sidewalk and barbershop image, reproduced in *Let Us Now Praise Famous Men*. Evans's black figures are sturdy if remote, proud if a bit mysterious, certainly not monolithic; this is no simple cast of entertaining yokels or wounded proletarians. The conservative, suit-and-tie dress and gentlemanly pose of the older man seated at the left is not matched by either of his colleagues, one of whom, leaning against a storefront with hands thrust in his pockets and his gaze challenging ours (or, potentially, that of the white man in the parked automobile), lends a touch of insouciance. Evans, envisioning both the complex sociological particulars of a time and a place (important gradations within black society) and the transcendental implications of Time and Place, is as respectfully revealing here as he is with many of his white subjects.

9. Angela Davis, "Photography and Afro-American History," in *A Century of Black Photography, 1840–1960*, ed. Valencia Hollins Coar (Providence: Rhode Island School of Design, 1983), 2.

10. Roy Stryker, interview by Richard Doud, 13 June 1953, transcript at Archives of American Art.

11. Thomas Bender, "Making History Whole Again," *New York Times*, 6 Oct. 1985, sec. 7, p. 43.

12. James Agee and Walker Evans, *Let Us Now Praise Famous Men* (1941; rev. ed., Cambridge, Mass.: Riverside Press, 1960), 11.

13. Alan Trachtenberg, "Introduction: Photographs as Symbolic History," in *The American Image* (New York: Pantheon, 1979), xxv.

14. Roland Barthes, "The Photographic Message," in *Image-Music-Text* (New York: Farrar, Straus, Giroux, 1977); reprinted in *The Camera Viewed: Writings on 20th Century Photography*, vol. 2, ed. Peninah R. Petruck (New York: Dutton, 1979), p. 198.

15. Fisher, *Let Us Now Praise Famous Women*, 153; Stein, *Marion Post Wolcott: FSA Photographs*, 9.

16. Clifford Geertz, *The Interpretation of Culture* (New York: Basic Books, 1973), 29.

17. Edith Kurzweil, *The Age of Structuralism: Levi-Strauss to Foucault* (New York: Columbia Univ. Press, 1980), 183 and 243. Psychoanalytic approaches to the visual arts in general have received a boost recently from the critical acclaim accorded Michael Fried's *Realism, Writing, Disfiguration: On Thomas Eakins and Stephen Crane* (Chicago: Univ. of Chicago Press, 1987). Fried's imaginativeness cannot be denied, yet the essential foundation for his reading of "The Gross Clinic" amounts to a suspicious combination of faith and arrogance. Fried's reliance, in a cen-

tral passage, on the logic of "inevitability" is a giveaway: "Altogether, then, the juxtaposition in a single, intensely dramatic composition of a dominant, authoritative older man, an intrusive, highly emotional older woman, and no less than two sons—the figures of Eakins and of the patient being operated on (I am eliding the younger Gross)—*makes it inevitable* that 'The Gross Clinic' be construed, sooner or later, in Freudian terms. With Gross's bloody scalpel before our eyes, it should be unnecessary to add that among those terms will be the issue of castration" (41, emphasis mine). For examples of post-structuralist obscurantism as applied to photography, see Fisher's readings of images other than the Wolcott "Drug Store" in *Let Us Now Praise Famous Women*, Victor Burgin's *End of Art Theory: Criticism and Post-Modernity* (Atlantic Highlands, N.J.: Humanities Press International, 1986), as well as his *Between* (New York: Basil, Blackwell, and London Institute of Contemporary Arts, 1986), and, to a lesser extent, Maren Stange's "Gotham's Crime and Misery: Ideology and Entertainment in Jacob Riis's Lantern Slide Exhibitions," *Views: The Journal of Photography in New England* 8 (Spring, 1987): 7–11.

18. John Szarkowski, *The Photographer's Eye* (New York: Museum of Modern Art, 1966), 70; Russell B. Nye, "History and Literature: Branches of the Same Tree," in *Essays on History and Literature*, ed. Robert H. Bremner (Columbus: Ohio State Univ. Press, 1966), 154.

19. Fisher, *Let Us Now Praise Famous Women*, 133.

20. Allan Sekula, "On the Invention of Photographic Meaning," in *Photography in Print: Writings from 1816 to the Present*, ed. Vicki Goldberg (New York: Simon and Schuster, 1981), 473.

21. Denis Donoghue, "The Strange Case of Paul de Man," *New York Review of Books*, 29 June 1989, 37.

22. Alan Trachtenberg, introductory essay in *Documenting America*, ed. Fleischhauer and Brannan, 70.

23. Roland Barthes, *Camera Lucida: Reflections on Photography* (New York: Hill and Wang, 1981), 107.

24. Maurice Mandelbaum, *The Problem of Historical Knowledge: An Answer to Relativism* (Freeport, N.Y.: Books for Libraries Press, 1971), 177.

25. Michael Walzer, "The Politics of Michel Foucault," in *Foucault: A Critical Reader*, ed. David Couzens Hoy (Oxford: Basil Blackwell, 1986), 61.

26. Virginia Shirley, "Kentucky Has Her Bit of the Deep South," *Louisville Courier-Journal Magazine*, 9 Oct. 1938, p. 3.

27. Alan Trachtenberg, "Albums of War: On Reading Civil War Photographs," *Representations* 9 (Winter 1985): 29. Relativist-absolutist tensions implicit in this essay can also be discerned in other Trachtenberg

articles collected in his *Reading American Photographs: Images as History, Mathew Brady to Walker Evans* (New York: Hill and Wang, 1989).

28. Quoted in Harvard Sitkoff, *A New Deal for Blacks: The Emergence of Civil Rights as a National Issue* (New York: Oxford Univ. Press, 1978), 49.

29. See, for example, John W. Blassingame, *The Slave Community: Plantation Life in the Antebellum South* (New York: Oxford Univ. Press, 1972); Herbert Gutman, *Work, Culture, and Society in Industrializing America: Essays in American Working-Class and Social History* (New York: Random House, 1977); William Foote Whyte, *Street Corner Society* (Chicago: Univ. of Chicago Press, 1955); John Dollard, *Caste and Class in a Southern Town* (New Haven: Yale Univ. Press, 1937); Horace Cayton and St. Clair Drake, *Black Metropolis: A Study of Negro Life in a Northern City* (New York: Harcourt, Brace, and Company, 1945).

30. Richard Wright, introduction to Cayton and Drake, *Black Metropolis*, xxxiv.

31. Peter L. Burger and Thomas Luckmann, *The Social Construction of Reality: A Treatise in the Sociology of Knowledge* (Garden City, N.Y.: Doubleday and Company, Inc., 1966), 153.

32. Sterling Brown, *The Negro in American Fiction* (1937; reprint, Port Washington, N.Y.: Kennikat Press, 1968), 194.

33. "50 Million Watermelons Go to Market," *Life*, 9 Aug. 1937, 52.

34. "The Homestead Entertaining Japanese Diplomats as Patriotic Duty," *Life*, 16 Feb. 1942, 70.

35. "Biggest Cotton Plantation in U.S. Is the 60 Square Miles of Delta and Pine Land Company of South Mississippi . . . ," *Fortune* 15 (Mar. 1937): 128; Joseph Alsop and Robert Kintner, "Ickes, the Man of Wrath," *Life*, 21 Nov. 1938, 59; "Negroes at War: All They Want Now Is a Fair Chance to Fight," *Life*, 14 June 1942, 87.

36. "Negroes: The U.S. Also Has a Minority Problem," *Life*, 3 Oct. 1938, 48.

37. Greene County, Georgia, official quoted in Ralph Bunche, *The Political Status of the Negro in the Age of FDR* (Chicago: Chicago Univ. Press, 1973), 412.

38. Elizabeth McCausland, "Art Notes," *Springfield Sunday Union and Republican*, 24 Oct. 1937, 15.

39. Julia Peterkin and Doris Ulmann, *Roll, Jordan, Roll* (New York: Robert O. Ballou, 1933), 18; see also photos on pp. 6, 15, 19, 117, 119, and 121.

40. Tom O'Connor and Leon Goodelman, "Here Are Some of the Things the Strike Is About," *PM*, 4 May 1941, 13.

41. Erskine Caldwell and Margaret Bourke-White, *You Have Seen Their Faces* (1937; rpt. New York: Modern Age Books, 1937), pp. 32–33, plate 7; pp. 16–17, plate 17; p. 1, plate 18, 15; pp. 32–33, plate 15.

42. Caldwell and Bourke-White, *You Have Seen Their Faces*, p. 1, plates 15 and 4.

43. James Borchert, *Alley Life in Washington: Family, Community, Religion, and Folklife in the City, 1850–1970* (Urbana: Univ. of Illinois Press, 1980), 223.

44. Harlem resident E. H. Davis, quoted in "Exhibitions: Feature Group's 'Toward a Harlem Document,'" *Photo Notes* (April 1939): 2.

45. In this regard, the major biographical surveys of black photographers have come up a bit short. These include: Valencia Hollins Coar, ed., *A Century of Black Photographers, 1840–1960*; Deborah Willis-Thomas, *Black Photographers, 1840–1940* (New York: Garland Press, 1985); and Jeanne Moutoussamy-Ashe, *Viewfinders: Black Women Photographers* (New York: Dodd, Mead, and Co., 1986).

46. Robert McNeill, interview with author, 26 June 1989.

47. Quoted in James Haskins, *James Van DerZee: The Picture Takin' Man* (New York: Dodd, Mead, 1979), 248.

48. Cayton and Drake, *Black Metropolis*, 559.

49. As Vera Jackson recently told an interviewer: "In order to forget [the] bad times . . . there was a showiness on the part of the most of us. We were most impressed with elegance, richness, or opulence in our homes, and our dress and all activities which we pursued." Quoted in Jeanne Moutoussamy-Ashe, *Viewfinders: Black Women Photographers*, 8.

50. Glenn S. Callaghan to Herbert Little, 24 Sept. 1940, Records of the National Youth Administration (RG 119), Correspondence of the Director and Others in his Office with State NYA Officials Concerning Publicity and Other Informational Matters, 1938–1942, Box 7, National Archives. See also, in Box 7, "South Charleston Resident Work Experience Project at U.S. Naval Ordnance Plant," NYA Information Bulletin, Summer 1940.

51. Alfred T. Palmer, interview with author, 18 Aug. 1990.

52. Chandler Owen, *Negroes and the War* (Washington, D.C.: Office of War Information, 1943), n.p. Memo, "Negroes and the War," 1943. Records of the Office of War Information, Domestic Branch, Foreign Language Section: Subject File of the Chief, Box 1079, folder "Negro Morale," National Archives.

53. Significantly, Hine's 1930s work for the Red Cross and the WPA is all but ignored in one of the recent revisionist studies of Hine; see Peter Seixas, "Lewis Hine: From 'Social' to 'Interpretive' Photographer," *American Quarterly* (Fall 1987): 381–409.

54. Among the Harlem residents' responses to the "Harlem Document," quoted in the Photo League's *Photo Notes*: "For pictures of every day life

in Harlem, I consider your exhibit the most natural and realistic that I have seen. Marium Bickford." "The pictures are true and factual but why show one side of the life of Harlem; what about the intellectual and cultural side such as the thousands at night schools, the various churches and forums, the library and its avid readers, etc. B. Bryan." Quoted in "Exhibitions: Feature Group's 'Toward a Harlem Document,' " *Photo Notes* (Apr. 1939): 2. For the Siskind comment, see Aaron Siskind, "The Drama of Objects," *Minicam Photography* 8 (June 1945), reprinted in Carl Chiarenza, *Aaron Siskind: Pleasures and Terrors* (Boston: Little, Brown, and Co., 1982), 65. See also Aaron Siskind, "The Feature Group," *Photo Notes* (June–July 1940): 6.

55. Robert McNeill interview with author, 10 Oct. 1986.
56. "From Ben Shahn, FSA Photographer," *Photo Notes* (June–July 1940): 2; see also "Lange Visits Photo League," *Photo Notes* (Sept. 1939): 3.

2. FSA Photography

1. Resolution of Adams County, Miss., Farmers Bureau, 27 Oct. 1938, included in letter, Dan R. McGhehee to C. B. Baldwin, 31 Oct. 1938, Records of the Farmers Home Administration, Record Group 96, Series 2 (Cincinnati Office, 1935–42), Complaints—Mississippi, National Archives, Washington, D.C.
2. Theodore C. Bilbo to M. T. Aldrich, 29 Oct. 1938, Records of the Farmers Home Administration, RG 96, Series 2, Complaints—Mississippi, National Archives.
3. Helen Stickney to Mrs. White, 16 Nov. 1938, Records of the Farmers Home Administration, RG 96, Series 2, Complaints—Mississippi, National Archives.
4. T. Roy Reid to Bilbo, 4 Nov. 1938, Records of the Farmers Home Administration, RG 96, Series 2, Complaints—Mississippi, National Archives.
5. Felix Bruner, "Utopia Unlimited: Executive Order Gives Tugwell Power to Administer Projects Calling for $364,790,000," *Washington Post*, 10 Feb. 1936, 1. See also, Bruner, "Utopia Unlimited: Homes for Workers Planned around Campuses; Factories Slow to Move in with Jobs," *Washington Post*, 11 Feb. 1936; Bruner, "Utopia Unlimited: Communities Planned to Relieve Residents of 'Stranded Towns' Are 'Stranded,' Too," *Washington Post*, 12 Feb. 1936; Bruner, "Utopia Unlimited: Resettlement Administration Cost Is 40¢ of Every Dollar Actually Spent to Date," *Washington Post*, 13 Feb. 1936.

6.   Frank L. Kluckhorn, "Tugwell Has Staff of 12,089 to Create 5,012 Relief Jobs, Pays His Aides $1,750,000 a Month While Workers on Projects Get $300,000," *New York Times*, 17 Nov. 1935, sec. 1, p. 1.

7.   Mrs. Ruby Pugh to George Mitchell, 9 Sept. 1941, and J. J. Pugh to John Rankin, 10 Aug. 1941, Records of the Farmers Home Administration, RG 96, Series 2, Complaints—Louisiana, National Archives.

8.   Milton Tainter, quoted in FSA district rural rehabilitation report by A. E. Robinson, 12 May 1941, Records of the Farmers Home Administration, RG 96, Series 2, Complaints—Louisiana, National Archives.

9.   Editorial, *Greensboro* (Alabama) *Watchman*, 8 Jan. 1942, included in Records of the Farmers Home Administration, RG 96, Series 2, Complaints—Alabama, National Archives.

10. Will W. Alexander, "Our Conflicting Racial Policies," *Harper's* 190 (Jan. 1945): 177.

11. Quoted in Sidney Baldwin, *Poverty and Politics: The Rise and Decline of the Farm Security Administration* (Chapel Hill: Univ. of North Carolina Press, 1968), 250.

12. Quoted in Wilma Dykeman and James Stokely, *Seeds of Southern Change: The Life of Will Alexander* (Chicago: Univ. of Chicago Press, 1962), 230–31.

13. Jack Bryan notes on regional information report by Garford Wilkinson, 15 June 1942, Records of the Farmers Home Administration, RG 96, Series 2, Box 142, National Archives.

14. Ed Trapnell, interview with author, 1 Nov. 1990.

15. Memorandum, John Fischer to regional information advisors, 24 Oct. 1940, Records of the Farmers Home Administration, RG 96, Series 2, Box 142, National Archives.

16. Constance E. H. Daniel, "Security for Farmers," *Crisis* 47 (Apr. 1940): 114.

17. Daniel to Stryker, 8 June 1940, Roy E. Stryker Papers, microfilm reel NDA 30, Archives of American Art.

18. Ed Trapnell, interview with author, 1 Nov. 1990.

19. "Eastern Press Follows Forum's Lead, Unearths History of This Fake Photo," *Fargo* (North Dakota) *Forum*, 31 Aug. 1936, 1; "Drought Photos in Files of RA Branded Fakes," *Chicago Tribune*, 29 Aug. 1936, 8; " 'Fake' Drought Photo Revealed in Tugwell Files, Skull and All," *New York Herald-Tribune*, 29 Aug. 1936, 5; "Drought Photo Branded Fake—North Dakota Newspaper Attacks RA Picture," *New York Sun*, 29 Aug. 1936, 3; "Explains Skull Use in Drought Pictures: RA Aide Says It Was Moved Only 110 Feet . . . Fargo Paper Renews the Attack," *New York Times*, 28 Aug. 1936, sec. 1, p. 3. On the "Tenant Madonna" controversy, see

Stryker to Lee, 21 June 1937, Roy E. Stryker Papers, microfilm reel NDA 31, Archives of American Art.

20. Stryker interview with Richard Doud, 13 June 1964, transcript at the Archives of American Art.

21. Fischer to Lee, 17 Sept. 1938, Roy Stryker Papers, 1912–1972, Series 1: Correspondence, microfilm reel 1 (Univ. of Louisville Photographic Archives; Sanford, N.C.: Microfilming Corporation of America, 1982).

22. John Vachon to Stryker, Oct. 1938, Roy E. Stryker Papers, microfilm reel NDA 26, Archives of American Art.

23. Stryker to Walker Evans, 10 Dec. 1935, Roy E. Stryker Papers, microfilm reel NDA 25, Archives of American Art.

24. Stryker to Arthur Rothstein and Lee, 19 Feb. 1942, Roy E. Stryker Papers, microfilm reel NDA 8, Archives of American Art.

25. Stryker to Marion Post Wolcott, 25 May 1939, Roy E. Stryker Papers, microfilm reel NDA 30, Archives of American Art.

26. Stryker to Lee, 3 Nov. 1939, Roy E. Stryker Papers, microfilm reel NDA 31, Archives of American Art.

27. Lee to Stryker, 2 June 1939, and Stryker to Lee, 3 Nov. 1939, Roy E. Stryker Papers, microfilm reel NDA 31, Archives of American Art.

28. Lange to Stryker, 2 May 1938, and Lange to Stryker, 12 Jan. 1938, Roy E. Stryker Papers, microfilm reel NDA 30, Archives of American Art.

29. Gordon Parks interview with Richard Doud, 30 Dec. 1964, transcript at Archives of American Art.

30. Esther Bubley, interview with author, 26 Feb. 1987.

31. Stryker to Jack Delano, 23 Apr. 1941, Roy Stryker Papers, 1912–72, Series 1: Correspondence, microfilm reel 3 (Univ. of Louisville Photographic Archives; Sanford, N.C.: Microfilming Corporation of America, 1982).

32. Robert Williams, interview with author, 10 June 1990.

33. Wolcott interview with Richard Doud, 18 Jan. 1965, transcript at Archives of American Art.

34. Rothstein to Stryker, 27 Jan. 1937, Roy E. Stryker Papers, microfilm reel NDA 26, Archives of American Art.

35. Edwin Locke to Stryker, 4 Feb. 1937, Roy E. Stryker Papers, microfilm reel NDA 25, Archives of American Art.

36. Wolcott, general caption, Orange County, N.C., 28 Sept. 1939, Resettlement Administration/Farm Security Administration/Office of War Information Written Records: Office Files, Caption Lists, Supplementary Reference files, 1935–43, microfilm reel 18, Library of Congress Prints and Photographs Division, Washington, D.C.

37. John Collier to Stryker, Sept. 1941, Roy E. Stryker Papers, microfilm reel NDA 25, Archives of American Art.

38. "*Life* did not like what we [Edwin and wife Louise] produced, oh boy did they not like it!" Rosskam later recounted. "It was a highly critical evaluation of [the American] position in Puerto Rico at that time, and among other things it foretold the election of Munos which was already pretty clear to anybody on the inside. *Life* didn't like that at all because they were backing somebody else." Edwin and Louise Rosskam interview with Richard Doud, 3 Aug. 1965, transcript at Archives of American Art.

39. Collier to Stryker, 11 Feb. 1943, Roy E. Stryker Papers, microfilm reel NDA 25, Archives of American Art. See also Collier to Stryker, Mar. 1943, Roy E. Stryker Papers, microfilm reel NDA 25, Archives of American Art.

40. Jean Lee, general caption, Hammond, La., Apr. 1939, RA/FSA/OWI Written Records, microfilm reel 19, Library of Congress.

41. John Vachon, "Tribute to a Man, an Era, an Art," *Harper's* 247 (Sept. 1973): 98.

42. Between 1939 and 1942, Delano, Collier, Wolcott, Vachon, Rothstein, Lee, and Louise Rosskam experimented with color photography for the FSA, amassing some 800 images that are currently stored on a Library of Congress videodisk. Blacks are as well represented in the color material (particularly Wolcott's in Florida and Delano's in Georgia) as they are in the main file. As for the noncolor photographs, I am not including in the black count Delano's 335 photos taken of dark-skinned Virgin Islands residents in 1941. Suffice it to say here that Delano, confronting numerous opportunities to exploit the "primitive black" angle, seems to have resisted them.

43. When I refer to "black representation" in the RA/FSA and other government files, I am including photographs in which both blacks and whites appear. One might argue here that resulting statistics are inflated by photos in which whites are prominent in the foreground, blacks consigned to a distant background presence. In the case of the RA/FSA file, however, the percentage of such images is negligible; among other files, only that of the Office of the Secretary of Agriculture would have an appreciable percentage.

44. My definitions of the Northeast, North Central, South, and West follow those used in the 1940 U.S. Census Reports. *Northeast* includes Maine, New Hampshire, Vermont, Massachusetts, Rhode Island, Connecticut, New York, New Jersey, and Pennsylvania. *North Central* includes Ohio, Indiana, Illinois, Michigan, Wisconsin, Minnesota, Iowa, Missouri, North Dakota, South Dakota, Nebraska, and Kansas. *South* includes Delaware, Maryland, District of Columbia, Virginia, West Virginia, North Carolina, South Carolina, Georgia, Florida, Kentucky, Tennessee, Alabama,

Mississippi, Arkansas, Louisiana, Oklahoma, and Texas. *West* includes Montana, Idaho, Wyoming, Colorado, New Mexico, Arizona, Utah, Nevada, Washington State, Oregon, and California. Readers may object to the rather broad definition of the South; where useful, the lower South (Florida, Georgia, Alabama, Mississippi, Louisiana, Texas, and South Carolina) will be distinguished from the upper South (Virginia, North Carolina, Delaware, Maryland, the District of Columbia, Arkansas, Tennessee, Kentucky, West Virginia, and Oklahoma).

45. Rosskam and Delano to Stryker, n.d. (ca. 1941), Roy E. Stryker Papers, microfilm reel NDA 8, Archives of American Art.

46. Stryker interview with Richard Doud, 13 June 1964, transcript at Archives of American Art.

47. Wolcott, general caption, Oxford, N.C., 22 Nov. 1939, RA/FSA/OWI Written Records, microfilm reel 18, Library of Congress.

48. From caption on Florida lynching photograph (LC-USZ62-35346) included in Lot 10647-13, NAACP Collection, Prints and Photographs Division, Library of Congress.

49. Lee to Stryker, 19 Mar. 1940, Roy E. Stryker Papers, microfilm reel NDA 31, Archives of American Art.

50. Jack and Irene Delano interview with Richard Doud, 12 June 1965, transcript at Archives of American Art.

51. Rothstein statement cited in Roy Stryker interview with Richard Doud, 13 June 1964, transcript at Archives of American Art.

52. Jack Delano, interview with author, 30 Oct. 1990.

3. Ben Shahn's Southern Meditations

1. Stryker to Rothstein, n.d. (ca. 1939), Roy E. Stryker Papers, microfilm reel NDA 8, Archives of American Art. See also memorandum, Stryker to all photographers, 18 Jan. 1941, Roy E. Stryker Papers, microfilm reel NDA 8.

2. Jack Lockhart, "AAA Defenders Paint Control for Cotton as Barrier to Chaos," *Memphis Commercial Appeal*, 12 Oct. 1935, 2.

3. Quoted in Donald H. Grubbs, *Cry from the Cotton: The Southern Tenant Farmers' Union and the New Deal* (Chapel Hill: Univ. of North Carolina Press, 1971), 49.

4. F. Raymond Daniell, "Arkansas Violence Laid to Landlords," *New York Times*, 16 Apr. 1935, sec. 1, p. 18.

5. Ed Trapnell, interview with author, 1 Nov. 1990. See also the comments of *New York Times* reporter F. Raymond Daniell: "To express sympathy

for the sharecropper is to invite trouble. . . . There are few planters or office-holders who will accept a visitor . . . without first looking him up in Elizabeth Dilling's *Red Network*, which lists Mayor F. H. LaGuardia and Jane Addams of Hull House as dangerous radicals." Daniell, "Arkansas Violence Laid to Landlords," *New York Times*, 16 Apr. 1935, sec. 1, p. 18.

6. John D. Morse, ed., *Ben Shahn* (New York: Praeger, 1972), 80–81. See also, Selden Rodman, *Portrait of the Artist as an American; Ben Shahn: A Biography in Pictures* (New York: Harper and Brothers, 1951), 99–101.

7. Ben Shahn interview with Richard Doud, 14 Apr. 1964, transcript at Archives of American Art.

8. Harriet Teresa Hassell, "Cotton-Pickers," *The Commonweal*, 2 July 1932, 330.

9. Morse, ed., *Ben Shahn*, 137.

10. For the comment on Lange's image, see J. Earl Moser, "Speaking of Government Workers: Modern Business," *Washington Times*, 2 Aug. 1938, 18.

11. Josiah Roberts, quoted in *First-Person America*, ed. Ann Banks (New York: Random House, 1981), 188–89. See also William Stout and N. T. Oliver, "Alagazam: Story of Pitchmen, High and Low," *Saturday Evening Post*, 19 Oct. 1929, 26–27.

12. Shahn interview with Richard Doud, 14 Apr. 1964, transcript at Archives of American Art.

13. Andre Sennwald, "The Screen: 'Hard Rock Harrigan,' " *The New York Times*, 30 July 1935, sec. 1, p. 16.

14. Caldwell and Bourke-White, *You Have Seen Their Faces*, p. 1, photo 2.

15. Damon Runyon, "Sensational Joe Louis Hangs K.O. on Max Baer in Fourth," *Charleston* (West Virginia) *Gazette*, 25 Sept. 1935, Sec. F, p. 10; Edward J. Neil, "Louis Knocks Out Baer in Fourth to Win Shot at Title," *Arkansas Gazette*, 25 Sept. 1935, 10.

16. "Youth Takes Its Place," *Chicago Defender*, 5 Oct. 1935, 16.

4. Arthur Rothstein and the Missouri Bootheel

1. Max White, Douglas Ensminger, and Cecil Gregory, "Rich Land, Poor People," 1940, RA/FSA/OWI Written Records, microfilm reel 17, Library of Congress.

2. Carl Harris, "Sharecropper Dies in Missouri Fight against Evictions," *Daily Worker*, 14 Jan. 1939, 5.

3. Harry S. Truman, speech in U.S. Senate, 16 Jan. 1939 (*Congressional*

Record), included in RA/FSA/OWI Written Records, microfilm reel 17, Library of Congress.

4. Louis Cantor, *A Prologue to the Protest Movement: The Missouri Sharecropper Roadside Demonstration of 1939* (Durham, N.C.: Duke Univ. Press, 1969), 88.

5. "Tread Highway Seeking Security," *Chicago Daily News*, 11 Jan. 1939, 1; "Families and Belongings Strung along Road," *Chicago Daily News*, 11 Jan. 1939, 34; "Blame Crop Law," *Chicago Daily News*, 11 Jan. 1939, 34; "Roadside Is Schoolroom for Children in Sharecroppers' Camps," *Chicago Daily News*, 13 Jan. 1939, 38; "All Is Not Beautiful in the Snow—Not Near New Madrid," *Chicago Daily News*, 14 Jan. 1939, 32.

6. "We Eat," *St. Louis Globe Democrat*, 12 Jan. 1939, 6A; "Evicted Missouri Sharecroppers," *St. Louis Post Dispatch*, 15 Jan. 1939, sec. 1, p. 2.

7. *St. Louis Post Dispatch*, 15 Jan. 1939, sec. 1, p. 2.

8. "Missouri Police Oust Sharecroppers," *Philadelphia Inquirer*, 15 Jan. 1939, 2.

9. "Moving Again," *St. Louis Post Dispatch*, 16 Jan. 1939, sec. D, p. 1.

10. "Sheriff Thwarts Sharecropper Riot," *St. Louis Globe Democrat*, 17 Jan. 1939, 1; Carl Harris, "Terror Reigns among Evicted Croppers as U.S. Begins Probe," *Daily Worker*, 23 Jan. 1939, 3.

11. Rothstein to Stryker, 11 Jan. 1939, Roy E. Stryker Papers, microfilm reel NDA 26, Archives of American Art.

12. "Washington Notes: Sharecroppers' Security," *New Republic* 98 (8 Feb. 1939): 15.

13. Rothstein to Stryker, 10 Jan. 1939, Roy E. Stryker Papers, microfilm reel NDA 26, Archives of American Art.

14. Rothstein to Stryker, 16 Jan. 1939, Roy E. Stryker Papers, microfilm reel NDA 26, Archives of American Art.

15. Ibid.

16. Ibid.

17. Ibid.

18. Ibid.

19. Ibid.

20. Constance E.H. Daniel, "The Missouri Boot-Heel," *Crisis* 47 (Nov. 1940): 348.

5. Russell Lee, Chicago, and the 1940s

1. Lee to Stryker, 14 Jan. 1937, Roy E. Stryker Papers, microfilm reel NDA 31, Archives of American Art.

2. Sterling North, "Book of the Week: Native Son," *Chicago Daily News*, 28 Feb. 1940, 15.
3. Peter Monro Jack, "A Tragic Novel of Negro Life in America," *New York Times*, 3 Mar. 1940, sec. 6, p. 20.
4. "244,000 Native Sons," *Look*, 21 May 1940, 10.
5. Roy Stryker, "From Roy Stryker, Head of the FSA Photographers," *Photo Notes* (June–July 1940), 2.
6. Louise Rosskam, interview with author, 15 Dec. 1987.
7. Stryker to Lee, 26 Apr. 1941, Roy E. Stryker Papers, microfilm reel NDA 31, Archives of American Art.
8. Lee to Stryker, 25 Apr. 1941, Roy E. Stryker Papers, microfilm reel NDA 31, Archives of American Art.
9. Cayton and Drake, *Black Metropolis*, 639.
10. Ibid., 382.
11. Lee to Stryker, 9 Apr. 1941, Roy E. Stryker Papers, microfilm reel NDA 31, Archives of American Art. For Rosskam's description, see general caption, "Face of the Black Belt," Chicago, Apr. 1941, RA/FSA/OWI Written Records, microfilm reel 17, Library of Congress.
12. Lee to Stryker, 9 Apr. 1941, Roy E. Stryker Papers, microfilm reel NDA 31, Archives of American Art.
13. Rosskam, general caption, "Face of the Black Belt," RA/FSA/OWI Written Records, Library of Congress.
14. "Easter Services at Coventry," *Chicago Daily News*, 14 Apr. 1941, 1.
15. William Cross, "The Land of Hope," *Chicago Defender*, 20 Feb. 1917, in Hampton Univ. Newspaper Clipping File (Alexandria, VA.: Chadwyck-Healey, 1988), microfiche no. 340.
16. Richard Wright, introduction to *Black Metropolis*, xx.
17. Cayton and Drake, *Black Metropolis*, 459.
18. Louise Rosskam, interview with author, 15 Dec. 1987.
19. Edwin Rosskam, general caption, "Recent Immigrants," Chicago, Apr. 1941, RA/FSA/OWI Written Records, microfilm reel 17, Library of Congress.
20. Edwin Rosskam, general caption, "Relief Family," Chicago, Apr. 1941, RA/FSA/OWI Written Records, microfilm reel 17, Library of Congress; Jacob Riis, *How the Other Half Lives: Studies among the Tenements of New York* (1890); reprint, New York: Dover Press, 1971), 152, 155.
21. For the Frazier thesis, see E. Franklin Frazier, *The Negro Family in the United States* (Chicago: Univ. of Chicago Press, 1939), 484–86; Ernest W. Burgess, introduction to Frazier, *The Negro Family in the United States*, ix–xvii; and Daniel Patrick Moynihan, *The Negro Family in America: The Case for National Action* (Washington, D.C.: U.S. Government Printing

Office, 1965). For critics of the Frazier thesis, see Herbert G. Gutman, *The Black Family in Slavery and Freedom, 1750–1925* (New York: Pantheon Books, 1976); Jerold Heiss, *The Case of the Black Family: A Sociological Inquiry* (New York: Columbia Univ. Press, 1975); Eleanor Engram, *Science, Myth, Reality: The Black Family in a Half Century of Research* (Westport, Ct.: Greenwood Press, 1982); Demitri B. Shimkin, Edith M. Shimkin, and Dennis A. Frate, ed., *The Extended Family in Black Society* (Chicago: Aldine Press, 1978); Carol B. Stack, *All Our Kin: Strategies for Survival in a Black Community* (New York: Harper and Row, 1974); Elmer P. and Jeanne Mitchell Martin, *The Black Extended Family* (Chicago: Univ. of Chicago Press, 1978); and Borchert, *Alley Life in Washington*.

22. Gutman, *The Black Family in Slavery and Freedom*, 465–66.
23. Rosskam, general caption, "Day of a Negro Doctor," Chicago, Apr. 1941, RA/FSA/OWI Written Records, microfilm reel 17, Library of Congress.
24. Rosskam, general caption, "Negro Church," Chicago, Apr. 1941, RA/FSA/OWI Written Records, microfilm reel 17, Library of Congress.
25. Ibid.
26. "244,000 Native Sons," *Look*, 21 May 1940, 11.
27. Stryker to Lee, 30 Apr. 1941, Roy E. Stryker Papers, microfilm reel NDA 31, Archives of American Art.
28. Lee to Stryker, 9 Apr. 1941, Roy E. Stryker Papers, microfilm reel NDA 31, Archives of American Art.
29. "244,000 Native Sons," *Look*, 21 May 1940, 13.
30. Cayton and Drake, *Black Metropolis*, 191.
31. "Pres. Patterson of Tuskegee," *Chicago Defender*, 5 Apr. 1941.
32. Gordon Parks interview with Richard Doud, 30 Dec. 1964, transcript at Archives of American Art.
33. Ibid.
34. Ibid.
35. Ibid.
36. Garrison and Catherine Shippen, "All Is Not Smooth Sailing in D.C., Prospective War Workers Told," *Baltimore Afro-American*, 29 Aug. 1942, 20.
37. Alden Stevens, "Washington: Blight on Democracy—Plain Talk About Our Capitol City," *Harper's* 184 (Dec. 1941): 54.
38. "White Haters Curse, Stone D.C. Golfers," *Baltimore Afro-American*, 1 Aug. 1942, 24.
39. "Post Office Cafe Closed by Jim Crow," *Baltimore Afro-American*, 25 July 1942, 24.
40. Stryker to Delano, 8 Apr. 1941, Roy E. Stryker Papers, microfilm reel

NDA 25, Archives of American Art; see also Stryker to Delano, 5 Sept. 1940, Roy E. Stryker Papers, microfilm reel NDA 25.

41. Stryker to Delano, 12 Sept. 1940, Roy E. Stryker Papers, microfilm reel NDA 25, Archives of American Art. See also Stryker to Delano, 26 May 1942, Roy E. Stryker Papers, microfilm reel NDA 25; Stryker to all photographers, memos, 3 Mar. 1942, 17 Aug. 1942, and 24 July 1942, Roy E. Stryker Papers, microfilm reel NDA 8; and Stryker to Rothstein, 11 Feb. 1942, and 4 Mar. 1942, Roy E. Stryker Papers, microfilm reel NDA 26.

42. FSA report on Eastern migrant agricultural workers, 1940, included in Delano general caption, Belcross, N.C., July 1940, RA/FSA/OWI Written Records, microfilm reel 18, Library of Congress.

43. "I Wonder Where We Can Go Now? . . . Migratory Labor—A Social Problem," *Fortune* 19 (Apr. 1939): 74.

44. Delano to Stryker, 2 July 1940, Roy E. Stryker Papers, microfilm reel NDA 25, Archives of American Art.

45. Ibid.

46. Irene Delano, general caption, Belcross, N.C., July 1940, RA/FSA/OWI Written Records, microfilm reel 18, Library of Congress.

47. Jack Delano, interview with author, 30 Oct. 1990.

48. Stryker to Delano, 26 Apr.1941, and Stryker to Delano, 30 Apr. 1941, Roy E. Stryker Papers, microfilm reel NDA 25, Archives of American Art.

49. Delano to Stryker, 11 June 1941, Roy E. Stryker Papers, microfilm reel NDA 25, Archives of American Art.

50. Jack Delano, interview with author, 30 Oct. 1990.

51. Delano to Stryker, 7 May 1941, Roy E. Stryker Papers, microfilm reel NDA 25, Archives of American Art.

52. Arthur Raper, *Tenants of the Almighty* (New York: Macmillan Co., 1943), 309.

53. Delano to Stryker, 7 May 1941, Roy E. Stryker Papers, microfilm reel NDA 25, Archives of American Art.

6. The FSA Black Image in the Marketplace

1. Hartley E. Howe, "You Have Seen Their Pictures," *Survey Graphic* 29 (Apr. 1940): 236.

2. Dorothea Lange interview with Richard Doud, 22 May 1964, transcript at Archives of American Art, Washington, D.C.

3. Stryker to Lee, 16 Apr. 1937, 21 Apr. 1937, 16 June 1937, and 12 Oct. 1937, Roy E. Stryker Papers, microfilm reel NDA 31, Archives of Ameri-

can Art; see also Stryker to Lange, 10 May 1937, Roy E. Stryker Papers, microfilm reel NDA 30.

4. Bernard A. Drabeck and Helen E. Ellis, eds., *Archibald MacLeish: Reflections* (Amherst: Univ. of Massachusetts Press, 1986), 95.

5. Stryker to Lee, 10 Aug. 1937, Roy E. Stryker Papers, microfilm reel NDA 31, Archives of American Art.

6. Archibald MacLeish, *Land of the Free* (1938; rev. ed., New York: Da Capo Press, 1977), 87; "Talking Pictures," *Time*, 25 Apr. 1938, 70.

7. MacLeish, *Land of the Free*, 81.

8. Peter Monro Jack, "Archibald MacLeish's Poem for Our Day," *New York Times*, 8 May 1938, sec. 7, p. 2; Ruth Lechlitner, "Now the Land Is Gone," *New York Herald-Tribune*, 10 Apr. 1938, sec. 9, p. 6; T. K. Whipple, "Land of the Free," *New Republic* 94 (13 Apr. 1938): 311.

9. Eugene Davidson, "American Faces," *Yale Review* 27 (Summer 1938): 838.

10. Stryker to Lange, 7 Oct. 1938, Roy E. Stryker Papers, microfilm reel NDA 30, Archives of American Art.

11. A few complaints came on aesthetic grounds (insufficient poetic depth and originality, observed Babette Deutsch in *Poetry*), on reformist political grounds (an indictment too tentative, objected Muriel Rukeyser in *New Masses* and Pare Lorentz in the otherwise conservative *Saturday Review of Literature*), and, very occasionally, on right-oriented political grounds (too much imitation-proletarian rebelliousness, sighed John Holmes in the *Boston Transcript*). See Babette Deutsch, "Meaning and Being," *Poetry* 52 (June 1938): 53; Muriel Rukeyser, "We Aren't Sure . . . We're Wondering," *New Masses* 27 (26 Apr. 1938): 26–28; Pare Lorentz, "We Don't Know . . . ," *Saturday Review of Literature* 18 (2 Apr. 1938): 6; John Holmes, "Poetry Now," *Boston Transcript*, 16 Apr. 1938, sec. 3, p. 2.

12. John Holmes, "Poetry Now," p. 2.

13. MacLeish, *Land of the Free*, 66.

14. Ibid., 7.

15. Ibid., 62.

16. "World's Greatest Photo-Mural Dramatizes Our Defense Effort in the Grand Central Terminal," *New York Herald-Tribune*, 14 Dec. 1941, sec. 7, p. 2.

17. Stryker to Herbert Mayer, 8 May 1939, RA/FSA/OWI Written Records, microfilm reel 3, Library of Congress.

18. Quoted in Cal Ward, Nebraska Regional Information Advisor's Report, 10 Sept. 1936, Records of the Farmers Home Administration, Record Group 96, Series 1 (Washington Office, 1935–38), Correspondence, Box 32, National Archives.

19. Stryker to John Fischer, 29 Aug. 1940, RA/FSA/OWI Written Records, microfilm reel 3, Library of Congress.

20. George Wolf to John Fischer, 16 Mar. 1940, Records of the Farmers Home Administration, Record Group 96, Series 2 (Cincinnati Office, 1935–42), Correspondence, Box 142, National Archives.

21. J.A. Oliver to Stryker, 1 Dec. 1939, Records of the Farmers Home Administration, RG 96, Series 23, Box 147.

22. Garford Wilkinson to Fischer, 18 Jan. 1940, Records of the Farmers Home Administration, RG 96, Series 2, Box 145, National Archives.

23. Wolf to Fischer, 17 Jan. 1940, Records of the Farmers Home Administration, RG 96, Series 2, Box 145, National Archives.

24. Elmer Isaksen to Fischer, 23 Jan. 1940, RA/FSA/OWI Written Records, microfilm reel 3, Library of Congress.

25. "Grand Central's Photo Mural," Time, 29 Dec. 1941, 33.

26. For the Cleveland show ("The Drama of America"), for example, the Historical Section submitted 147 photographs and a Stryker statement of general theme; museum curators made the final cuts and, fortunately from the black standpoint, disregarded the advice of one official who, Stryker was told, "is a Southerner of the old school, and can't stand the sight of the pictures." The government photographer and occasional curator Peter Sekaer figured prominently in the choices for the College Art Association exhibit, while Edward Steichen drew up the final list for MOMA's "Road to Victory" show. On the Cleveland exhibit planning, see Helen Foote to Stryker, 20 Mar. 1939, Records of the Farmers Home Administration, RG 96, Series 2, Box 148, National Archives.

27. Unsigned comments collected at First International Photographic Exposition, New York, April 18–24, 1938, included in Roy E. Stryker Papers, microfilm reel NDA 8, Archives of American Art.

28. Ed Trapnell, interview with author, 1 Nov. 1990. For the curious selection of migrant pictures, see "Oakies at Our Door," Washington Daily News, 1 Mar. 1940, RA/FSA/OWI Written Records, microfilm reel 21, Library of Congress.

29. "Truly Rural America That Faces Resettlement—Out in the Country, USA," Washington Post, 4 Mar. 1936, 16; Washington Evening Star, 15 Mar. 1936, Gravure Section, p. 2.

30. "The New South Facing Its Knotty Land Tenure Problem," Mid-Week Pictorial, 4 July 1936, RA/FSA/OWI Written Records, microfilm reel 21, Library of Congress.

31. Ibid.

32. John Temple Graves, "The Big World at Last Reaches Gee's Bend," New York Times, 22 Aug. 1937, Magazine, p. 12.

33. Theodore Pratt, "Land of the Jook," Saturday Evening Post, 26 Apr. 1941,

20, 21, 43.

34. Ibid., 20, 21.

35. Joseph H.B. Evans, "Race Has Major Part in Resettlement Drive," *Pittsburgh Courier*, 31 Oct. 1936, 10.

36. "When the Army Moves, Farm Families Must Move Out; The Government Lends a Hand," *Atlanta World*, 1 Aug. 1941, 1; Delano to Stryker, 9 Apr. 1941, Roy Stryker Papers, 1912–72, Series 1: Correspondence, microfilm reel 3 (Univ. of Louisville Photographic Archives; Sanford, North Carolina: Microfilming Corporation of America, 1982).

37. Edward Steichen, "The FSA Photographers," in *U.S. Camera: 1939* (New York: William Morrow and Co., 1939), 43–66.

38. Anderson, *Home Town*, 5.

39. Ibid., 37.

40. Ibid., 8.

41. Ibid., 45, 56, 44, 26.

42. R. L. Duffus, "The Small Towns of America: Sherwood Anderson, Assisted by the Camera, Captures Their Quality," *New York Times*, 27 Oct. 1940, sec. 6, p. 30.

43. John C. Cort, "Home Town," *The Commonweal* 33 (20 Dec. 1940): 233.

44. Lewis Gannett, "Books and Things," *Boston Transcript*, 23 Oct. 1940, 11.

45. Henry Seidel Canby, "Home Town," *Saturday Review of Literature*, 11 Jan. 1941, 21.

46. Ralph Steiner, "The Small Town: A New Book Presents Great Pictures of Rural America Taken by U.S. Government Photographers," *PM*, 13 Oct. 1940, 46–49; "The Small Town: Sherwood Anderson Writes about It, Government Pictures It," *Des Moines Sunday Register*, 3 Nov. 1940, sec. 11A, pp. 2–3.

47. Edwin and Louise Rosskam, interview with Richard Doud, 3 Aug. 1965, transcript at Archives of American Art.

48. Herman Clarence Nixon, *Forty Acres and Steel Mules* (Chapel Hill: Univ. of North Carolina Press, 1938), 95, 23, 30, 679.

49. Dorothea Lange and Paul Taylor, *An American Exodus: A Record of Human Erosion* (1939; reprint, New York: Russell and Russell, 1971), 265, 180.

50. Arthur Raper and Ira DeA. Reid, *Sharecroppers All* (1941; reprint, New York: Russell and Russell, 1971), 265, 180.

51. Nixon, *Forty Acres and Steel Mules*, 77.

52. Raper and Reid, *Sharecroppers All*, 196, 133.

53. Ibid., 149.

54. Virginius Dabney, "Georgia's Doughty Stepchildren," *The New York Times*, 18 July 1943, sec. 7, p. 20.

55. Raper, *Tenants of the Almighty*, plate 18.

56. Stryker to Raper, 28 May 1942, RA/FSA/OWI Written Records, microfilm reel 6.

57. Raper, *Tenants of the Almighty*, plate 75.

58. Jack Delano, interview with author, 30 Oct. 1990.

59. Lange and Taylor, *American Exodus*, 41, 58.

60. Richard Crandell, "They Were Off for California: An Album That Illustrates *The Grapes of Wrath*," *New York Herald-Tribune*, 21 Jan. 1940, sec. 9, p. 5.

61. Jonathan Daniels, "Slavery Misnamed," *Saturday Review of Literature*, 1 Mar. 1941, 10.

62 Leon Whipple, "Interrogation Southward," *Survey Graphic* 27 (Sept. 1938): 468.

63. Edward Alden Jewell, "Camera: Aspects of America in Three Shows," *The New York Times*, 2 Oct. 1938, sec. 9, p. 9.

64. William Carlos Williams, "Sermon with a Camera," *New Republic*, 12 Oct. 1938, 283.

65. Richard Wright note on FSA stationery, n.d., Papers of Richard Wright, Miscellaneous Notes on *12 Million Black Voices*—Folder 919, James Weldon Johnson Collection, Beinecke Library, Yale Univ.

66. Louise Rosskam, interview with author, 15 Dec. 1987. Richard Wright and Edwin Rosskam knew what one another was up to. After receiving a draft of Wright's text and doing a preliminary layout, Rosskam wrote Wright: "I started [the layout] Monday, and expect to see you in New York with the pictures and dummy before the end of the month. . . . I wish you would do me one favor—Please don't revise the city part before I see you. Let me do the lay-out according to available picture material, available space, and the best of my editing ability and then do your changing and chopping with lineage and exact wordage at your disposal. You'll be surprised how the pictures will help you. In the meantime, the interval will give your mind a rest—and I wouldn't be astonished if it needed it." Rosskam to Wright, n.d. (ca. Summer 1941), Papers of Richard Wright, Miscellaneous Correspondence Box, James Weldon Johnson Collection, Beinecke Library.

67. Rosskam to Leonard Lyons, 26 Sept. 1941, Papers of Richard Wright, Miscellaneous Correspondence Box, James Weldon Johnson Collection, Beinecke Library.

68. Richard Wright and Edwin Rosskam, *12 Million Black Voices* (New York: Viking Press, 1941), 46, 111, 146, 5; Richard Wright note, n.d., Papers of Richard Wright, Miscellaneous Notes on *12 Million Black Voices*—Folder 919, James Weldon Johnson Collection, Beinecke Library.

69. Wright and Rosskam, *12 Million Black Voices*, 15, 25, 31, 671, 60, 108. See also John Rogers Puckett, *Five Photo-Textual Documentaries from the Great Depression* (Ann Arbor: UMI Research Press, 1984), 61-81.

70. Charles Curtis Munz, "12 Million Black Voices," *The Nation* 153 (13 Dec. 1941): 620.

71. Wright and Rosskam, *12 Million Black Voices*, 30, 44–45, 132–33.

72. Ibid., 92.

73. Ibid., 76–77, 119, 60, 109.

74. Ibid., 110, 9. See William Stott, *Documentary Expression and Thirties America* (New York: Oxford University Press, 1973), 232.

75. George Streator, "12 Million Black Voices," *The Commonweal* 35 (28 Nov. 1941): 147.

76. "12 Million Black Voices," *New York Age*, 31 Jan. 1942, 6; Ben Davis, Jr., "Wright's New Book Powerful," *Atlanta World*, 1 Dec. 1941, 2; J. A. Schuyler, "12 Million Black Voices," *Pittsburgh Courier*, 6 Dec. 1941, 7; Beatrice M. Murphy, "Wright's New Book Biased, Depressing," *Baltimore Afro-American*, 22 Nov. 1941, 9.

77. Richard Crandell, "Dark Thoughts on Dark Citizens," *New York Herald-Tribune*, 23 Nov. 1941, sec. 9, p. 8; reader to Richard Wright, 11 Feb. 1942, and reader to Wright, 28 Sept. 1942, Papers of Richard Wright, Miscellaneous Letters from Readers—*12 Million Black Voices Box*, James Weldon Johnson Collection, Beinecke Library.

78. Ben Davis, Jr., "Wright's New Book Powerful," *Atlanta World*, 1 Dec. 1941, 2.

79. William Shands Meacham, "The Bitter Saga of the Negro: The Drama of Centuries Compressed into a Short Book Written in Astringent Prose," *New York Times*, 23 Nov. 1941, sec. 6, p. 11.

80. David R. Lindsay, "Negro 'Folk History,' " *PM*, 2 Nov. 1941, 56. Rosskam was appalled by the *PM* review, apologizing to Wright for what he called the "debacle." See Rosskam to Wright, n.d. (ca. Nov. 1941), Papers of Richard Wright, Miscellaneous Correspondence Box, James Weldon Johnson Collection, Beinecke Library.

81. Wright and Rosskam, *12 Million Black Voices*, 10.

82. Lou Gittler to Stryker, 27 July 1941, RA/FSA/OWI Written Records, microfilm reel 3.

83. Jack Delano, interview with author, 30 Oct. 1990.

84. Alfred Palmer, interview with author, 18 Aug. 1990.

85. Paul Vanderbilt, interview with author, 20 Aug. 1986. Steve Wright, interview with author, 19 Aug. 1990.

86. Esther Bubley, interview with author, 26 Feb. 1987.

87. W. Eugene Smith, "Nurse Midwife: Maude Callen Eases Pain of Birth, Life, and Death," *Life*, 3 Dec. 1951, 135–45.

88. Robert Frank, *Les Americaines* (Paris: Encyclopedie Essentielle, 1958), 13, 31.

89. Levitt photos from the 1940s–50s reproduced, along with a perceptive introduction by James Agee, in *Helen Levitt: A Way of Seeing—Photographs of New York* (New York: Viking Press, 1965).

90. Rondal Partridge, interview with author, 5 Aug. 1990.
91. Steve Wright, interview with author, 19 Aug. 1990.
92. James Alinder, ed., *Roy DeCarava: Photographs* (Carmel, Ca.: Friends of Photography, 1982), plates I, II. See also Roy DeCarava and Langston Hughes, *The Sweet Flypaper of Life* (New York: Simon and Schuster, 1955).
93. Griffith Davis, "Coast-to-Coast Ambition of Walls," *Ebony*, Apr. 1948, 23–28; Richard Saunders, "Coal Mining: It's Still Dirty and Dangerous," *Ebony*, June 1948, 39–43; David Jackson, "Steel City Family: Stove Tender's Job is Hot and Dirty, But Pays the Bills," *Ebony*, Sept. 1957, 45–49.
94. Robert Williams, interview with author, 10 June 1990.
95. Robert McNeill, interview with author, 26 June 1989.

Selected Bibliography

Books and Parts of Books

Agee, James. Introduction to *Helen Levitt: A Way of Seeing— Photographs of New York*. New York: Viking Press, 1965.

Agee, James, and Walker Evans. *Let Us Now Praise Famous Men*. New York: Houghton-Mifflin, 1941. Rev. ed. Cambridge, Mass.: Riverside Press, 1960.

Anderson, James, Calvin Kytle, and Robert Doherty. *Roy Stryker: The Humane Propagandist*. Louisville: Univ. of Louisville Photographic Archives, 1977.

Anderson, Sherwood. *Home Town*. 1940. Rev. ed. Mamaroneck, N.Y.: Paul P. Appel, 1975.

Appel, Alfred. *Signs of Life*. New York: Knopf, 1983.

Baldwin, Sidney. *Poverty and Politics: The Rise and Decline of the Farm Security Administration*. Chapel Hill: Univ. of North Carolina Press, 1968.

Barthes, Roland. "The Photographic Message." In *Image-Music-Text*. New York: Farrar, Straus, Giroux, 1977. Rpt. in *The Camera Viewed: Writings on 20th Century Photography*, vol. 2. Edited by Peninah R. Petruck. New York: Dutton, 1979.

Beals, Carleton, and Walker Evans. *The Crime of Cuba*. Philadelphia: J. B. Lippincott and Co., 1933.

The Black Photographer, 1908–70: A Survey. New York: James Van DerZee Institute, 1971.

Borchert, James. *Alley Life in Washington: Family, Community, Religion, and Folklife in the City, 1850–1970*. Urbana: Univ. of Illinois Press, 1980.

Brown, Sterling. *The Negro in American Fiction*. 1937. Reprint. Port Washington, N.Y.: Kennikat Press, 1968.

Brown, Sterling, ed. *The Negro in Washington, D.C.* Washington, D.C.: Federal Writers Project, 1937.

Bunche, Ralph. *The Political Status of the Negro in the Age of FDR*. Chicago: Univ. of Chicago Press, 1973.

Caldwell, Erskine, and Margaret Bourke-White. *You Have Seen Their Faces*. 1937. Reprint. New York: Modern Age Books, 1937.

Cantor, Louis. A Prologue to the Protest Movement: The Missouri Sharecropper Roadside Demonstration of 1939. Durham, N.C.: Duke Univ. Press, 1969.

Chiarenza, Carl. Aaron Siskind: Pleasures and Terrors. Boston: Little, Brown, and Co., 1982.

Coar, Valencia Hollins, ed. A Century of Black Photographers, 1840–1960. Providence: Museum of Art, Rhode Island School of Design, 1983.

Coles, Robert. Dorothea Lange: Photographs of a Lifetime. Millerton, N.Y.: Aperture, 1982.

Curtis, James. Mind's Eye, Mind's Truth: FSA Photography Reconsidered. Philadelphia: Temple Univ. Press, 1989.

Daniel, Pete, Merry Foresta, Maren Stange, and Sally Stein, eds. Official Images: New Deal Photography. Washington, D.C.: Smithsonian Institution Press, 1987.

Davis, Allison. Children of Bondage: The Personality Development of Negro Youth in the Urban South. Washington, D.C.: American Council on Education, 1946.

Davis, Allison, Burleigh Gardner, and Mary Gardner. Deep South: A Social Anthropological Study of Caste and Class. Chicago: Univ. of Chicago Press, 1941.

Doherty, Robert. Social Documentary Photography in the USA. Garden City, N.Y.: AMPHOTO, 1976.

Dollard, John. Caste and Class in a Southern Town. New Haven: Yale Univ. Press, 1937.

Dykeman, Wilma, and James Stokely. Seeds of Southern Change: The Life of Will Alexander. Chicago: Univ. of Chicago Press, 1962.

Elliott, George. Dorothea Lange. New York: Museum of Modern Art, 1966.

Engram, Eleanor. Science, Myth, Reality: The Black Family in a Half Century of Research. Westport, Conn.: Greenwood Press, 1982.

Evans, Walker. American Photographs. New York: Museum of Modern Art, 1938.

_____. Walker Evans. Millerton, N.Y.: Aperture, 1979.

_____. Walker Evans: First and Last. New York: Harper and Row, 1978.

Featherstone, David. Doris Ulmann, American Portraits. Albuquerque: Univ. of New Mexico Press, 1985.

Federal Writers' Project. These are Our Lives: As Told By the People and Written by Members of the Federal Writers' Project of the Works Progress Administration in North Carolina, Tennessee, and Georgia. Chapel Hill: Univ. of North Carolina Press, 1939.

Fisher, Andrea. Let Us Now Praise Famous Women: Women Photographers for the U.S. Government, 1935–1944. New York: Pandora Press, 1987.

Fleischhauer, Carl, and Beverly Brannan, eds., Documenting America. Berkeley: Univ. of California Press, 1988.

Frank, Robert. *Les Americaines*. Paris: Encyclopedie Essentialle, 1958.

Frazier, E. Franklin. *The Negro Family in the United States*. Chicago: Univ. of Chicago Press, 1939.

Fried, Michael. *Realism, Writing, Disfiguration: On Thomas Eakins and Stephen Crane*. Chicago: Univ. of Chicago Press, 1987.

Ganzel, Bill. *Dust Bowl Descent*. Lincoln: Univ. of Nebraska Press, 1984.

Garver, Thomas, ed. *Just Before the War*. New York: October House, 1968.

Geertz, Clifford. *The Interpretation of Culture*. New York: Basic Books, 1973.

Green, James. *Grassroots Socialism*. Baton Rouge: Louisiana State Univ. Press, 1982.

Grubbs, Donald H. *Cry from the Cotton: The Southern Tenant Farmers' Union and the New Deal*. Chapel Hill: Univ. of North Carolina Press, 1971.

Gutman, Herbert G. *The Black Family in Slavery and Freedom, 1750–1925*. New York: Pantheon Books, 1976.

Gutman, Judith M. *Lewis Hine and the American Social Conscience*. New York: Walker, 1967.

Harnan, Terry. *Gordon Parks: Black Photographer and Filmmaker*. Champaign, Ill.: Garrard Publishing Company, 1972.

Heiss, Jerold. *The Case of the Black Family: A Sociological Inquiry*. New York: Columbia Univ. Press, 1975.

Heyman, Therese Thau. *Celebrating a Collection: The Work of Dorothea Lange*. Oakland, Calif.: Oakland Museum, 1978.

Hurley, F. Jack. *Portrait of a Decade: Roy Stryker and the Development of Documentary Photography in the Thirties*. Baton Rouge: Louisiana State Univ. Press, 1972.

———. *Russell Lee, Photographer*. Dobbs Ferry, N.Y.: Morgan and Morgan, 1978.

———. *Marion Post Wolcott: A Photographic Journey*. Albuquerque: Univ. of New Mexico Press, 1989.

Johnson, Charles S. *Shadow of the Plantation*. Chicago: Univ. of Chicago Press, 1934.

Kirby, John. *Black Americans in the Roosevelt Era: Liberalism and Race*. Knoxville: Univ. of Tennessee Press, 1980.

Kurzweil, Edith. *The Age of Structuralism: Levi-Strauss to Foucault*. New York: Columbia Univ. Press, 1980.

Lange, Dorothea, and Paul S. Taylor. *An American Exodus: A Record of Human Erosion*. 1939. Reprint. New York: Russell and Russell, 1971.

Lee, Russell. Autobiographical essay. In *Russell Lee: Retrospective Exhibition, 1934–1964*. Austin: Univ. of Texas, 1965.

Levine, Lawrence W. *Black Culture and Black Consciousness: Afro-American Folk Thought from Slavery to Freedom*. New York: Oxford Univ. Press, 1977.

Locke, Alain. *The Negro in Art*. New York: Hacker Art Books, 1971.

MacLeish, Archibald. *Land of the Free*. New York: Harcourt, Brace, 1938.

Mandelbaum, Maurice. *The Problem of Historical Knowledge: An Answer to Relativism*. Freeport, N.Y.: Books for Libraries Press, 1971.

Marling, Karal Ann. *Wall-to-Wall America: A Cultural History of Post-Office Murals in the Great Depression*. Minneapolis: Univ. of Minnesota Press, 1982.

Martin, Elmer P., and Jeanne Mitchell Martin. *The Black Extended Family*. Chicago: Univ. of Chicago Press, 1978.

McElvaine, Robert S. *Down and Out in the Great Depression: Letters from the "Forgotten Man."* Chapel Hill: Univ. of North Carolina Press, 1983.

McKay, Claude. *Harlem: Negro Metropolis*. New York: Dutton, 1940.

Meltzer, Milton. *Dorothea Lange: A Photographer's Life*. New York: Farrar, Straus, Giroux, 1978.

Morse, John, ed. *Ben Shahn*. New York: Praeger, 1972.

Moutoussamy-Ashe, Jeanne. *Viewfinders: Black Women Photographers*. New York: Dodd, Mead, and Co., 1986.

Moynihan, Daniel Patrick. *The Negro Family in America: The Case for National Action*. Washington, D.C.: U.S. Government Printing Office, 1965.

Mydans, Carl. *Carl Mydans: Photojournalist*. New York: Abrams, 1985.

_____. *More Than Meets the Eye*. Westport, Ct.: Greenwood Press, 1974.

Myrdal, Gunnar. *An American Dilemma: The Negro Problem and American Democracy*. New York: Harper and Brothers, 1944.

Nixon, Herman Clarence. *Forty Acres and Steel Mules*. Chapel Hill: Univ. of North Carolina Press, 1938.

Odum, Howard. *Southern Regions of the United States*. Chapel Hill: Univ. of North Carolina Press, 1936.

Ohrn, Karin. *Dorothea Lange and the Documentary Tradition*. Baton Rouge: Louisiana State Univ. Press, 1980.

O'Neal, Hank. *A Vision Shared: A Classic Portrait of America and Its People 1935–1943*. New York: St. Martin's Press, 1976.

Owen, Chandler. *Negroes and the War*. Washington, D.C.: Office of War Information, 1942.

P.H. Polk. Birmingham, Ala.: Birmingham Museum of Art, 1983.

Park, Marlene and Gerald Markowitz. *Democratic Vistas: Post Offices and Public Art in the New Deal*. Philadelphia: Temple Univ. Press, 1984.

Parks, Gordon. *The Gordon Parks Collection*. Manhattan, Kans.: Kansas State Univ. Department of Art, 1983.

_____. Foreword to *Harlem Document: Photographs 1932–1940*. Edited by Ann Banks. Providence, R.I.: Matrix Publications, 1981.

_____. *Voices in the Mirror: An Autobiography*. New York: Doubleday, 1990.

Peterkin, Julia, and Doris Ulmann. *Roll, Jordan, Roll*. New York: Robert O. Ballou, 1933.

Petruck, Peninah R., ed. *The Camera Viewed: Writings on 20th Century Photography.* New York: Dutton, 1979.

Plattner, Steven W. *Roy Stryker: USA, 1943–1950.* Austin: Univ. of Texas Press, 1983.

Pratt, Davis. *The Photographic Eye of Ben Shahn.* Cambridge, Mass.: Harvard Univ. Press, 1975.

Puckett, John Rogers. *Five Photo-Textual Documentaries from the Great Depression.* Ann Arbor: UMI Research Press, 1984.

Raper, Arthur. *Preface to Peasantry.* Chapel Hill: Univ. of North Carolina Press, 1936.

_____. *Tenants of the Almighty.* New York: Macmillan Co., 1943.

Raper, Arthur, and Ida DeA. Reid. *Sharecroppers All.* 1941. Reprint. New York: Russell and Russell, 1971.

Reid, Robert L. and Larry A. Viskochil, eds., *Chicago and Downstate: Illinois As Seen by FSA Photographers.* Urbana: Univ. of Illinois Press, 1989.

Riis, Jacob. *How the Other Half Lives: Studies among the Tenements of New York.* 1890. Reprint. New York: Dover Press, 1971.

Rodman, Selden. *Portrait of the Artist as an American: Ben Shahn, A Biography in Pictures.* New York: Harper and Brothers, 1951.

Rosskam, Edwin. *Washington, D.C.: Nerve Center.* New York: Alliance Corporation, 1939.

Rothstein, Arthur. *Arthur Rothstein's America in Photographs, 1930–80.* New York: Dover, 1984.

_____. *Photojournalism: Pictures for Magazines and Newspapers.* Philadelphia: Chilton, 1965.

Shahn, Bernarda Bryson. *Ben Shahn.* New York: Abrams, 1972.

Shapiro, David. *Social Realism: Art as a Weapon.* New York: Ungar, 1973.

Shimkin, Demitri B., Edith M. Shimkin, and Dennis A. Frate. *The Extended Family in Black Society.* Chicago: Aldine Press, 1978.

Sitkoff, Harvard. *A New Deal for Blacks: The Emergence of Civil Rights as a National Issue.* New York: Oxford Univ. Press, 1978.

Soby, James Thrall. *Ben Shahn, Paintings.* New York: Braziller, 1963.

Sontag, Susan. *On Photography.* New York: Farrar, Straus, and Giroux, 1973.

Sosna, Morton. *In Search of the Silent South: Southern Liberals and the Race Issue.* New York: Columbia Univ. Press, 1977.

Spivak, John. *Georgia Nigger.* New York: Brewer, Warren, Putnam, 1932.

Stange, Maren. *Symbols of Ideal Life: Social Documentary Photography in America: 1890–1950.* New York: Cambridge Univ. Press, 1989.

Steichen, Edward, ed. *The Bitter Years 1935–1941: Rural America as Seen by the Photographers of the Farm Security Administration.* New York: Museum of Modern Art, 1962.

Stein, Sally. *Marion Post Wolcott: FSA Photographs.* Carmel, Calif.: Friends of Photography, 1983.

Sterner, Richard. *The Negro's Share*. New York: Harper and Brothers, 1943.

Sternsher, Bernard. *Rexford Guy Tugwell and the New Deal*. New Brunswick, N.Y.: Rutgers Univ. Press, 1964.

Stott, William. *Documentary Expression and Thirties America*. New York: Oxford Univ. Press, 1973.

Stryker, Roy, and Nancy Wood, eds. *In This Proud Land: America, 1935–1943, as Seen in the FSA Photographs*. Greenwich, Conn.: New York Graphic Society, 1973.

Szarkowski, John. *Walker Evans*. New York: Museum of Modern Art, 1971.

_____. *The Photographer's Eye*. New York: Museum of Modern Art, 1966.

Thompson, Jerry, ed. *Walker Evans at Work*. New York: Harper and Row, 1982.

Trachtenberg. Alan. Introduction to *America and Lewis Hine: Photographs 1904–1940*. New York: Aperture, 1977.

_____. Introduction to *The American Image*. New York: Pantheon, 1979.

_____. *Reading American Photographs: Images as History, Mathew Brady to Walker Evans*. New York: Hill and Wang, 1989.

Tugwell, Rexford. *To the Lesser Heights of Morningside: A Memoir*. Philadelphia: Univ. of Pennsylvania Press, 1982.

Tugwell, Rexford, Thomas Munro, and Roy Stryker. *American Economic Life*. New York: Harcourt, Brace, 1925.

Warner, William Lloyd. *Color and Human Nature*. Washington, D.C.: American Council on Education, 1941.

Weiss, Margaret. *Ben Shahn, Photographer: An Album from the 1930s*. New York: DeCapo Press, 1973.

Weiss, Nancy. *Farewell to the Party of Lincoln: Black Politics in the Age of FDR*. Princeton: Princeton Univ. Press, 1983.

Whelan, Richard. *Double Take: A Comparative Look at Photographs*. New York: C. N. Potter, 1981.

Willis-Thomas, Deborah. *Black Photographers, 1840–1940: An Illustrated Bio-bibliography*. New York: Garland Press, 1985.

Wolters, Raymond. *Negroes and the Great Depression: The Problem of Economic Recovery*. Westport: Greenwood Publishing Co., 1970.

Woodward, C. Vann. *The Strange Career of Jim Crow*. New York: Oxford Univ. Press, 1974.

Wright, Richard. *Native Son*. New York: Harper, 1940.

_____. *Uncle Tom's Children: Five Long Stories*. New York: Harper, 1938.

Wright, Richard, and Edwin Rosskam. *12 Million Black Voices: A Folk History of the Negro in the U.S.* New York: Viking Press, 1941.

Manuscript Collections, Archives, and Interviews

Alexander, Will W. Reminiscences of Will Winton Alexander. Columbia Univ. Oral History Collection, 1952.

Cook, Fannie. Fannie Cook Papers—Miscellaneous Related Photographs. Missouri Historical Society, St. Louis, Mo.

Doud, Richard. Transcribed interviews with U.S. Resettlement Administration/Farm Security Administration/Office of War Information personnel. Archives of American Art, Washington, D.C.: C.B. Baldwin (24 Feb. 1965); John Collier, Jr. (18 Jan. 1965); Jonathan Daniels (14 June 1965); Jack Delano (12 June 1965); Dorothea Lange (22 May 1964); Russell Lee (2 June 1964); Robert Hudgens (1 June 1965); Carl Mydans (29 Apr. 1964); Gordon Parks (30 Dec. 1964); Edwin Rosskam (3 Aug. 1965); Arthur Rothstein (25 May 1964); Ben Shahn (14 Apr. 1965); Roy Stryker (17 Oct. 1963; 13–14 June 1964; 23 Jan. 1965); Rexford Tugwell (21 Jan. 1965); John Vachon (28 Apr. 1964); Paul Vanderbilt (10 Nov. 1964); Marion Post Wolcott (18 Jan. 1965).

Hampton Univ. Newspaper Clipping File. Hampton Univ. Library, Hampton, Va. Alexandria, Va.: Chadwyck-Healey, 1988. Microfilm.

Harlem Renaissance Photograph Collection. Schomburg Center for Research in Black Culture, New York Public Library.

Harmon Foundation Collection. Kenneth Space Photographic File. Record Group 200. National Archives, Still Picture Branch, Washington, D.C.

Johnson, James Weldon. James Weldon Johnson Collection. Richard Wright Papers. Beinecke Library, Yale Univ., New Haven, Conn.

Natanson, Nicholas. Interviews with Esther Bubley (26 Feb. 1987); Jack Delano (30 Oct. 1990); Robert McNeill (10 Oct. 1986, 26 June 1989, and 10 Apr. 1990); Alfred T. Palmer (18 Aug. and 6 Sept. 1990); Rondal Partridge (5 Aug. 1990); Louise Rosskam (15 Dec. 1987); Ed Trapnell (1 Nov. 1990); Paul Vanderbilt (20 Aug. 1986); Robert Williams (10 June 1990); Steve Wright (19 Aug. 1990).

National Association for the Advancement of Colored People Photographic Collection. Library of Congress, Prints and Photographs Division, Washington, D.C.

Siskind, Aaron. Harlem Document Photograph Collection. Library of Congress, Prints and Photographs Division, Washington, D.C.

Stryker, Roy E. Papers, 1924–72. Univ. of Louisville Photographic Archives, Louisville, Ky. Sanford, N.C.: Microfilming Corporation of America, 1982. Microfilm.

Stryker, Roy E. Papers, 1935–43. Archives of American Art, Washington, D.C. Microfilm.

U.S. Department of Agriculture, Bureau of Agricultural Economics. Photographic Files. Record Group 83. National Archives, Still Picture Branch, Washington, D.C.

U.S. Department of Agriculture, Extension Service. Photographic Files. Record Group 33. National Archives, Still Picture Branch. Washington, D.C.

U.S. Department of Agriculture, Office of the Secretary of Agriculture. Photographic Files. Record Group 16. National Archives, Still Picture Branch, Washington, D.C.

U.S. Farmers Home Administration. Records of the Washington Office, 1938–1942; Records of the Cincinnati Office, 1935–1942. Record Group 96. National Archives, Suitland, Md.

U.S. Housing Authority. Photographic Files. Record Group 196. National Archives, Still Picture Branch, Washington, D.C.

U.S. National Youth Administration. Photographic Files. Record Group 119. National Archives, Still Picture Branch, Washington, D.C.

U.S. Office of War Information. Domestic Branch: General Records of the News Bureau; Correspondence of the Chief, Negro Press Section; Correspondence of the Chief, Division of Photography. Record Group 208. National Archives, Suitland, Md.

U.S. Resettlement Administration/Farm Security Administration/Office of War Information: Photographic Files, 1935–1943. Library of Congress Prints and Photographs Division, Washington, D.C.

U.S. Resettlement Administration/Farm Security Administration/Office of War Information Written Records: Office Files, Caption Lists, Supplementary Reference Files, 1935–1943. Library of Congress Prints and Photographs Division, Washington, D.C. Microfilm.

U.S. Solid Fuels Administration. Photographic File: Medical Survey of the Bituminous Coal Industry. Record Group 245. National Archives, Still Picture Branch, Washington, D.C.

U.S. Works Progress Administration, Division of Information. Photographic Files. Record Group 69. National Archives, Still Picture Branch, Washington, D.C.

U.S. Works Progress Administration, Division of Research. Photographic Files. Record Group 69. National Archives, Still Picture Branch, Washington, D.C.

U.S. Works Progress Administration, Federal Arts Project—New York. Photographic File. Record Group 69. National Archives, Still Picture Branch, Washington, D.C.

Index